THE BARE BONES INTRODUCTION TO INTEGRATED MARKETING COMMUNICATION

THE BARE BONES INTRODUCTION TO INTEGRATED MARKETING COMMUNICATION

Robyn Blakeman

ROWMAN & LITTLEFIELD PUBLISHERS, INC.
Lanham • Boulder • New York • Toronto • Plymouth, UK

ROWMAN & LITTLEFIELD PUBLISHERS, INC.

Published in the United States of America
by Rowman & Littlefield Publishers, Inc.
A wholly owned subsidiary of The Rowman & Littlefield Publishing Group, Inc.
4501 Forbes Boulevard, Suite 200, Lanham, Maryland 20706
www.rowmanlittlefield.com

Estover Road
Plymouth PL6 7PY
United Kingdom

British Library Cataloguing in Publication Information Available

Library of Congress Cataloging-in-Publication Data:

Blakeman, Robyn, 1958–
    The bare bones introduction to integrated marketing communication / Robyn
Blakeman.
      p.   cm.
    Includes bibliographical references and index.
    ISBN-13: 978-0-7425-5540-2 (cloth : alk. paper)
    ISBN-13: 978-0-7425-5541-9 (pbk. : alk. paper)
    ISBN-10: 0-7425-5540-2 (cloth : alk. paper)
    ISBN-10: 0-7425-5541-0 (pbk. : alk. paper)
    1. Communication in marketing.   I. Title.
    eISBN-10: 0-7425-6479-7
    eISBN-13: 978-0-7425-6479-4
HF5415.123.B5568   2008
658.8'02—dc22   2008013548

Printed in the United States of America

∞ ™ The paper used in this publication meets the minimum requirements of
American National Standard for Information Sciences—Permanence of Paper for
Printed Library Materials, ANSI/NISO Z39.48-1992.

CONTENTS

Part I: Understanding Integrated Marketing Communication

1 The Roots of Advertising and the Evolution of Integrated Marketing
Communication   3

2 Where Do We Find the Answers? Research and Targets   45

3 The Making of an Image: Branding and Positioning   61

4 Marketing Plans and Creative Briefs: How Marketers and Creatives
Work   75

5 Media   91

Part II: The Creative Process

6 Creative: Determining the Product's or Service's Visual/Verbal Tone of
Voice   111

7 Digital Prepress: Putting the Pieces in Place   133

**Part III: Media Use: How IMC Uses Diverse Media Vehicles to Speak
and Reach the Target Audience**

8 Public Relations   153

9 Print Advertising: Newspapers   167

10 Print Advertising: Magazines   177

11 Out-of-Home Advertising   189

12 Broadcast Advertising: Radio   201

13 Broadcast Advertising: Television   213

14 Direct Marketing   229

15 Sales Promotion   243

16 The Internet   255

17 Alternative Media: Guerrilla and Viral Marketing   275

Glossary   291

Bibliography   299

Index   301

About the Author   305

PART ONE

UNDERSTANDING INTEGRATED MARKETING COMMUNICATION

CHAPTER ONE

THE ROOTS OF ADVERTISING AND THE EVOLUTION OF INTEGRATED MARKETING COMMUNICATION

playfully posh.

F·A·O·SCHWARZ

Eric Burroughs

If I were starting life over again, I am inclined to think that I would go into the advertising business in preference to almost any other. . . . The general raising of the standards of modern civilization among all groups of people during the past half century would have been impossible without the spreading of the knowledge of higher standards by means of advertising.

—Franklin Delano Roosevelt, quoted in David Ogilvy,
Confessions of an Advertising Man, 132.

Understanding **advertising** today requires a look at where advertising began and its evolution in the United States. **Integrated marketing communication** (IMC) is a renewed twist on an old idea and can trace its roots to long before the invention of computers and industrialized manufacturing, to one-on-one trade between friends and neighbors.

The concept of advertising is very old. Some of the first and most rudimentary forms of advertising can be traced back centuries to wall, rock, or cave drawings. The Egyptians, Greeks, and Romans used papyrus to advertise political messages, announce gladiator games, make lost-and-found inquiries, and give directions. Later, during medieval times, word of mouth was used to spread the advertised message by town criers, followed later by print, thanks to the invention of the printing press.

Early in the settlement of the United States, the majority of the population lived and worked in small, tight-knit communities. While word of mouth was probably the first official form of communication between seller and potential buyers, it was personal selling that built and retained relationships between local consumers and merchants.

Local citizens could rely on area craftsmen for handcrafted items such as furniture, and goods such as boots and shoes that were custom made to meet buyers' individual needs. Household goods such as pots, pans, coffees, teas, ammunition, and tobacco were sold by, or could be ordered through, the resident grocer, while local farmers supplied the community with a variety of meats, fruits, vegetables, and dairy products.

The mid-nineteenth century ushered in the Industrial Revolution, and for the first time mass-produced goods, often manufactured in far-off places, were sold to a wide audience, via catalog or mail-order advertising. The custom work of the craftsman was all but replaced with machine-produced products, effectively ending the two-way dialogue between local merchants and residents. Taking its place was a generic one-way statement from an anonymous manufacturer to an unknown, uninvolved consumer. Limited competition and media options made advertising efforts simple and wide exposure more or less guaranteed—for a while.

The effects of the Industrial Revolution led the way to changes that would eventually expand media options and encourage competitive growth. Product categories once dominated—often for generations—by one brand were suddenly inundated with multiple equivalent products. Features once considered unique or cutting-edge in one brand could now be easily and economically copied by other brands within a category, so that what was once a selling point for a particular brand became a routine product feature within months. Without any distinguishing features or meaningful differences between individual products, brand image erodes—along with consumer brand loyalty. The unqualified number of diverse and often misused or incorrectly used media options contributed to this erosion by splintering consumer attention further—offering too many media options to successfully guarantee reaching a specific target audience—and diluting brand awareness.

When radio ushered in the broadcast era in the early 1920s, it carried no advertising at all. Needing a way to increase profits, broadcasters began looking for program sponsors. Initially, sponsors would pay to receive little more than a brief mention at the beginning and ending of each program. Later, individual advertisers were retained to sponsor entire programs, increasing their exposure.

Television's introduction in the 1940s was slow to catch on with advertisers and consumers alike. The cost of owning a television set was still relatively high, and programming options were few. But by the time the economy improved during the 1950s, the sale of TV sets was increasing, along with the quality and quantity of both programming and advertising. Originally, television relied on individual program sponsors in much the same way radio did. The idea of selling smaller blocks of advertising space to multiple sponsors came about in response to the dictatorial power that individual sponsors wielded over program content, which was often written or censored by the individual sponsor or its advertising agency. Individually sponsored programming, however, was anything but obsolete and continued to be popular for several decades.

To find modern advertising's visual/verbal roots we must turn to the 1960s. Targets were more defined and creativity was the name of the game. Every successful brand touted a **position,** an idea or image that the consumer would associate with a product or service. The advertising developed during this decade was unique, visually attractive, and revolutionary; it sold as well as entertained the reader or viewer, visually and verbally. Advertising had evolved from a "just the facts" type of sales message to one creatively focused on building the product's brand image and its relationship with the consumer. The founding fathers of what has been dubbed the "creative revolution" included Bill Bernbach, founder of Doyle Dan Bernbach in New York; Leo Burnett, founder of Leo Burnett in Chicago; and David Ogilvy, founder of Ogilvy and Mather, also in New York.

The ever-changing advertising industry's next major movement involved the introduction of cable television, and later satellite television, in the 1980s and 1990s. Though cable and satellite TV were responsible for creating additional advertising opportunities and more programming than ever before, they were also responsible for fractionalizing the target audience more than ever before. Consumers now had a hundred viewing options, where historically only three or four existed. On the upside, cable introduced advertising programming that consumers actually elected to tune into, in the form of **infomercials** and home-shopping channels like QVC or Jewelry Television.

The idea of elective advertising continued to develop throughout the 1990s and into the twenty-first century, with the introduction and explosion of the Internet.

This elective media vehicle was used not only for entertainment purposes but also as a product research tool for expanding consumer knowledge, and as a means of making purchasing easier than when it entailed traveling to a mall, visiting a showroom, or dealing with salespeople. For the first time, **marketers** and advertising no longer controlled the flow of information to the consumer.

INTEGRATED MARKETING COMMUNICATION: THE NEW ADVERTISING

IMC, also known as **relationship marketing**, works to interactively engage a specific individual, using a specific message, through specific media outlets. The goal is to build a long-term relationship between buyer and seller by involving the targeted individual in an *interactive*, or two-way, exchange of information. Expertly placed media efforts and the use of computer **databases** play a big role in getting the message to the right target audience, as does the development of a consistent visual/verbal image for a product or service.

It wasn't until the mid-1990s that IMC first began to attract and hold the attention of marketers. Up to this point, most advertising dollars were spent on more traditional mass-media advertising, such as *print* (newspapers and magazines) and *broadcast* (radio and television), which sent a more generalized message to a large audience. IMC, in contrast, focuses on the use of alternative or promotional media, such as **direct marketing** or **sales promotion**, to reach individual consumers with a personalized message. Consumers in today's marketplace are inundated with hundreds of advertising messages daily; they must pick and choose which will be remembered and which will be ignored. IMC attempts to ensure that the message will be remembered by replacing unwanted "one-size-fits-all" tactics with a customized message to members of a much smaller target audience, in a language they can understand and relate to, and via media they are sure to see and use.

Messages used in an IMC campaign must be tailor-made to fit a specific targeted audience's needs, wants, and lifestyle. The goal is to reach one individual within the target with a specially designed message that will create a lasting relationship and develop a brand-loyal consumer, who will continue to purchase that brand without the need for continuing advertising efforts.

Each brand or product must be as individualized as the target. The enormous number of media options and virtual product anonymity in many product categories make it necessary for marketers to create an identity for a brand or service, so it will stand out from the competition.

It is important that a product's image match the target's image of him- or herself, and the advertised message must get and hold the target's attention among the clutter of the competition.

If it sounds like it's more expensive to get a message to individual targets as compared to a mass audience, it is. IMC is often more expensive to employ than traditional advertising methods, but the results can be worth the expense.

Communicating with a target that has a known interest in the product or service increases **reach**, or the number of interested people who will see the message, and reduces the **frequency**, or number of times an ad or promotion will need to be used. Exposure to the message is more or less guaranteed when placed in a special-interest medium the target is known to use, making purchase more likely.

The initial steps required to attract a brand-loyal consumer are more expensive than those needed to retain a brand-loyal customer. Once the consumer thinks of a brand as her only choice, the need for additional communication efforts is reduced, minimizing costs.

Traditional advertising, on the other hand, takes longer to build loyalty. Because it is less likely a given target will have repeated exposure to a mass-media vehicle, the amount of time it takes to educate the target on the features and benefits of the product or service is increased. The result is a target that is often unable to recall the product's name at the time of purchase.

Basic Reasons for the Growth of IMC

Technology has changed the way corporations market their products and services. The customer is now in control of what he buys, when he buys, and where and how he buys. Computerized databases have given names and personalities to segments of the mass audience. Advertised messages can be addressed to an individual and feature products he or she has a known interest in, based on past purchase behavior. The Internet and other interactive media make it easy to purchase virtually any item without leaving the house, at any time of the day or night, with a credit card, via a toll-free number or Internet site. Consumers are better educated about products and can seek out additional information at their leisure. Marketers realize consumers have many product options from which to choose when making a purchase. Because of this, thinking has gone from being sales oriented to being customer driven in a relatively short period of time.

Before IMC, traditional marketing efforts were simple, aimed at making sales and increasing profits. This type of tactic, where the seller does no more than deliver a message to a buyer, is known as an *inside-out approach*. IMC, on the other hand, is consumer driven and understands that the consumer has many choices available in any single product category. Marketers are now focusing on an *outside-in approach* in which products are designed to meet consumers' individual needs and wants.

Successfully employing IMC requires a change in corporate philosophy, or a different way of thinking about and planning for strategically effective marketing communications. To be effective, IMC must be looked at as a process for building a relationship with the target and developing a product or offering a service that meets her specific needs. Product performance and quality is also a critical component to success. Each time the target repurchases, the product or service must match her expectations and consistently deliver reliable results.

Why IMC Fails

IMC fails when it is seen as just another communication effort, rather than a corporate philosophy expressed both inside and out.

Most people think of IMC as just the equivalent of conventional advertising, with its one-image/one-tone-of-voice approach. However, unlike traditional advertising, IMC really comprises all aspects of planned or unplanned communication between the brand, service, or corporation and the target audience, at all interaction points, and it is affected by both inside and outside influences.

Planned contact is external and includes outside advertising and promotions employed to reach the target. **Unplanned contact** is internal, or focused within a corporate context on employees and vendors, and is the less controllable of the two. Because of this, it must be the most flexible form of contact, in order to adjust to changing market, corporate, or consumer conditions. Corporate philosophy plays a major role in unplanned contact, which includes (or can arise in conjunction with):

- Employee gossip
- Word of mouth
- Governmental or media investigations
- Management style and/or philosophy
- Sales tactics
- Management performance
- Customer service initiatives
- Sales associate practices in greeting clientele
- Delivery driver conduct
- Dress codes
- Employee uniform policy and design
- Product quality and performance
- In-store and out-of-store displays
- Packaging
- Distribution
- Deliveries
- Pricing
- Decisions regarding store locations

All of these will have a direct impact on how the target views the product or service and will affect both initial and repeat sales.

Any change in corporate philosophy brought about by IMC efforts must be communicated internally as well as externally. Even the smallest details affect the success of IMC, and for IMC to work, every individual in the company, from the top down, must buy into the message being delivered to the consumer. If this is not the case, the target will receive mixed messages: a disconnect between what he hears in communication efforts and what he actually experiences when dealing with a company representative. Consider the following example: If the message to the public is "Fly the Friendly Skies," every employee with access to the public must be made aware of, and understand, this message. Nothing will kill the momentum of this advertising campaign faster than an encounter between the target and an angry ticket agent or snooty customer service representative.

What Drives IMC?

To successfully use IMC, a corporation must absorb the message into its corporate philosophy, to ensure that the target receives a consistent message and a reliable product or service. But this is only one of many initiatives that drive IMC. In order to be truly consumer driven, IMC planning must also involve the following:

- Research
- Database development
- Use of the Internet
- Employment of correct media tactics
- The building of brand-loyal consumers
- Creation of an interactive relationship
- Brand development
- Projection of a consistent visual/verbal image
- Attention to the promotional mix and media mix
- Evaluation

Meghan Campbell

Research: It's All about Knowing Who You Are Talking To

IMC can't work without an intimate knowledge of the intended **target audience**—those individuals research has determined most likely to buy the product or use the advertised service. Research is key to understanding what the target audience wants, how they will use the product or service, where and how they live, what media vehicles they use or see, and what they are looking for in a customer-brand relationship. Information gathered in the research phase will be used to determine the best promotional and media mix to reach the intended target audience, and what type of message will motivate purchase.

Database Development Tells the Tale

The growth of IMC can be traced to the development of **database marketing.** Database marketing uses a computer to store personal information about individuals and their past purchase history. Unlike traditional advertising methods, which focus communication efforts on a large group of targeted members, IMC targets individuals. Every time a consumer makes a credit card or grocery store purchase, visits a website, subscribes to a magazine or trade organization, or fills out a warranty or rebate form, personal information about the consumer is gathered and stored on a database. This information is used to direct future communication to only those individuals known to be interested in a product or service, eliminating message waste and allowing for a more personalized appeal.

The ability to talk to a target audience member by name is not all that new. What is new is how much is known about a targeted individual and his or her special interests. Because messages can be designed to specifically address issues of importance to the target, the question "What's in it for me?" can be answered for every target group or smaller niche market. Database information also plays a role in determining the best media and promotional mix, creative strategy, and overall message strategy needed to reach the intended target.

Use of the Internet

The use of computer databases to identify targeted audiences and the growth of the Internet as an information source are behind the initial and ongoing success of IMC. The Internet has personalized communication efforts between seller and buyer, moving the seller from talking *at* the target to talking *with* the target. As an educational and informational tool, the Internet can persuade and motivate consumers to take the next action-oriented step—such as picking up the phone and dialing a toll-free number to speak directly to a customer service representative; requesting additional information; making a purchase; giving feedback; asking for coupons; requesting sales promotion materials; or entering a contest or sweepstakes—all on their own time, from their own homes or offices, and with few distractions. The use of credit cards and the availability of multiple quick-and-easy contact options have made interaction and purchase immediate and, most importantly, interactive.

Employing Correct Media Tactics

It's no longer necessary for IMC to depend only upon traditional advertising vehicles to reach the intended target audience. Modern IMC is about using any type of communication vehicle to reach the target audience.

It's impossible to develop a relationship if the target never sees the message. Students of advertising often think only of traditional advertising vehicles when deciding what media to use in developing their IMC programs. The options are so much more diverse than that. The IMC media grab bag also includes public relations, direct marketing, sales promotion, the Internet, and—new to the media mix—alternative media sources such as guerrilla-marketing and viral-marketing tactics, to name only a few.

The focus in IMC is on getting a coordinated message out to the right target via the best media. The advertised message must appear in the right place at the right time, no matter how unusual that "place" may be. If the target can see it or hear it, it is a potential advertising vehicle. It doesn't matter if it's a bathroom stall, the sidewalk, athletic wear, a T-shirt, a shopping cart, a shopping bag—everything has message potential. The message can be scrawled on a curb, dropped from the sky, or communicated through product placement on television or in a movie. This kind of advertising is known as **guerrilla marketing** or use of **alternative media**. The role guerrilla marketing plays is small compared to that of the promotional or traditional mass-media vehicles, but it is no less important. Although traditional media vehicles are where the majority of advertising is still placed, the times are a-changin', and traditional vehicles might not be the best place to find the target.

If the message doesn't reach target audience members where they are, the budget is wasted, and, unless it is utterly unique, the product will not gain enough acceptance to survive in a cluttered product category. The increasing cost of mass-media advertising makes the old hit-or-miss ways of advertising obsolete. The message must be placed in those media that research has proven are seen or used by the target audience on a regular basis. The media that ought to be used will depend on the target, the objectives or goals that need to be accomplished, and the overall strategy.

Building Brand-Loyal Consumers: The Long Road to Loyalty

For decades, the middleman—the retailer—has successfully silenced communication between buyer and seller. IMC removes this barrier by encouraging consumers to actively participate in communication with the seller.

Individually targeted buyers can order products built to their individual specifications, make suggestions, and/or give feedback about a product or service or a customer service initiative. This two-way dialogue between buyer and seller solicits brand loyalty by allowing the consumer to receive a product tailor-made to his or her needs, and function as a major contributor to ongoing product and corporate development. *Brand loyalty* means that the target will not only favor the advertised product or brand over all the others in the category, but also do this reliably, building the lasting, long-term relationship that the seller needs in order to increase brand equity or become the product leader in any one category.

By concentrating communication efforts on a specific group of individuals, advertising efforts develop an approach that consistently and effectively speaks to the target's needs. Message development based on a target's needs, wants, and special interests sets a product or service apart from its competition, and is the basis for an effective creative approach.

Creating an Interactive Relationship

It took a long time for today's product and corporate leaders to understand that it is less expensive to retain old customers than it is to constantly look for new ones. Communication tactics used in an IMC approach shift communication efforts away from the traditional mass-media monologue to a dialogue between buyer and seller. This approach builds a relationship by allowing the target to give feedback, discuss ideas, and register complaints as an involved consumer.

Building a relationship between buyer and seller is a necessary precursor to building a brand-loyal consumer. Brand-loyal consumers require less advertising effort, and this leads to rising profit margins.

Relationships are built on dialogue. One feature that distinguishes IMC from traditional advertising efforts is that advertising speaks *at* a group of individuals, through mass-media vehicles, about perceived problems or special interests, while IMC speaks *to* (or with) a single individual about his known problems or special interests.

Brand Development and Image

Because today's consumers are exposed to hundreds—if not thousands—of diverse advertising messages on a daily basis, it is important that a product or service have a personality, or *brand image*. A *brand* is a product's identity: its name, symbol, and image that distinguish the brand from others. A brand's name is something the consumer trusts based on her past history with the product. If the product tastes the same, works the same, or fits the same every time the consumer buys, she no longer spends time thinking about or looking for a replacement. This is brand loyalty.

Brand value is the sum of every experience the consumer has—not only with the product, but also with the company that makes the product. Are the sales associates courteous every time the target enters the store? Do delivery drivers drive cautiously and make deliveries at times that don't inconvenience consumers? Is the product always as fresh as the advertising says it will be? These are the type of influencers that affect brand image. Every experience between the seller and the target will affect the brand's image and brand equity.

All communication efforts should work to anchor or position the brand's identity and image in the target's mind. If the brand's image mimics that of the consumer, it creates a tie that binds the product to the consumer's lifestyle. A reliable brand offers reliable results and will be the first product the target thinks of, and recognizes, when purchasing. With all the similar brands available in any one category, the goal is to make the brand a familiar face to the consumer among a crowd of strangers.

Today, IMC has resurrected the relationship between buyer and seller by recreating an environment of consumer-focused communication efforts. IMC's ability to strategically deliver a consistent message to the right audience, through the correct media, is crucial to the successful implementation of an IMC creative series.

The Visual/Verbal Voice of the Message

Advertising is more than a creative idea: it is the end result of months of planning and strategizing. Advertising encapsulates a study of the product or service, the competition, and the target audience into an effective and coordinated business and creative strategy.

The results seen on television or in print media are just a small part of the business of advertising. At its most basic, advertising is a process that reacts to the client's or marketer's business needs by finding a creative way to sell a product or promote a service.

Traditional advertising is no longer the most strategically effective way to reach a media-blitzed, often apathetic audience. To reach today's savvy and educated consumer with the right message requires a message that relates to the target's life experiences, reflects the target's image of him or herself, and is repeated enough to develop an identity or relationship with the target.

It is important that all pieces in an IMC creative series have a consistent *visual* identity and send a consistent *verbal* message that is easily recognized as the tone, or voice, of the product or service. The visual/verbal identity must talk the talk and look the part consistently from media vehicle to media vehicle. This is not to say the ads are repetitive—that would be boring—but they do need to have some kind of tie that binds them together visually, such as the layout style, typeface, headline style, color, or spokesperson or character representative.

The bottom line is that every communicated experience should look and sound familiar. The ability to strategically direct a cohesive message to the right audience, through the correct media, is crucial to the successful implementation of an IMC creative series.

The Promotional and Media Mix

The ability to reach the targeted audience using the best promotional and media mix available is another of IMC's many strengths. The **promotional mix** includes public relations, advertising, direct marketing, sales promotion, the Internet, and any alternative media vehicles.

Communication efforts are often directed at different audiences, each requiring its own message and promotional mix. Determining which combination of promotional vehicles to use often depends on the target's overall knowledge about the product or service. For example, those who know little about a brand will need a different promotional mix than will those who are more regular users.

The **media mix** breaks the promotional mix down into specific media vehicles such as newspaper, magazine, direct mail, and so on. The media mix can be either concentrated or assorted. A *concentrated* media mix places all advertising efforts into one medium. An *assorted* media mix employs more diverse media. Like the promotional mix, the type of media mix employed will depend on the budget, on the overall objectives for the ad or campaign, and on the target audience and their degree of brand knowledge and loyalty.

Let's take a brief look at a few of the major players that make up the promotional mix that we will be studying in more detail later in this text:

1. Public relations
2. Advertising (including newspaper, magazine, radio, and television)
3. Sales promotion
4. Direct marketing
5. Internet and viral marketing
6. Guerrilla marketing
7. Personal selling

PUBLIC RELATIONS

The job of *public relations* is to give a product or service news value. The most common form of information distribution is issuing a news release, but news conferences and interviews are also useful. Such exposure is often free, but it is not always guaranteed. Information sent to local news outlets is not always picked up and used, and, when it is, the news staff often rewrites content. Not all forms of public relations rely on the ability to generate news; others, like event sponsorships or brochures, are paid for, have guaranteed message content, and occur on a predetermined schedule.

Strategically, public relations can be used to inform, to tantalize, or to build curiosity around a product or service launch; to deliver testimonials; or to whet the consumer's appetite for upcoming promotional events. Public relations can also be an effective way to announce events or repair a damaged reputation.

ADVERTISING

Advertising can be defined as a paid form of nonpersonal, mass-media communication in which the sponsor of the message is clearly identified. Advertising uses persuasion to sell, inform, educate, remind, and/or entertain the target about a product or service. The term is often used to generically describe all forms of marketing communication. In reality, it covers only communication appearing in print media, including newspapers and magazines, and in broadcast media, including radio and television. Known as a mass-media vehicle, advertising can reach a large, less-targeted audience. And because it must be paid for, media placement and message content are guaranteed. Advertising is still the best choice for building brand awareness and developing brand image.

SALES PROMOTION

Sales promotion uses incentives or motivators as an enticement for consumers to buy or use a product or service. Typical incentives are coupons; rebates; samples; contests; sweepstakes; buy-one-get-one-free offers; and premiums such as T-shirts, pens, pencils, and calendars, to name just a few.

Sales promotion incentives can generate interest, and are best used for new product launches or "try me" opportunities, or when attempting to resurrect an aging brand.

DIRECT MARKETING

Direct marketing, also known as *direct response*, employs such media vehicles as direct mail, catalogs, infomercials, and telemarketing. Because direct marketing uses databases to reach an exclusively targeted audience, it is one of the best ways to talk to the target on an individual level and induce an immediate response. The availability of credit cards, toll-free numbers, order forms, and websites makes purchasing from home convenient, fast, and easy. Both sales promotion and direct marketing are considered *promotional vehicles*, and are great ways to build brand awareness and encourage purchases.

THE INTERNET AND VIRAL MARKETING

The *Internet* allows the target the opportunity to gather information or shop from the comfort of home, at a time when he is exposed to fewer distractions. Products can be purchased online, and targets can seek out additional information interactively through chat rooms with other product users or by talking one-on-one with customer-relations or technical representatives.

Viral marketing, the newest form of Internet word of mouth, is a great way to build brand awareness and to reach a large number of consumers. Viral marketing uses interactive and/or entertaining Internet advertising, often delivered via e-mail or secondary websites, to inform and "infect" targets with enough interest about a product or service to visit the host website. The success of viral marketing depends on each receiver passing the interactive message along, "infecting" a friend or family member with information about that particular site. Viral advertisements can take many forms, but the most common include innovative and/or entertaining video streams or audio, interactive games, and text messaging.

GUERRILLA MARKETING

Guerrilla marketing refers to the use of any clean, printable, and innovative surface that can be used to deliver a message (or similar use of an event). Surfaces appropriate for guerrilla marketing campaigns include, but are not limited to, sidewalks, transportation vehicles, parking meters, building sides, and bathroom stalls. These unique media vehicles often reach the target audience more effectively than advertisements in print or broadcast media, so advertising efforts and costs are often minimized, while maximum exposure is achieved. This nontraditional approach looks at the demographic, psychographic, behavioristic, and geographic profile of the target audience and determines whether traditional media will, or will not, reach them.

PERSONAL SELLING

Since this text deals exclusively with consumer promotions and personal selling is usually found in corporate environments, it will not be discussed in detail here. But as a member of the promotional mix, it is worth mentioning. Personal selling is face-to-face selling between a buyer and a seller, the ultimate interactive relationship. However, its very one-to-one nature makes it very expensive, relegating its use almost exclusively to the corporate environment.

In choosing the most appropriate media mix for reaching the target, the point is to know the target: where she is and what she sees or hears. Employing alternative media like the Internet, or viral or guerrilla marketing techniques, opens up a whole range of communications possibilities. The right media mix for the client's product or service might include any of the following: newspaper or magazine articles; remote radio broadcasts; outdoor boards; banners; transit advertising, including both interior and exterior options, on bus sides or taxis; small airplane banners; building signs; caps and cups; messages stuffed in the pockets of new garments; grocery-store receipts or packaging, or window or in-store displays; table tents; posters; shopping bags; bill or credit-card-statement stuffers; freestanding inserts; text messages; home pages; and banner ads or pop-up ads. These are only a few of the alternative media options available for use in an IMC campaign. The target and the product determine which ones are the most appropriate for an individual campaign.

Evaluation

Evaluating the results of traditional advertising efforts was fairly easy: Did we realize a **return on investment** (ROI)? Very basically, ROI is determined by how much money was spent on advertising versus how much money was made.

Agencies use evaluation techniques to determine if all goals or objectives for the IMC campaign have been met. If they were, great—they keep doing what they're doing. If not, it must be determined what outside or inside influences got in the way—such as competitors' advertising, the use of an incorrect message, a failure of the target audience to see or understand the message, and so on.

Evaluation can be a rejuvenator or an annoyance. There are many who feel the evaluation techniques used in IMC are inadequate and do not accurately assess results. However, as it stands right now, evaluation is the best indicator of what worked, what should be used again, what should be given a rest, where additional attention needs to be directed, and what needs to be changed, in order to accomplish the overall objectives.

IMC is designed to make money, but additional ROI is not enough: survival in today's competitive market requires more than a strong profit margin. For this reason, it is also important to determine such things as brand awareness, how the target views or positions the product or service against leading competitors in the category, and smaller but no less important factors such as the quantity of new contacts made, the number of responses resulting from direct mail efforts, or the number of participants in the most recent sales promotion, to name a few.

Everything Is Done on a Budget

After discussing everything a successful IMC campaign must do, it's important to look at how much it costs to deliver a message or series of messages to the consumer.

An advertising budget can best be described as a bank with very little money in it. Marketers determine how much money will be deposited, and agencies determine how the money will be distributed and spent on items such as research, creative, production, and so on. Because the bank is limited, agencies must be sure monies are spent on media that will reach the target with the correct message, effectively eliminating waste.

Dissecting the Differences between Advertising and IMC

Traditional, or mass-media, advertising uses conventional print and broadcast media such as newspapers, magazines, radio, and television to get a message across to a mass audience that may or may not be listening. Because the messages are general rather than personalized in nature, this sort of advertising does not build a relationship with the target audience, and it takes longer to build brand loyalty.

Successful relationships require nurturing, a component missing in traditional advertising efforts. Without dialogue, information can only travel one way, as a monologue from a seller to an often passive and distracted buyer.

With all that being said, when pure message is all that needs to get out, traditional advertising methods are still the best way to build awareness or influence consumer attitudes about a product or service.

Traditionally, advertising has always taken a lead role, with public relations, sales promotion, and direct marketing used as support media. IMC, on the other hand, analyzes the various options available and chooses only those that will most effectively and consistently reach the target audience. *Advertising is no longer a marketer's first—or even best—media option, and oftentimes is not used at all.*

IMC differs from traditional advertising in the way it chooses media, uses databases to talk to individual members of the target audience, tailors messages to the target's self-interest, and creates consistency between advertising pieces via layout and message delivery.

IMC is everything traditional advertising methods are not. IMC is about communicating the client's message, or the key benefit of the product or service, both consistently and cohesively. It's about developing an image that is recognizable to the target no matter what medium it appears in.

Traditional advertising knows the target audience; IMC knows the targeted individual and uses a message that relates specifically to that audience member's needs or wants. Unlike traditional advertising, IMC vehicles can be personalized to speak to one person within a target group, or to other shareholders such as employees, retailers, or tradespeople.

Media choices are based on the target's lifestyle, and IMC messages appear in media vehicles the target is sure to see and use. The brand's overall image should be expressed consistently in the choice of creative strategy and message, as well as being reflected in the product name, logo design, packaging, price, and overall layout design. No internal or external customer interaction point should be overlooked. These images will further reflect the image and reputation of both the consumer and the store where the product can be purchased or the service can be used. In many cases, traditional advertising methods do not coordinate these elements, sending multiple or unrelated messages to the target. IMC strategically coordinates these elements, both inside and out, into one consistent brand image targeted to a very specific audience.

In IMC it is important for the marketer or client to build a relationship with prospective targets. Today's marketers focus on a customer-driven approach, where research determines customer needs and then, with the customer's input, develops a product to satisfy these needs. The Internet has taken customer-driven product development one step further by enabling custom-made products for individual consumers.

Today, IMC has resurrected the relationship between buyer and seller by recreating an environment of consumer-focused communication efforts. IMC's ability to strategically deliver a consistent message to the right audience, through the correct media, is crucial to the successful implementation of an IMC creative series.

Who Drives the IMC Machine

Marketing begins the advertising process with the need to sell a good or offer a service. The American Marketing Association (AMA) defines *marketing* as "an organizational function and a set of processes for creating, communicating and delivering value to customers and for managing customer relationships in ways that benefit the organization and its stakeholders." But I think the best definition as it applies to advertising is one by marketing strategists Al Ries and Jack Trout that states, "Marketing is simply 'war' between competitors."

A **marketer** or *advertiser* is the seller of a product, who provides a good or a service for money. In advertising the marketer is known as the *client*, and clients

Brian Starmer

hire advertising agencies to market, sell, or promote their products or services to the buying public.

To develop a competitive advantage, marketers and their agencies will appeal directly to the needs, wants, and image of their target. To be successful, their product must be better than (or be perceived as better than) that of the competition. In IMC, extensive research (covered in more detail in chapter 2) and the use of database marketing make determining behaviors and needs easier.

THE ROLE OF ADVERTISING IN SOCIETY, ECONOMICS, AND POLITICS

Advertising Drives Trends and Social Values

Advertising, along with art, music, television, fashion, and movies, forms part of the voice of American—and, thanks to the Internet, global—pop culture. Advertising messages affect not only society but also the economy, culture, and political system within any free-market system.

Advertising is a powerful force in developing societal values and defining who we are as individuals. It is what most people know about a business and its products. Amounting to over $36 billion in expenditures in 2006, advertising touches our lives thousands of times each day, making it one of the most powerful informational and educational tools available. Yet ads do more than educate us on a product's or service's features and benefits. Advertising sells self-image and lifestyle, as well as shaping our views on success, family, and social acceptance.

The messages and imagery used in advertising define social ideologies and cross cultural boundaries when consumers assimilate products into their lives. Slogans become part of everyday vocabulary, and manufactured trends and fads dictate what we wear, drive, eat, and listen to. The very existence of advertising satisfies individual demand by placing a multitude of same, similar, or new and unique products into the hands of consumers. These choices allow consumers to select the products that best match their lifestyles and fulfill their financial, social, and psychological needs and wants.

With that said, critics blame advertising for contributing to the erosion of societal values, the increase in childhood obesity, and the continued propagation of stereotypes against women and minority groups.

Marketers, on the other hand, wholeheartedly endorse the benefits of advertising, believing it validates the development of new products and the reinvention of old ones. Healthy competition among products brings variety to the marketplace, and not only lowers prices but also offers a range of prices among competing products. Advertising creates jobs, improves the standard of living, subsidizes the news media, and can be used to deliver public service announcements.

Today, over $350 billion per year is spent on advertising worldwide, to educate the public about thousands of products and services and to help differentiate competing products. But is the consumer reading, viewing, or listening to the advertised message? With all the new options that help the consumer edit out advertising, it might seem as though advertising's time has come to evolve or die. This might be a bit melodramatic. It is unlikely that advertising as a sales and promotional tool has breathed its last, since consumers both want and need products that are good investments and social validators.

It is difficult to predict how advertising will evolve in the future, but evolve it will. Economically, we need advertising to move products through the marketplace. Socially, we need advertising to tell us what's hot and what's not, and what product has the best features, value, and performance evaluation.

The Effect of Advertising on the Economy

Conservative market conditions create conservative consumers, who are more likely than ever before to comparison shop before making a purchase. During economic downturns, advertising should concentrate on issues important to the consumer—

such as price; value; and what the product or service brings to his life, and how it will fulfill his immediate needs. Keeping the channels of communication open by encouraging consumers to call in, or log on, for additional product information or tips will offer an extra amount of customer service, which is critical when consumers are making product decisions.

From an economic standpoint, a brand that continues to advertise during economic downturns increases visibility, strengthens consumer confidence, and builds or strengthens its place in the product category.

Arguably, without advertising there would be little economic growth. Without information, consumers would not be able to recognize products, make informed choices, or engage products. When the economy is good, advertising can spotlight a brand, setting it off from the competition. During economic slowdowns, advertising helps a product from being eliminated by competitors.

Economists differ on the economic impact of advertising. Many believe that advertising has a positive impact because it encourages purchasing, increases demand, and, as a result, strengthens the economy. A competitive environment and a strong economy encourage product development, which, in turn, leads to lower prices and better quality products. It is also believed that by encouraging purchases, advertising increases the number of products sold, resulting in lower production costs and thus a lower price.

Economists critical of advertising believe advertising to be cost-ineffective, thus contributing to the costs of products and services. They believe advertising does nothing more than separate one product from the pack of competitors, in effect doing little to stimulate the economy.

Spending by both advertisers and consumers is affected by local, national, and international events such as hurricanes, high energy prices, terrorism, war, and rising interest rates, all of which can impact budgets and personal income. Economic slowdowns directly affect consumer confidence and, as a result, consumer spending habits. When the economy is up, consumers spend, and they often spend more than their take-home pay or accumulated savings and investments.

Other events, like World Cup soccer, the Olympics, and major political elections, increase advertising spending and in turn help the economy. Smaller, locally advertised events, such as annual festivals, bring much-needed tourist dollars into a community, boosting the local economy and affecting sales at local restaurants, retail establishments, and hotels.

Beyond influencing consumer purchases and stimulating supply and demand, advertising also subsidizes the media by providing working capital. For most media, advertising revenue is a major source of income. Conventional broadcast radio and television rely solely on advertising. Magazines and newspapers often make their money from both advertising and subscription revenues.

The Reaction of Advertising to Recessionary Conditions

During an economic recession, it is not uncommon for marketers to cut or eliminate ad budgets. The theory is that consumers have less money and so will spend less, and spend it more wisely. Cutting or eliminating budgets may seem like the right thing to do, but in reality those who continue to advertise come out ahead in the long run. The best course of action is not to eliminate advertising altogether, but to cut back on the amount of advertising placed. Marketers need to think creatively and consider reducing the size and amount of their print advertising, or moving prime-time television buys to cable or less expensive time slots.

History has proved that those who continue to advertise come out of recessionary periods ahead of their competitors. Recession-period goals are simple: increase both short- and long-term profits and increase market share. To do this, marketers need to concentrate on branding, customer service, and defining a brand's features and their benefits. During recessionary times, consumers are not as focused on their wants as on their needs. Generic messages do not touch the target's needs.

Recessionary studies conducted over the last fifty years suggest that reducing or eliminating advertising budgets during recessionary periods can have immediate and long-term effects on both sales and profit margins. Failure to continue advertising during economic downturns can jeopardize present and future profit margins, and will make it necessary to do more advertising later on to rebuild image, brand loyalty, and equity. Marketers who hold out and hang on to their sales goals during economic downturns will be rewarded with increased sales and profits when things improve. Those who remain silent will not only lose both market share and consumer loyalty; they will also take a backseat to those who continue to advertise. A marketer who maintains or even increases her current level of advertising stands out from the silent voices of competitors, which makes her advertising more memorable.

Advertising that continues during economic downturns gives the product, service, or corporation an air of stability in unstable times, and allows the advertiser to shout the product's or service's benefits into the minds of consumers with increased memorability.

There are opportunities for marketers during recessionary times. A marketer who retains a strong advertising presence is in a position to build his customer base and capture business from less aggressive competitors, resulting in a strong foundation for future growth during recovery.

Additionally, an economic downturn is a great time to introduce a new product. This is a great opportunity to be first in some type of product development. Market conditions are slow and the competition is weak, making product parity less likely for some time.

Continued advertising during a recession is probably most important to small businesses. Although cutting or eliminating advertising is the most painless way to save money in the short run, it has the most long-lasting effects, often affecting employee salaries, hours, and eventually jobs.

Savvy marketers realize it is less expensive, especially in bad economic times, to retain a brand-loyal customer than to continually search for new ones. Brand-loyal consumers require less advertising to ensure repurchase than do new customers, who need to be repetitively reminded about a product's features and benefits. Marketers who don't panic and stay with their advertising agencies can call on their expert knowledge about their products or services to analyze consumers' recessionary needs and reposition their products or services to meet those needs. Not only will this build equity and market share, but it will also create brand awareness and increase a brand's image.

Political Consequences of Advertising

Political Influence

You can't talk about advertising without talking about political influence, political interest groups, and public opinion.

Various government agencies regulate many products and the companies who sell them in order to protect the public interest. Products that are deemed harmful or dangerous in some tangible way often come under scrutiny, first by consumer groups and then by the U.S. government. In order to protect the public, the government may pass laws that prohibit or restrict a product's manufacture and distribution, or that ban advertising efforts to certain groups and/or in particular locations.

When the government steps in to regulate product distribution, development, or advertising by placing political pressure on businesses with the threat of legislation, this is known as *political influence*. In opposition to legislative efforts, big business can respond by building political support through political contributions; funding opposition programs; filing lawsuits; and employing lobbyists.

A **lobbyist** is a person hired to influence the legislative process. A lobbyist not only puts pressure on political leaders to hear her employer's side of an issue, but, if successful, she can also protect a company's position and message in the marketplace.

Some of the most influential lobbyists are associated with the tobacco and pharmaceutical industries.

Historically, advertisers such as the tobacco industry who do not respond to customer or government concerns lose both brand equity and profits in the long run, and/or they become subject to heavy-handed regulations. One good example of this is the Master Settlement Agreement, imposed upon the tobacco industry, which focused specifically on issues facing young consumers. This agreement severely restricted where tobacco ads could appear and what they could say, and it permanently banned sponsorships at athletic and concert events. Additional restrictions banned the sale of tobacco products to teenagers, prohibited the use of cartoon characters in promotional efforts, regulated the size of the package, outlined where samples could be distributed, and required health issues to be clearly represented on packaging. Beyond the federal regulations, many states attempt to control the continued purchase of tobacco-related products by attaching high taxes and by banning their use in public places.

In spite of the regulations the tobacco industry faces in most traditional media vehicles, that is not the case with the Internet. Young people, the very ones regulations attempt to protect, are easily manipulated with intrusive and creative ads that prey on their consumer vulnerabilities. It is not unusual for marketers to use games, contests, and prizes to entice children to their websites. Often the rules for entering or participating require children to enter the e-mail addresses of friends and family. Regulators are working on varied levels of restrictions, but as yet the Internet has no regulations against targeting children.

Another corporate giant currently under the governmental microscope is the pharmaceutical industry.

Pharmaceutical companies spend over $4 billion annually on *direct-to-consumer* (DTC) advertising, or advertising that skips the middleman (in this case the doctor) to talk directly to the consumer. The United States is one of the few industrialized nations to allow DTC prescription-drug advertising. The pharmaceutical industry believes that advertising is important because it informs consumers about new drugs and educates them about health risks and possible side effects.

Critics, on the other hand, believe that these same advertising efforts are strictly profit-driven and encourage consumers to ask for only the most expensive drugs, which they may or may not need, and that this drives up health costs. Critics also believe that DTC advertising is so engaging to consumers that it interferes with the doctor-patient relationship by giving consumers an apocryphal degree to self-prescribe.

The explosion of pharmaceutical advertising is a direct result of a reevaluation by the Food and Drug Administration (FDA) of its rules concerning television advertising. Prior to 1997, pharmaceutical ads appearing in both print and broadcast forms had to include lengthy and detailed copy about the drugs discussed. You can still find this type of detailed copy in magazine ads. But in 1997, the FDA removed the requirement for this lengthy copy in broadcast ads, now requiring only that an ad make a statement detailing the risks and encouraging consumers to seek additional information at the manufacturer's website or from their personal physicians.

In response to these relaxed restrictions, the House of Representatives Ways and Means committee has been asked to look into the economic impact of consumer advertising on drug spending. Current advertising efforts have gained attention from other legislative groups and from health-care organizations because of their effects on consumer spending and because of the dangers of self-diagnosis.

Additionally, the FDA has introduced a bill that would ban drug companies from advertising any new drug for up to three years and require packaging to inform consumers that the drug is new to the marketplace.

The FDA does not sanction individual pharmaceutical advertisements, as many consumers believe. It does not have the power to prescreen for content. The best it can do is request compliance. The FDA cannot impose a fine or any other type of punishment if a company does not comply, although most companies do. The FDA can, however, defer the matter to the judicial system for further action. The FDA's biggest hammer comes from the negative publicity investigation brings, and its effect on both image and sales.

As consumers advocate for lower prescription-drug costs by appealing to their state and federal representatives, they are combating the pharmaceutical companies, who are using their substantial financial clout to fight legislation every step of the way.

Other industries under scrutiny include the fast-food industry, which is currently feeling both consumer and regulatory pressure to prepare healthier products and to reduce the amount of advertising aimed at children. Early self-regulation will assist the industry in escaping additional consumer and governmental pressures and allow it to begin erasing the stigma of single-handedly fattening children with unhealthy portions and trans fats.

Also feeling the heat of scrutiny is the entertainment industry, with respect to the current level of explicit and violent programming directed at children.

The Political Process in Advertising Revenue

The advertising industry is often used as a communications scapegoat. It is accused of promoting consumerism and materialism, and of using its large budgets to bias the content of the news and entertainment industries. However, the ultimate goal of advertising has always been to give a product an image the consumer can relate to. This image reflects value to both the product and the consumer. The growth of advertising in the United States over the last hundred years or so has been phenomenal. Advertising spending in the late nineteenth century was only $30 million per year. By the early twentieth century, new products such as electricity, rubber, and certain foods sent advertising revenues soaring to $600 million per year. In modern times, annual spending on advertising in the United States has risen to over $120 billion. The increased spending is most commonly associated with the rise of *consumerism*, or increased purchasing power due to rising salaries, availability of credit cards, the use and popularity of increased leisure time, and the invention of the shopping mall.

The first governmental agency to promote the idea of consumerism was the U.S. Commerce Department, established in 1921 under the guidance of President Herbert Hoover. The Department of Commerce encouraged businesses to advertise, both internally and externally, and helped determine the best ways for them to deliver merchandise to consumers; suggested ways to improve parking and transportation situations; and provided guidance regarding how to attractively display merchandise. The goals were to reach consumers and make it easy for them to buy.

Today, the stability of the economy relies more and more on the increased spending habits of citizens. For example, in an attempt to boost consumer confidence and avoid a recession after September 11, President George W. Bush urged Americans to go out and spend money—by taking a trip to Disney World, for instance. This economic mindset is in stark contrast to the mentality of earlier generations. President Franklin D. Roosevelt, in his inaugural address in 1941 envisioning the nation's possible entry into World War II, ruminated on the fact that American democracy was strong "because it is built on the unhampered initiative of individual men and women joined together in a common enterprise." As a unifying force for stability in the marketplace, individualism is no longer as strong as the mob mentality of consumerism.

The Internet and Consumer Political Influence

Before the Internet, politicians reacted to issues partly as a result of public pressure. Today, the Internet supplies the public with information, blogs, and e-mails that help individuals spread the word about political issues and any number of infractions by corporations. This movement of information has put more power for change into the hands of the public.

Socially, the Internet allows an individual to voice her concerns, hear the opinions of others, make a decision, or demand a response from politicians or corporate America.

A recent opportunity to see the power behind public opinion occurred following the 2007 Super Bowl. Several ads that aired during the game had used suicide themes, not just to sell their products but also to entertain. In order to stand out from the crowd, today's advertising spends more time entertaining and shocking than informing. A shock message from General Motors had featured a robot who was so depressed over losing his factory job that he jumped off a bridge. Volkswagen had shown a man so despondent over world affairs that he stepped out onto the ledge of a building. Washington Mutual had shown various bankers working their way toward the edge of a roof in response to the company's free-checking offer. CareerBuilder.com had shown a group of office workers diving off a cliff to avoid a training seminar.

Even the makers of beer ads, which were once known for focusing on noncontroversial social gatherings, jumped on the "shock-message" bandwagon. A Bud Light commercial that ran during the 2007 Super Bowl, for example, showed a man hitting his friend in the head with a rock during a game of rock-paper-scissors. Coors Light showed a man at a wedding, beheading an ice sculpture of the bride in order to chill his beer. This type of shock-advertising imagery is meant to attract the valued 18-to-39-year-old viewers, and to keep them from avoiding or ignoring the message.

Not surprisingly, this type of imagery attracted the attention of the American Foundation for Suicide Prevention and the American Psychiatric Association, who successfully put pressure on both General Motors and Volkswagen to stop running the controversial spots: both marketers complied. (Washington Mutual and CareerBuilder.com reported no adverse publicity surrounding their advertising.)

There are those who believe these responses were nothing more than a reflection of a "politically correct" world. Right or wrong, reactions of this type have to be taken into consideration if public opinion matters at all to a marketer.

Issues that continue to be hot political topics include violence on television; advertising to children; and the portrayal of women in advertising, which some perceive to be negative and characterized by an inappropriate sexual provocativeness.

Using Advertising to Sell a Candidate's Features and Benefits

Advertising can bring a political candidate's message to the people, making it a very influential part of the democratic process. More than $467 million was spent on various campaigns during the 1998 elections.

Political advertising allows candidates to express their positions on important issues, respond to opponents' positions or criticisms, and educate voters on who they are, where they have been, and what they believe in. Political ads that run on television can take advantage of its mass-media status to reach voters both locally and nationally.

Political advertising is a great example of what's known as *image advertising*, leading critics to believe that television ads sell image rather than presenting a discussion on the issues.

With advertising becoming more global every day, it must be able to sell a product to an individual's needs and wants more than ever before. These needs and wants are similar across cultural boundaries. The universal appeal of some campaigns has been able to successfully negate cultural differences. Advertising not only promotes political campaigns, it has become intrinsic to them. It is not unusual for political candidates to turn to popular culture to make a point voters can relate to. Never was this more obviously used than when Walter Mondale asked Gary Hart, in a 1984 presidential primary debate, *"Where's the beef?"*—a slogan made popular by the Wendy's fast-food chain—to suggest his campaign lacked substance.

Regulatory Agencies: Who's Watching Advertising's Every Move?

Throughout the history of advertising there has always been deceptive or misleading advertising. In the United States this issue came to a head in the 1930s, when the government began regulating advertising. These actions and the subsequent legislation have made advertising one of the most heavily regulated forms of free speech.

Increasingly, efforts to regulate advertising are looked upon by many in the industry as an intrusion, or a way to squash freedom of speech. Advertising agencies believe the issues can be handled better through self-regulation than through federal regulatory agencies. Self-regulation keeps creative options open; once federal regulations are in place, a product's voice can be all but silenced.

The success of self-regulation over federal regulation is again being tested, in the area of children's advertising and the fast-food industry. A 2004 report issued by the Keiser Foundation suggested that food advertising to children played a major role in the growth of childhood obesity in the United States.

Self-regulation is the advertising industry's way of avoiding any additional federal regulations, and it creates a more controlled form of self-policing. By binding advertising efforts to a self-prescribed code of ethics, the industry attempts to inhibit bad taste, misrepresentation, and deception, both visually and verbally, as well as any unfair depictions of competitors' products. Yet marketers continue to push the envelope with more and more sexually explicit advertising, the continued use of stereotype images depicting women and minorities, and beefed-up advertising to children.

All organizations associated with advertising have some form of ethical code that they adhere to. The advertising industry has four groups associated with self-regulation issues: The American Advertising Federation, the American Association of Advertising Agencies, the Association of National Advertisers, and the Institute of Outdoor Advertising. These groups act as the overseers of the advertising industry, focusing on any deceptive or misleading practices, puffery, child- and drug-related issues, and stereotyping imagery, to name just a few of their concerns.

Beyond what advertising agencies do, various media groups often establish their own codes of ethics. Newspapers and magazines for example, regulate advertising copy and can refuse to run sexually explicit advertising or ads for controlled substances such as alcohol and tobacco. Radio and television companies make an effort to investigate brands before airing, in an attempt to prevent any controversial material from reaching the public.

The tobacco industry was one of the first to be federally regulated, with the banning of all television and radio cigarette advertising. This resulted from advertising efforts aired in the 1950s and 1960s, where it was not unusual for tobacco companies to sponsor television programs geared toward children, such as *The Beverly Hillbillies* and *The Flintstones*. Characters from *The Flintstones* were not only used in the early 1960s as spokespersons, but were actually shown using the product.

The Federal Trade Commission (FTC) is the federal agency that acts as a business watchdog for consumers. The FTC does not act on behalf of an individual consumer, which would be the job of the Better Business Bureau (BBB), but it can react to repetitive consumer complaints against individual businesses. The Federal Communications Commission (FCC) regulates the broadcasting and telecommunications industries.

THE FEDERAL TRADE COMMISSION

The FTC regulates advertising in the United States. The FTC's role in advertising is to make sure that advertised messages are not deceptive or overly "puffed up," and that all claims are fair and accurate and can be substantiated. The terms *unsubstantiated claims* and *deceptive advertising* describe ads that include information, or purposely omit information, with the intention of misleading the consumer or interfering with his ability to make a purchasing decision. *Puffery*, although not illegal, makes a claim that cannot be substantiated, such as "the best," "greatest tasting," and so on.

Advertising that makes claims such as "nine out of ten dentists recommend," or "tests prove," must be able to prove any statements or back up any research. The term *misleading information* refers, not to the research, but to the "spin" of that research. For example, if research finds that a slice of bread has fewer calories than competitors' slices, this conclusion must be based on nutritional findings, not on the fact that the advertiser's bread was sliced more thinly than the other brands.

Overall, the FTC can do little more than act as a consumer watchdog. For one thing, the downsizing of the FTC has made it difficult for them to keep up with traditional regulatory efforts within the United States. In addition, the authority of the FTC is limited. For example, the FTC fined four marketers of weight-loss drugs a grand total of $25 million, claiming they knowingly made false assertions in their advertising; yet the FTC had no power to remove the products from store shelves. So they did the next best thing: they used the media to effectively reach consumers and at the same time generate negative publicity.

The ineffectuality of the FTC in properly governing advertising has caused state attorney generals to step up their efforts to regulate both local and national advertising campaigns. All this scrutiny has resulted in additional regulation by a larger number of government agencies.

Adding to their already-heavy workload, the FTC must actively keep up with the ever-growing number of alternative media outlets available to marketers. The Internet, for example, has opened up a global market, not only to major corporations but also to a legion of small companies that have the same global reach but may have less knowledge about FTC regulations. Any problems or concerns resulting from local complaints will be relegated to the proper state, county, or city agency. For more information on FTC practices you can go to their website, www.ftc.gov.

THE BETTER BUSINESS BUREAU

Probably the regulatory agency with the most clout is the BBB. This watchdog agency is responsible for investigating and exposing unethical or misleading advertising by local businesses. Their proximity to the problem and the parties involved puts them in a good position to resolve the problem. Traditional problem-solving tactics include persuasion, publicity, and, as a last resort, legal action. It is important to note that the very people it watches, such as local and national businesses and the media, also subsidize local and national branches of the BBB.

THE FEDERAL COMMUNICATIONS COMMISSION

The FCC regulates television, radio, and the telecommunications industry. The FCC has the authority to issue or revoke broadcast licenses, but has no authority over content. The FCC is also responsible for any international services developed within the United States.

The FCC's role is slowly diminishing, as technology exposes the public to greater amounts of broadcast material via the Internet, cable stations, and satellite radio. Fighting for its survival, the FCC would love to get its regulatory hands on these alternative media sources. More information on the FCC can be found on their website, www.fcc.gov.

Other governmental watchdogs include the FDA, in charge of regulating packaging and labeling; the United States Postal Service, which regulates the direct mail industry; and the Bureau of Alcohol, Tobacco, Firearms and Explosives, which watches over the distribution and sale of alcohol and tobacco products.

Editorial Control

Advertising is the economic pulse behind mass media. It is the job of mass media to deliver a definable audience to advertisers. Mass media works not only for the people, but also for the advertisers, who pay not only for advertising space, but also for positive press and for popular news that will not depress the reader or viewer out of a buying frame of mind.

Some advertisers have so much clout today that newspapers and magazines may

Stick With the Clear Winner.

Don't be left in an uncomfortable situation. Band-Aid Liquid Bandage covers small cuts and scrapes discreetly when a regular bandage just won't do.

Your Seal of Approval

Get Results Fast

BAND-AID
LIQUID
BANDAGE
Invisible, Anywhere Protection

Amanda Sherrod

think twice before publishing anything negative about major advertisers. Negative press can result in advertisers withdrawing their advertising or threatening to do so. For this reason, it's not unheard of for newspaper and magazine editors to choose content that does not adversely affect or negatively portray advertisers, their main source of revenue.

Advertisers may also react negatively when controversial content makes them fear the stigma of *tainted sponsorship*. A good example of tainted sponsorship occurred recently when radio personality Don Imus made derogatory comments about the Rutgers University women's basketball team. Advertisers, including General Motors, American Express, Sprint Nextel, GlaxoSmithKline, and others, announced they would not be associated with the show in the future. Results like this often occur because sponsors associated with a program do not want the negative press associated with controversial comments or actions to attach itself to their products or corporate image.

Mass-media advertising is still a powerful advertising tool. Its wide coverage gives corporate giants a strong economic arm; and, as much as they are loath to acknowledge it, they need mass media not only to get their message out to the public, but also to manage their economic clout and their political influence.

The Ethics of Advertising

Advertising ethics, according to Bruce G. Vanden Bergh and Helen Katz in their book *Advertising Principles: Choice, Challenge, Change,* can be explained in the following way: "Ultimately, advertising ethics depend to a large extent on your beliefs about the purpose of advertising and your view of consumers. If you believe that consumers are rational, skeptical, and self-aware, and accept that advertising is designed to persuade the audience to think, feel, or act in a certain way in order to increase sales, then you will probably not find advertising inherently unethical . . . On the other hand, if you think that consumers are completely innocent with regard to the ads they see, hear, or read, then you are likely to find advertising, by and large, to be unethical with its promises of leaner bodies, cleaner homes, faster cars, or money-saving credit cards."

Advertising to Children

Today's modern media machine has set its sights on our children. Considering them a consumer group, marketers are looking to develop the purchasing habits children will use throughout their lives, a strategy they refer to as "building cradle-to-grave brand-loyal consumers." The way it works goes something like this: if the child loves the product, she will use it into her teens and twenties, buy it for her children in her middle years, and continue to purchase it for her grandchildren.

In order to better understand how children perform as consumers, advertising agencies are hiring clinical psychologists and cultural anthropologists to interview and study children between the ages of 6 and 19.

Psychological research, for instance, has shown that nagging is a great way to boost sales. Research has also shown retailers how to exploit this natural childhood tendency, and has identified the types of parents (mostly divorced) who are most likely to respond positively to nagging techniques. Products that top the "nag" list include fast-food visits and home-video rentals.

Children are capable both of purchasing and of influencing parental purchases, making them a viable advertising target. Strategies aimed at children (ages 2–7), tweens (aged 8–12), and teens (aged 13–19) have not only increased but have become much more sophisticated than ever before. Catchy jingles and recognizable characters are used to promote products to children. The majority of products advertised to children are foods, and most of this advertising is for unhealthy products like nutritionally poor snack foods.

Researchers divide the children's market into three distinct areas: primary, influence, and future. The *primary market* refers to the more than $28 billion a year that children actually spend. The *influence market* refers to the possible $500 billion spent by parents on products as a direct result of influence by their children. The *future market* refers to the unlimited dollars children will spend on products throughout their lives.

Until recently, advertising appearing during children's programming was directed at parents. Today's sophisticated marketing efforts appeal directly to children, who at an early age identify themselves as consumers. But research has concluded that preschool-age children in particular have difficulty differentiating between commercials and regular programming. Confusion results because (1) children tend to believe what they are told, (2) characters from current programming are present in commercials, and (3) children do not understand that advertising can often be misleading or untrue until closer to the age of 8.

Older children understand the concept of advertising but not the repercussions surrounding wants and needs. Advertising's message to preteens and teenagers is social acceptance; this image is built into the product's message, and thus into its overall image. These cynical yet inexperienced consumers are vulnerable to advertising because they are responsive to peer pressure and are still developing their values and roles as consumers.

Advertising tactics in this area concentrate on developing small commandos who will lead successful assaults on unsuspecting parents, who are incapable of warding off the slick pitches of Madison Avenue. No matter how much parental control is available, they cannot overcome the more than $12 billion a year marketers spend to educate our children on the value of materialism. Marketers deliver the knockout blow to parents by offering children incentives such as playgrounds, collectible toys, contests, and club memberships to visit their fast-food restaurants or purchase their products.

WATCHING ADVERTISING DIRECTED AT CHILDREN

Although advertising directed at children lacks any meaningful type of regulation, several U.S. regulatory agencies and consumer groups have pointed out that advertising appearing during children's programming is heavily weighted toward fast food, soft drinks, candy, and cereals; advertising for healthy foods is around 4 percent. What's a healthy product to do when fast-food chains spend over $3 billion a year reaching out to children? The answer is to create an advertising balance, ensuring that an equal number of ads appear for healthy foods and junk food—thus creating educated consumers, who can in turn make educated decisions.

The FCC is responsible for television advertising appearing during children's programming, and for the amount of advertising allowed in each program. In 1990 Congress passed the Children's Television Advertising Practice Act. Its focus is on limiting the amount of advertising included in children's programming. Advertising is currently limited to no more than twelve minutes per hour of children's programming on weekdays and ten and one-half minutes on weekends. A study by the Kaiser Family Foundation found that programming aimed at tweens age 8–12 contained the most food ads, followed by programming aimed at children age 2–7.

Marketers and their advertising agencies believe that the policing of children's programming for content is best left up to the parents. However, the enormous number of advertising vehicles and the sophistication of today's marketing techniques make keeping up with the psychological and social hype difficult. Controlling access to media is more difficult than it sounds. The Consumers Union reports that children see anywhere from 18,000 to 30,000 commercials a year in school, on clothing, on billboards, in computer and video games, and in movies and on television, to name just a few vehicles. As a result, they become very savvy consumers at an early age, choosing favorite products and influencing family purchases.

OUR KIDS ARE GETTING FATTER

Over the past decade, childhood obesity has become an important public-health issue. A 2002 study published in the *Journal of the American Medical Association* found that over nine million American children were overweight. This figure is three times what it was only two decades ago.

Childhood obesity is considered a marketing-related disease. Politicians and consumer groups are not pointing the finger directly at advertising as a potential cause of childhood obesity, but rather as a contributing factor to choices made by children concerning food and drink. Additional contributors to childhood obesity, beyond advertising, include a sedentary lifestyle in which American children watch between four and five hours of television a day. Companies who ignore government and consumer concerns could end up like the tobacco industry—battling the courts, Congress, state legislatures, and school boards for control of their message and choice of media vehicles. Self-regulatory efforts need to come in the form of improved nutritional content in foods and a reduction in the amount of advertising aimed at children.

In tune with recent concerns about childhood obesity, companies like Kellogg's have announced that by the end of 2008, their advertising efforts for any cereals that do not meet a new set of self-imposed nutritional standards will no longer target children under 12. Advertising for those products that don't meet these new standards will target an older demographic. Kellogg's also reports that they currently do not advertise to children under the age of 6.

Reflecting possible future legislation, the FTC in 2007 asked the food, beverage, and fast-food industries for information on their current marketing efforts aimed at children. Specifically, the FTC wants to find out more about efforts concerning in-store promotions, packaging, event sponsorships, and various product-placement efforts.

The FCC, on the other hand, is taking a "wait and see" attitude toward regulation, while the food and beverage industries consider self-regulatory measures. Many, like Kellogg's, are already voluntarily working with government agencies and consumer groups to advertise and deliver healthier products. Several are going a step further, working with media and government officials to develop guidelines to assure self-regulation.

Health concerns, due in part to advertising, have led to political, medical, and legal concerns for marketers, as the issue of childhood obesity has expanded beyond U.S. borders to become a worldwide public-health issue.

ADVERTISING IN U.S. SCHOOLS

Most marketers see education-directed marketing as a cost-effective and memorable way to develop cradle-to-grave brand-loyal consumers.

Whether outside or inside the school building, advertising bombards school-age children. Buses, hallways, and lunchrooms buzz not only with children's chatter but also with sponsored radio programs; scoreboards, billboards, bulletin boards, public telephone booths, urinals, and book covers all announce corporate sponsors.

Corporate America is allowed to "sponsor" education because state-supported funds for education are declining. Funding issues create an ongoing motivation for educators to search for and use corporate-sponsored materials, which are often free or available for a small fee. This type of sponsorship, known as **sponsored educational messages** (SEMs), may include cash contributions, time, expertise, equipment, multimedia kits, videos, software, or other available teaching aids, all of which are good examples of cradle-to-grave advertising economics.

Taking advantage of this captive audience, corporations use the educational environment to build brand loyalty, to introduce or test new products, to deliver samples, and to encourage trial and eventual purchase. Not surprisingly, corporate materials used in the classroom are often biased toward the contributing sponsor.

Some of the top corporate marketers employing educationally directed marketing techniques are Anheuser-Busch, Kellogg's, Upjohn, Dow, and Procter & Gamble.

Another way in which marketers reach beyond children to parents and others is by sponsoring old-fashioned school fund-raisers. Students may be required to collect labels or UPC codes from products, which can then be redeemed for cash or school-based supplies. These school-endorsed fund-raisers require students to sell the product. In return, schools or school-supported organizations receive a percentage of each sale.

ADVERTISING CAN MAKE A DIFFERENCE

It's important to point out that advertising doesn't have to be all negative, and that it can positively alter children's behavior. Companies in the alcohol industry, for example, use a percentage of their advertising expenditures to warn about the dangers of drinking and driving. The milk industry's advertising efforts have increased the amount of milk kids consume, providing further proof that children are in fact directly influenced by what they see and hear.

The Effects of Advertising on Women

Children are not the only group negatively affected by advertising. Advertising geared toward women often pushes the boundaries of good taste and walks a fine line between what is sexy and what is pornographic. Stereotypical images used in advertising often define society's values, attitudes, prejudices, behaviors, and beliefs, and shape how both men and women look at, and live in, society. Critics speculate that because of this, image-based advertising has played a role in the increase in violence against women.

Practically all sexually based images sell. Typically they portray unrealistic, unattainable, and unhealthy images of women and their roles in society. These visual icons of professionalism, domestication, or sexual impossibility are never ugly, old, overweight, or poor, and they are rarely disabled or unhealthy, either mentally or physically.

Young women who grow up believing in the imagery they see in advertising often develop negative body images, which often leads to low self-esteem, depression, excessive dieting, and, in the most extreme instances, eating disorders.

NO MATTER HOW MUCH THINGS CHANGE . . .

Over the last fifty years, the domesticated image of women in the media has slowly been sexually manipulated. Also over the last half-century, the characterization of women in advertising has evolved to reflect women's diverse roles in society. Their move from traditional role of wife and mother has coincided with the sexual manipulation and exploitation of female images used in advertising. Women appearing in advertising are often decoration, with no obvious relation to the product or service. When portrayed as central characters, they appear sexier than their male counterparts, with a woman typically exuding a more alluring persona.

Sexually explicit advertising specifically targeted to young girls can be traced back to the deregulation of children's programming in the mid-1980s. Resulting advertising efforts used gender roles, appearance, and sexual imagery to sell both young and older women on what a "perfect" woman should look like.

INDUSTRIES THAT EXPLOIT WOMEN

The fashion industry's use of sexually suggestive ads featuring wafer-thin models is one of the biggest exploiters of women in advertising and promotion. Not only do these ads not promote a healthy mental and physical lifestyle, but they also do not represent actual women across the globe. The size 0 or 2 models used in advertising do not accurately depict the average American woman, who is a size 14.

Italy, home to some of fashion's biggest names and shows, is leading the way in changing fashion's image of perfection. In the United States, there is pressure to remove gaunt models not only from magazine covers but from all fashion advertising, based on a belief that these changes will reflect a more reality-based image of women in society.

Fashion imagery can be subtle or brash, and can push the limits of social acceptance. Calvin Klein, most notably, always pushes the envelope, treading the fine line between fashion novelty and what is often considered fashion pornography. In a 1995 campaign, Klein featured child-aged-looking models, portrayed in a sexually provocative way, in print, outdoor, and electronic media. Outraged at the imagery, parent groups, retail outlets, child-welfare groups, and religious groups attacked the campaign. An eventual investigation launched by the Federal Bureau of Investigation (FBI) found that models used in the ad were all above the age of 18, some as old as 29.

Images used in advertising for Bennington often portray both social and controversial issues. Examples of such imagery have included a nun kissing a priest, and a man dying of AIDS. Dolce & Gabbanna shocked the fashion industry when it chose to use imagery that possibly represented a gang rape. Critics wonder how this type of negative, violent, and/or demeaning imagery can sell fashion. Although provocative, it sends a very negative message about a woman's appearance and relationships between men and women.

VISUAL/VERBAL IMAGING IS POWERFUL

Campaigns directed at women should reflect a realistic view of their ideas of personal beauty and inner strength. Mental and physical well-being is not a political or cultural issue, but a personal choice whose multifaceted options should be reflected both visually and verbally in an ad's message.

The visual/verbal images used in advertising define gender roles and propagate stereotyping by setting the rules for behavior and appearance, for both men and women.

Imagery used in advertising needs to look beyond the physical beauty of the target; it should attempt to reflect character and values.

Dove is changing how women and the media see beauty. Dove's "Celebrating Curves" European campaign is changing how beauty is defined, by changing not only how the beauty industry defines a beautiful woman, but also how women define themselves. Dove's repositioning campaign focuses on the inherent beauty all women possess despite their shapes or sizes. Traditionally, advertising for products within this category featured women younger than the targeted market and in perfect physical shape, reflecting a nontraditional user. Dove ultimately chose to use real women in their ads rather than the traditional "anorexic-looking" models. This cutting-edge approach not only broke new ground by featuring women within the targeted age group, but also featured those most likely to need, and subsequently use, the product. Dove's advertising is meant to empower women by exposing the beauty within and by explaining that conventional beauty is not something you settle for, but something you celebrate.

Unilever, makers of Skippy peanut butter and Lipton teas, has joined the growing number of businesses refusing to use excessively thin models or actors in their advertising. Their decision is an attempt to fight the growing number of eating disorders among teenage boys and girls.

A WOMAN'S PURCHASING PROFILE

Women make up over 50 percent of the population and influence the majority of all purchases. Women are known to bond with brands that do not use a heavy-handed promotional approach. Women respond to details and unique approaches. Research is important when making product decisions, and thus women rarely make impulse buys when it comes to major purchases. Women are quick to adapt to changing social conditions and make many purchases based on word of mouth, received through their networks of friends, family members, and colleagues. Advertised messages targeting the female consumer should relate to her lifestyle and, when possible, make use of testimonials to make an important point. Messages should also include relevant details, and they should avoid puffery, to which she will respond negatively.

Understanding Advertising Agencies

Volney B. Palmer established the first advertising agency in Philadelphia in 1841. Initially, advertising agencies did little more than secure ad space for their clients in local newspapers. Expanded services beyond media buying, including research and creative, were introduced in 1869 by N. W. Ayer and Sons, making them the first full-service, commission-based ad agency.

Today's advertising agency is still multifunctional and supplies expertise beyond just the basic services. Diversification in the areas of business, creative, technology, and promotion is what helps agencies keep up with, and evolve within, an ever-changing market environment.

Madison Avenue in New York has long been the home of some of the biggest advertising agencies in the United States, but not necessarily the best agencies. Successful agencies do not need to be in New York or even large cities; many are scattered across the country, often in midsized cities, and have fewer than 100 employees. A Madison Avenue agency, on the other hand, can employ thousands.

The Departmental Structure of Advertising Agencies

An agency's infrastructure is comprised of multiple and disparate departments made up of business- and creative-savvy professionals in research, media (planners and buyers), account services (executives and planners), creative (art directors and copywriters), production, and traffic. Agency size will determine the number of departments.

Once a project is received by the agency, it will move from department to department until it is ready to be produced or printed. Each department is made up of specialists in a particular area, who concentrate on developing and producing advertising that sells. One of the first departments to become involved in an ad's development is research.

Researcher

In order for creative to be successful, art directors and copywriters need information on the product, the target, and the competition. Advertising without information cannot reach the target with a message that piques his interest, and successfully encourages him to buy. Understanding a product's strengths and weaknesses and the opportunities that can influence purchase are critical to the success of advertising. Once a campaign is released, agencies will often require additional research to evaluate results.

Media Planner

The *media planner* develops the media plan and determines what vehicles will reach the target and best deliver the message.

Media Buyer

Building a relationship with the consumer is more difficult in today's media maze. Audiences are fragmented, and media options are fragmented; there is no single straight line anymore from advertiser through media to consumer. Understanding who and where the targeted consumer is and what the message is, and determining what combination of media vehicles will reach the right audience with the right message, is the *media buyer*'s job.

Account Executive

The job of the *account executive* (AE) is to work as a liaison between the client and the agency. The AE is in charge of developing the creative strategy, defining budgets, and working closely with the creative team on direction. The AE is also in charge of securing approvals and setting deadlines.

Account Planner

Building relationships with the consumer is the *account planner*'s job. Using research to represent consumers' needs and wants, the account planner ensures that the message represents their point of view (as opposed to the AE, who brings a business mentality to the task of representing the client's needs and wants).

Creative Director

This title probably varies the most across the country; but basically this person is the boss or team leader. He or she handles administrative and/or management functions and is most often involved with television or high-profile projects.

Art Director

Job titles range from junior through senior levels. *Art directors* are the workhorses of the advertising agency; they have their hands in everything. On any given day, an art director could be working on newspaper, magazine, point-of-purchase, direct-mail, or television advertising, for any number of products or clients. The person in this position needs to know a lot about the creative process, from conceptual development through photo shoots and production.

Copywriter

These very talented and creative team members focus on writing ad content, and like art directors they have a range of titles. *Copywriters* on any given day can find themselves brainstorming and/or writing copy for multiple media vehicles, and even more diverse product types.

Production Artist

A *production artist* works closely with the art director assigned to the project, using a computer to assemble an ad's multiple elements (such as headline, copy, visuals, and logo) in order to prepare them for printing.

Traffic Manager

The traffic department works as the liaison between creative and account services. They are the drill sergeants of deadlines, and they keep the work flowing through creative by setting up work schedules and watchdogging the approval and production processes.

How Advertising Agencies Work

Advertising agencies control the flow of information between the client and the consumer, and/or wholesalers and distributors. Agencies can offer specialized or generalized services; they can be small, medium, or large in size, and local, national, or international in scope. Size can be measured on the basis of billings, number of employees, or both.

The advertising process begins when a marketer introduces a new product or service, or for one reason or another ends or modifies her relationship with her current agency by putting her entire advertising account, or a select portion of the available business, up for review, asking several agencies to pitch creative ideas and business proposals.

Alternatively, an agency can withdraw its services to a client. Reasons may include a deteriorating relationship, compensation-based issues, or the lure of a more lucrative account that is up for review.

Additionally, agencies may retain clients through formal presentations, referrals, community involvement, and good old-fashioned networking.

Until recently, the agency-client relationship was a stable one that often lasted for years. Today, clients change agencies regularly and often have more than one agency on the payroll. In instances such as this, the several agencies might handle different portions of the business, different geographical regions, or different phases of a campaign. Once an agency secures a piece of business, it will assign an AE to handle the business and act as liaison between the agency and the client.

Advertising Development and Delivery Options

Marketers have three ways in which to develop and deliver advertising. The first is to create and staff an in-house advertising department. In-house agencies are made up of company employees who work in a company-supported environment.

The second is to employ the use of a full-service advertising agency, made up of experts who can take a product from development through production and shipping. For a fee, full-service agencies use their expertise to coordinate advertising and marketing efforts; to deliver the right message to the right target; and to do follow-up evaluations of campaign results.

The third option is to use independent suppliers on a per-job basis. This option allows marketers to use the services of many different suppliers, who specialize in specific areas such as creative, media buying, production, and so on.

Seeking Help or Expertise through Independent Contractors

Marketers and agencies alike will often go outside the in-house or agency environment by hiring independent contractors known as *freelancers* when (1) the marketer's or agency's company is too small to have a full staff, (2) experts in a specific area are needed, or (3) the volume of work exceeds what can be handled by current staff.

FREELANCERS

Freelancers are independent creative, media, or research contractors hired by advertising agencies or marketers on a project-by-project basis. Specialists in copywriting, art direction, illustration, photography, and graphic design are the most commonly used types of freelancers.

CREATIVE BOUTIQUES

When art directors, copywriters, graphic designers, and/or illustrators set up a communal business, it's known as a *creative boutique*. Here creative specialists sell their individual talents on a freelance or individual-product basis to advertising agencies and marketers.

MEDIA BUYING

Much like creative boutiques, *media buying* services began with a few experienced media people working together to broker large media buys at a discount based on volume. These companies resell to agencies or marketers at a reduced price.

INTERACTIVE AGENCIES

The *interactive agency* is staffed by creative technological wizards who specialize in designing and developing Web-related projects.

GUERRILLA MARKETING

Guerrilla-marketing agencies develop unusual or unique "WOW" campaigns that use untraditional tactics to create interest, attract a target's attention, or add excitement to an event.

Other independent suppliers to an agency or marketer might include printers, production studios, or research developers. Other specialist agencies that will be discussed in detail in later chapters include public relations agencies, direct response agencies, and sales promotion agencies.

The Role of Advertising in Business

Marketers look for agencies that can help them reach their targeted consumer or business-to-business organization with the right message, placed in the best media environment.

Consumer advertising deals directly with the public, whereas **business-to-business advertising** focuses on wholesalers or distributors. This text will deal exclusively with consumer-based advertising.

Due to its broad focus, consumer advertising can be broken down even further into local, national, and international advertising. Local advertising focuses on a particular area or city, often uses local events in promotional efforts, and lets consumers know where a product or service can be purchased in their area. Its main job is to encourage purchase now. National advertising promotes a more generic type of product, such as shampoo or paper towels, that can be purchased anywhere in the country. The main job of national advertising is to build awareness and promote or reinforce brand loyalty. International advertising represents American products worldwide or brings internationally produced products to the United States.

The Buying and Selling of Services

Clients can compensate agencies by means of several different mechanisms, including commission, fee/commission, retainer, incentive, and ownership.

COMMISSION

Agencies used to charge their clients a standard 15 percent commission on media buys and ad production. Today, agencies are gravitating more toward what's known as a *straight fee*. A straight fee allows agencies to charge their clients for all services rendered. This change was a direct result of clients asking agencies to provide more than just media buys and creative execution.

FEE/COMMISSION

Very simply, a *fee/commission* combination is when the agency charges its clients a monthly fee for any and all services performed and also collects the standard media commissions.

RETAINER

The *retainer method* allows agencies to charge by a preset amount of time, and no media commissions are paid to the agency by the client.

INCENTIVE

The *incentive method* is tied to a campaign's success. Compensation is predetermined based upon successfully meeting specific goals.

OWNERSHIP

The newest form of billing is taking stock in a brand; here, agencies are actually awarded a percentage of sales. This form of billing allows agencies to partner with their clients, allowing them to retain and eventually profit from their creative work. This is in stark contrast to the traditional time-sheet models, where time spent on a client's individual project or campaign was documented for later billing, and all creative rights were surrendered to the client. Revenues in this model are based solely on the successful marketing of the client's product.

WORK BEYOND ADVERTISING AGENCIES

The newest way to present a message to the public is known as freelance advertising.

Freelance advertising is a public competition sponsored by the marketer where individuals enter their ideas for the company's product or service. This turned out to be very successful for products like Doritos, Dove, and Chevrolet, some of whom presented their winning consumer ideas during the 2007 Super Bowl.

SUCCESS COMES AT A PRICE

And finally, we can't talk about advertising without discussing awards and legendary campaigns. Both marketers and their agencies win big when all communication vehicles are creative and entertaining, and linked by the same tone of voice, layout style, and copy style. All of these factors make it is easier for consumers to navigate the message and become intimate with the brand, and these elements all build brand equity and brand loyalty.

Awards

Success breeds awards, and some of the best worldwide advertising recognition awards include the One Show, the ANDY, the ADDY, the EFFIE, the Design and Art Direction (D&AD) Awards (United Kingdom), and Cannes Film Festival; and placement in *Communications Art Advertising Annual*. Some of the better-known media specific awards are:

- OBIE Awards. Presented by the Outdoor Association of America for the best in out-of-home media.
- Athena Awards. Presented by the News Association of America for the best newspaper ads of the year.
- Radio-Mercury Awards. Determined by category and given for the best radio spots of the year.
- ECHO Awards. Presented by the Direct Marketing Association for the best direct-marketing efforts in various categories.
- Clio Awards. Given at the international level for the best in such categories as radio and television, print, outdoor, and package design.

Agencies and Marketers Work to Create the Best of the Best

Awards are great, but legendary status that endures is better. *Advertising Age* selected the following campaigns as the twentieth century's ten best:

1. Volkswagen: "Think Small," Doyle Dane Bernbach, 1959
2. Coca-Cola: "The Pause That Refreshes," D'Arcy, 1929
3. Marlboro: the Marlboro Man, Leo Burnett, 1955
4. Nike: "Just Do It," Wieden and Kennedy, 1988
5. McDonald's: "You Deserve a Break Today," Needham, Harper & Steers, 1971
6. DeBeers: "A Diamond is Forever," N. W. Ayer & Son, 1948
7. Absolut Vodka: the Absolut bottle, TBWA, 1981
8. Miller Lite Beer: "Tastes Great, Less Filling," McCann-Erickson Worldwide, 1974
9. Clairol: "Does She . . . or Doesn't She?" Foote, Cone & Belding, 1957
10. Avis: "We Try Harder," Doyle Dane Bernbach, 1963

Cultural integration and the globalization of advertising require advertising agencies to decide whether they will be communication specialists or generalists.

The decision will affect whether they concentrate efforts on developing advertising or developing IMC; whether they will offer a full range of services or use freelancers; whether their services will reach out to local, national, or international clients; and whether they will offer both interactive and traditional media and creative services, or just traditional broadcast and print.

Advertising agencies of the twenty-first century must understand, and be able to execute, creative and media buys that cross cultural and international boundaries. Addressing cultural differences in both media and message development increases the reach of a product or service.

CHAPTER TWO

WHERE DO WE FIND THE ANSWERS?

RESEARCH AND TARGETS

Travel Through Time
with East Tennessee's
History

All members can now take pleasure in a relaxing exhibit of East Tennessee's
art history with perks that non members cannot be a part of.

Be a Member of History.
KNOXVILLE MUSEUM OF ART

Michelle Hanson

There is no such thing as a Mass Mind. The Mass Audience is made up of individuals, and good advertising is written always from one person to another. When it is aimed at millions it rarely moves anyone.

—Fairfax Cone, of Foote, Cone & Belding, quoted in John O'Toole, 48.

WHERE TO BEGIN: RESEARCH

Research is all about solving problems and answering questions. It helps determine whom advertising efforts need to talk to, what needs to be said, where it needs to be said, and what the competition is saying. Marketers and advertising agencies utilize information gathered in very different ways. Marketers use research to determine sales direction, whereas agencies use research to help with message and media decisions.

In order to develop sales direction, marketing research needs to look at the product, the consumer, and any competitive data, in order to assist with the definition and dissection of current market conditions.

There are two types of developmental information available to researchers: primary data and secondary data. **Primary data** is not preexisting—its acquisition requires that original research be conducted through techniques such as surveys, interviews, focus groups, observations, or experiments.

Secondary data is already available and can be found from external sources like the public library, websites, trade associations, and the U.S. Census.

Data, especially primary data, helps marketers identify and build brand-loyal consumers. Successfully building and maintaining loyalty begins with a thorough understanding of the targeted consumer's behavior patterns, values, beliefs, and lifestyle. To help develop this knowledge further, marketers are adding anthropological, sociological, and psychological research to their traditional data-mining tactics.

Anthropology uses observation to determine and understand customer behavior, and evaluates the level of emotional connection between products and consumer beliefs and values. Sociology looks at consumer values and beliefs and how they are manipulated and shaped by family, friends, media use, and cultural values. Psychology looks at human behavior and how a product or service fits into a consumer's lifestyle, and how it will be viewed and used.

This type of research allows advertisers to see readers and viewers as people they are informing rather than consumers they are selling to, and it will ultimately assist them in delivering a message that is a reflection of both the target's image and that of the brand.

ADVERTISING RESEARCH METHODS

Advertising research uses both primary and secondary data to develop a consumer profile and determine message and media development. Research must be translated into a creative idea that touches consumer interests, values, beliefs, and lifestyle.

There are five categories of advertising research: developmental research, strategic research, conceptual research, pretesting research, and posttesting research.

Developmental research looks at the target to determine personal and lifestyle characteristics. *Strategic research* helps determine concept, product image, target profile, visual/verbal message, and the most appropriate media vehicles. *Conceptual research* is used to determine the target's receptiveness to various creative ideas at the concept stage. *Pretesting research* roots out any potential problems with creative ideas before a campaign begins; it is often conducted by means of focus groups, to test elements like copy before an ad appears on the air or in print. And *posttesting research* is used to evaluate results after a campaign runs.

The development and organization of research take place before any ad is designed or any media purchased. Primary research vehicles can be either qualitative or quantitative in nature. When agencies want to find out what is going on in the marketplace, they will use qualitative research. **Qualitative data** are collected by means of open-ended questions that can be distributed through interviews, convenience polling, and focus groups. A **focus group** gathers together a representative sample of the target audience, usually ten to twelve people, who will use or try the product in a controlled environment. Information gathered in a session can be used to determine such things as creative development, product design, or the effectiveness of product attributes.

The negative aspects of using a focus group are cost and size. Because focus groups bring participants together in a social atmosphere, participants' responses may be affected if individuals feel the need to go along with the more outspoken members of the group, or to express opinions that make them look good to the group.

Quantitative data, on the other hand, is comprised of closed-ended or controlled surveys, where participants must choose their answers from a preselected set of responses. There are two types of surveys: formal and informal. **Formal surveys** include closed-ended questions where participants choose from a predetermined set of responses such as "strongly agree," "agree," "strongly disagree," and so forth. **Informal surveys** are open-ended, allowing participants to give their opinions.

Surveys need not be completed in a sterile office environment; they can be conducted at malls and shopping centers, in parking lots, online, over the phone, or through the mail. Surveys are often subject to bias based on the way a question is written or asked. An interviewer's body language can also bias results, as can the attempt to use a small number of respondents as a representative sample. Researchers should not concentrate their efforts on only one type of research technique, but should consider using multiple options. Ultimately, the types and forms of research employed will depend on what needs to be accomplished, the product or service to be advertised, and the target audience.

Other research methods might include one-on-one personal interviews, consumer observation, and cohort analysis.

A *one-on-one personal interview* is a great way to ask in-depth questions and receive in-depth answers from an individual about his or her experience with a product or service. IMC's consumer-oriented approach makes the use of personal interviews a great method for building a relationship and learning more about the target's needs and wants. The downside is that personal interviews are expensive, take a great deal of time, and can result in unintentional interviewer bias.

Consumer observation techniques can also be very helpful. Observations may take place, for example, in a grocery store, where an observer might study how much time consumers spend comparing prices or examining labels.

Another research technique (discussed in more detail in the next section) is *cohort analysis*. This developmental research technique breaks the population of consumers down, segmenting them into demographic, geographic, behavioristic, and/or psychographic groups, or *profiles*.

SEGMENTING TARGET MARKET PROFILES

Segmenting means dividing consumers into specific categories or groups that are made up of individuals with similar characteristics and/or lifestyles. The more that is known about who will be using a product, the easier it will be to target the message directly to those people.

Segmenting allows marketers and agencies to focus message development on areas of particular relevance to a group, such as product variety, price, or media use, with attention to such factors as a product's distribution in places the target is likely to frequent. Let's look at four of the most common ways to segment a target audience.

Demographics breaks down personal attributes such as age, sex, income, marital status, professional status, occupation, education, and number of children. For example, a blue-collar worker and a college graduate might have different goals and limitations. They use and are exposed to different media and often require different messages.

Geographics defines where the target lives, and how that affects who he is, how he thinks, his goals, and his limitations. Geographics can be broken down by region, by state, by city, or by ZIP code. Where a person lives often influences the type of product she will buy and where the product should be advertised.

Once a target group has been broken down demographically and geographically, each segment can be given a brand identity, just like a product. In his book *The Clustering of America*, Michael J. Weiss discusses forty different lifestyle segments, including "Blue Blood Estates" (upscale and affluent); "Black Enterprise" (African American middle class); "Grey Power" (retired and living somewhere in the Sunbelt); "Blue-Collar Nursery" (working-class, young and married, with children); and "Pools & Patios" (prosperous and in the "empty nest" phase of life).

Behavioristic profiles look at why a person buys: is it loyalty, social acceptance, brand name, or need?

Psychographics looks at personal attributes that affect the target's lifestyle, such as cultural, emotional, social, health-related, and family-related characteristics, as well as hobbies and overall beliefs. Psychographic considerations affect how the consumer will view the product and advertising.

When determining the correct target audience for a client's product or service, any one, or any combination, of the above segmentation practices can be used. Demographic and geographic information, for example, can be combined to determine if the target audience has sufficient disposable income available to purchase the product. Likewise, a combination of psychographic and behavioristic data can be used in the creative-development stage.

Using psychological characteristics helps the creative team with message development and media planners with choosing the best media vehicles to deliver those messages. For example, if a psychographic group loves dogs, it is likely they also read dog magazines and visit dog-related websites.

Studying the consumer most likely to buy a product or use a service allows both marketers and agencies to understand:

- How consumers think and feel about, and select among, various products and services.
- How family, friends, culture, and the media influence consumers.
- How consumers make purchasing decisions.
- How consumers think about products whose purchase is rationally motivated or need-based (e.g., food, shelter) versus products whose purchase is emotionally motivated or want-based (e.g., jewelry, technology).

The Values and Lifestyles (VALS) questionnaire is a tool that marketers and agencies use to try and pinpoint a consumer's psychographic profile with a greater level of accuracy. VALS can be broken down into two separate typologies, VALS 1 and VALS 2.

First developed by the Stanford Research Institute in 1978, VALS 1 deals with demographic and psychographic information by breaking the American consumer down into four basic consumer groups: Need-Driven (sustainers and survivors); Outer-Directed (achievers, emulators, and belongers); Inner-Directed (societally conscious, experientials, and "I-Am-Me's"); and Combined Outer- and Inner-Directed (i.e., integrateds).

Need-Driven Consumers

Need-driven consumers have a low-level income and have a difficult time making ends meet. This group can be subdivided into two separate categories: survivors and sustainers. *Survivors* include the elderly and *sustainers* are young and driven, with little disposable income.

Outer-Directed Consumers

Those falling into the outer-directed group typically live in the middle section of the country and are socially conscious. This group can be further broken down into three separate categories: achievers, emulators, and belongers. *Achievers* are leaders, and are very successful. *Emulators* are image conscious, upwardly mobile, and competitively driven. Belongers are conservative, with traditional tastes and lifestyles.

Inner-Directed Consumers

Inner-directed consumers are egotistical and self-centered. This group can be broken down into three different categories: societally conscious, experientials, and "I-Am-Me's." Societally conscious consumers are down-to-earth types who often support social and environmental causes. "I-Am-Me" types are emotionally strong, young, inventive, independent, and individualistic. An experiential consumer is an older version of an "I-Am-Me" and is interested in self-growth.

Combined Outer- and Inner-Directed (Integrated) Consumers

Integrateds are self-assured, psychologically mature, and tolerant. Integrateds are the group most likely to try new products and influence others.

In the 1980s, VALS 2 was introduced as a more comprehensive version of the original VALS 1. VALS 2 breaks the consumer profile down even further by looking at education, health, income, and need, and it focuses specifically on the consumer decision-making process.

VALS 2 segments the American population into three consumer groups: principle-oriented (holding set views); status-oriented (influenced by friends and family, etc.); and action-oriented (seeking adventure and variety).

Principle-oriented consumers are self-motivated and rely on their own opinions and beliefs. Status-oriented consumers seek the approval of others before making a decision, and then act upon those opinions. Action-oriented consumers look for variety, socially and personally, and are often risk takers.

Once consumer groups are categorized, they are then broken down into eight different lifestyle groups: actualizers, fulfillers, believers, achievers, strivers, experiencers, makers, and strugglers. Each category can be analyzed in two areas: self-orientation and resources. *Self-orientation* looks at consumer buying habits, income level, education, self-confidence, health, and need to purchase. *Resources*, or income, pertains to the rise and/or fall of consumer income as the consumer ages.

Actualizers are successful, well-off financially, and concerned with self-image. Fulfillers look for practical, durable products; they are older, and financially and personally secure. Achievers are career oriented, stable, and self-disciplined. Experiencers are young risk takers; they are easily impressed and love to spend money. Believers are traditional, with a conservative view of the world that makes them more comfortable with well-known, experienced brands. Strivers, like achievers, are successful, business-oriented consumers. However, they are financially less secure than achievers, and they seek approval from others. Makers are self-sufficient, energetic consumers. Strugglers are usually elderly and struggle to make ends meet.

The second level of segmentation is based on product benefits, and the third looks at consumer behavior. Direct marketing is a great way to use segmentation, because marketers can buy lists containing information on a consumer's personal life, allowing messages to be personalized to those most likely to buy the product or use the service.

If IMC is to successfully build a relationship and develop advertising materials that are consumer focused, research needs to take a thorough look into the lives of the target audience members. It is just too expensive and wasteful to advertise to anyone who is not interested in buying or using a particular product or service. Because IMC is intended to develop a personal relationship and build a loyal client base, advertising must talk to those most likely to buy the product or use the service.

In order to personalize a message, we need to know what media the targeted consumers are most likely to use and what motivates and interests them. The success or failure of advertising depends on whether the information gathered will help determine the following things: the type of combination of media vehicles that will reach the target audience; and the kinds of messages that will offer solutions to their problems, address their concerns regarding image or social status, or promise to satisfy particular needs or wants.

HOW ARE CERTAIN TARGET AUDIENCES CHOSEN?

It is important to find a reason a target audience needs the product or service being advertised. What does the target want that is currently unavailable? How can the product or service meet that want? What does the client's product or service offer that the competition doesn't? Who are the people who are in need of the product or service? How do they live, and where do they live? What do they buy now? What are their purchasing and media-use habits? These questions and more can be answered through target profiling.

In his book *Strategies for Implementing Integrated Marketing Communication*, Larry Percy breaks five potential target-audience groups down into two categories. Knowing where your target audience falls will determine message development and media choice.

Noncustomer groups:

1. New category users—those trying the product for the first time
2. Other-brand loyals—those loyal to competitors' brands
3. Other-brand switchers—those who have loyalty to no particular brand and will switch based on a sale or promotion

Customer groups:

1. Favorable-brand switchers—those who favor the brand but will consider switching
2. Brand loyals—those who are using the brand and will never switch

Narrowing the Target Down Further

Target audiences can be further broken down into small specialty and/or age groups. In some cases a product that never reaches mainstream popularity nonetheless has a very strong and loyal group of users. When advertising efforts concentrate specifically on keeping the attention of a small group of mostly affluent consumers loyal to one specific product, it is known as **niche marketing**. The limited number of consumers keeps competitors from entering the market or trying to copy the product, because it would not be profitable.

Target audiences can be further classified into four distinct age groups. These groups respond to different kinds of advertising. Since they have social and financial differences, it is important to keep group classifications in mind. Differentiating one target group of consumers from another is crucial; see table 2.1.

Identifying Ethnic and Influential Consumer Groups

The type of advertising used should reflect both the lifestyle and the buying habits of the targeted consumer. Different segments will respond to advertising differently and purchase differently; some will greet advertising more openly, while others will greet it more skeptically. Each group requires an approach that speaks to their lifestyle. Knowing how members of the target audience think and act, what their needs and wants are, what excites them, and what offends them makes addressing their issues and concerns easier. This knowledge helps in building a loyal customer base and allows the product or service to grow and change as the target changes.

Changes may be based on the growth of a specific ethnic group; on the aging of a target population; or on changes in the purchasing power, geographical distribution, or interests of the targeted group. No matter what the condition may be, issues associated with these changes may affect various influential consumer groups—including various ethnic groups—differently. Three of the largest influential ethnic consumer groups in the United States are African Americans, Hispanics, and Asian Americans. The baby boomers are another influential group that we will look at.

Each group, although often part of a larger target profile, requires a message designed especially for its members. Culture is an external influence that affects consumer purchasing behavior. Cultural matters comprise lifestyle, language, music, morals, art, food, religion, and more. Advertising must often address a spe-

Table 2.1.   The Four Age Groups

Matures	*Born 1909–1945*
Baby Boomers	*Born 1946–1964*
Generation X	*Born 1965–1984*
Generation Y or Millenniums	*Born 1985–present*

cific *subculture* (i.e., a culture within a culture)—for example, teenagers within the Hispanic community. Information is often defined on the basis of demographics. Brand loyalty throughout ethnic and other influential groups is higher if communication efforts use members of the target group, are written in the group's native language, and appear in print or broadcast media targeted to that specific demographic group. Let's look at how these very different markets break down.

African Americans

According to the 2000 U.S. Census, African Americans make up just over 12 percent of the population. According to the latest edition of *The Buying Power of Black America*, African Americans spend more per capita than any other ethnic group in almost all product and service categories; are traditionally very brand loyal; and have a median income of just over $29,000 and rising. Additional statistics show African American women to be the leading force behind this spending growth. More than 17 percent of African Americans have a bachelor's or advanced degree, and approximately 47 percent of African American householders own their own homes.

The African American population is expected to show a rate of increase for the period from 2000 to 2020 that is twice the rate of growth of the European American population. The median age of the population is 30, making them younger than the average American population. Nearly half are married, and over 50 percent live in the South. Community involvement plays a big role, as do women family members. Almost half of the African American population is married with no children, allowing for discretionary buying. Major expenditures include food and clothing, cars and trucks, home decor, and travel.

Non-prime-time media use encompasses 94.6 percent of the population; prime-time, 86 percent; and cable-television viewing, 71.4 percent. Radio listening is at 84 percent, newspaper readership is at 83.4 percent, and Internet use is at 48.2 percent.

Hispanics

The Hispanic market includes Mexican Americans, Puerto Ricans, Cuban Americans, South American immigrant families, and other subgroups. The 2000 U.S. Census reported the Hispanic population at just over 14 percent. Hispanics are the fastest-growing ethnic group in the United States, with 75 percent of the population under age 45. More than 55 percent of Hispanic Americans are married, and this group has the second-largest median household size overall, at 3.25 members. The median household income is $33,103, and almost 12 percent are college graduates. Most, just over 70 percent, are bilingual.

The Hispanic community is very family oriented, hardworking, and success oriented, and Hispanics as a group proudly embrace their heritage. Image is important to Hispanic consumers. Very responsive to advertising efforts, they are often impulsive buyers who are willing to try new brands, and who will switch brands to keep up with current styles, or if pop culture dictates change. Family involvement plays a major role in Hispanic life, with multiple generations often sharing the same living space. Family considerations can often outweigh individual interests. Ads appearing in Spanish are five times more likely to be persuasive. However, research is showing that more native-born Hispanics prefer to receive information in English. The most heavily purchased items include children's products, health and beauty aids, fashion, and personal electronics.

Non-prime-time media use encompasses 94.4 percent of the population; prime-time, 81.4 percent; and cable-television viewing, 69.9 percent. Radio listening is at 85.9 percent, newspaper readership is at 64.7 percent, and Internet use is at 47.4 percent. Young Hispanics, between 18 and 34, are heavy magazine readers.

The growth of Hispanic advertising is expected to outgrow the general market, tapping $5.5 billion in advertising revenue by 2010.

Bryan Starmer

Asian Americans

The Asian American population includes Chinese Americans, Filipino Americans, Indian Americans, Japanese Americans, Korean Americans, and Vietnamese Americans, among other subgroups. The 2000 U.S. Census places the Asian American population at 4 percent. Of the three ethnic groups discussed here, Asian Americans are the second-fastest-growing group and the most affluent, with a median income of $52,626. They are also the best educated, with almost 50 percent having college degrees. Asian Americans often have several generations living under one roof, making their average household size the largest, at 3.98 members.

Asian Americans are brand-conscious consumers. They are generally geographically concentrated, making them an easy and cost-effective group to reach.

Media use is less than that of the other ethnic groups mentioned here. Non-prime-time encompasses 90.5 percent of the population; prime-time, 75.7 percent; and cable-television viewing, 68.3 percent. More than 78 percent listen to the radio; newspaper readership is at 69.8 percent; and 76.4 percent use the Internet. Asian American homes are the most "wired," and represent the highest Internet use of the ethnic groups discussed here.

Baby Boomers

The aging baby boomers make up 28 percent of the U.S. population but have 50 percent of the discretionary income. This underprofiled demographic will make up 45 percent of the adult population by 2015. Baby boomers are the most affluent of any demographic segment discussed thus far, with an average income of $60,000. They hold the majority of all net worth, at 91 percent.

This market is open to new brands and is willing to try new products. They purchase 41 percent of all new cars, represent 80 percent of all luxury travelers, and account for 65 percent of all cruise passengers. As grandparents, they purchase 25 percent of all toys, and in general they spend more in virtually all categories.

As "boomers" decide how they are going to spend their retirement years, marketers are rushing to advertise products that will make them as comfortable as possible. The 50+ consumer is living longer, is more physically active, is better educated, and is more financially secure than previous generations at this age. The majority of boomers are married, 80 percent own their own homes, and 80 percent are still employed. The majority of boomers are white, with only 8.1 percent being African American, 2.7 percent Asian American, and 5.5 percent Hispanic American.

Boomers watch more TV than 18-to-49-year-olds and spend more money online than teenagers—$7 billion annually. Baby boomers routinely spend time listening to the radio and are heavy users of all forms of print. They are profuse catalog purchasers, which makes them a great direct-mail target.

Baby boomers do not see themselves as old and worn out, but rather as healthy, independent, active, and successful, and any advertising efforts should reflect that lifestyle.

TALKING TO AN OLD FRIEND

It is critical that advertising efforts never lose sight of who the target audience is, since they are the ones the advertising needs to reach and affect.

Talking to the right target audience doesn't guarantee success (which also depends on the right message and the right media), but it does highly increase the chances for success. The bottom line is that the creative team should know the target audience member so well, after deciphering the research, that they are able to address their creative efforts to an old friend.

PRIMARY- AND SECONDARY-TARGET-AUDIENCE PROFILES

The *primary target* is identified based on research as the most likely prospect to buy the product or use the service. **Secondary audiences** are influencers whose opinions the primary target audience member trusts or seeks out. Take, for example, a campaign for iPod. Advertising efforts may focus on a primary target of 15-to-28-year-olds, with a secondary audience of parents or grandparents of the primary target audience members. Messages targeted to the primary audience may focus on image and features, while advertising targeted to the secondary audience may add information on price or purchasing options.

A thorough understanding of both audiences will help the creative team determine the answers to some important questions: What do the target consumers want? Are they aware of the product or service? What will influence their decision to purchase? How will the product be used in their lives? Are they currently using a competitor's product? If so, what do they like or dislike about that product? What will it take to convince them to switch brands? Are there any major influencers, or secondary-target-audience members, who also have to be reached?

Advertising to a single target audience no longer has the impact it once had to deliver the brand's image and promise. Many purchases require little or no thought; while others, especially high-dollar purchases or products that reflect a target's lifestyle, the wish to fit in, or a desire to be the first to own, are influenced by other individuals trusted by the primary target. These individuals are known as **outside influencers**.

In his *Strategies for Implementing Integrated Marketing Communication*, Percy identifies roles an individual can play that can positively or negatively affect her own decision or another individual's decision to buy:

1. Initiator: the individual who originally considers purchasing a product or using a service
2. Influencer: an outside person (or group of people) who recommends or discourages the purchase of a product or use of a service

Cole Mauer

3. Decider: the person who ultimately determines what will actually be purchased
4. Purchaser: the individual who actually initiates the purchase or use of the product or service
5. User: the individual who will use the product or service

It's important to remember that IMC talks not to a target audience but to a single individual within that targeted audience. Every time the target considers a particular type of purchase, he assumes a mindset or plays a role. That role will determine the type of message the target receives. Initiators must be made aware of the product or service and the benefits that come with ownership or use. Influencers, such as family and friends, salespeople who may or may not recommend the product or service, or any professional influencers such as doctors or financial advisors, must understand the reason a product or service should be recommended. The decider must have the answer to the question, "What's in it for me?" before deciding whether or not to purchase. The user must not only use the product but also be willing to recommend and repurchase the product or service.

CAUSE AND EFFECT

Consumers purchase products for any number of reasons. Some need to spend time doing research before undertaking any purchase; others are more impulsive and buy based on feelings and/or immediate need.

Consumer behavior can be defined as the response to a message or visual that ignites a sense of need, want, or emotional interest regarding an attainable product or service.

Ideally, purchase decisions are made in a logical manner with the study of a product's features and an understanding of the benefits they will bring to the consumer. Satisfaction with a purchase is the ultimate outcome, with the product supplying a solution to the target's perceived problem.

Actions that affect purchase decisions include:

1. Need
2. Research
3. Purchase
4. Reflection

Need

The *need* for a product or service can be either rational or emotional. Rational needs involve life's most basic issues, such as food and shelter. Emotional needs are related to lifestyle issues, often involving image or status. Purchases made in response to emotional needs have the goal of making the target feel better or look better to himself and others.

Research

Information gathering begins with an interest in a product or service and the hope that it can fulfill a need or solve a problem. *Research* can be undertaken in any number of ways: by seeking expert or professional advice; by seeking advice from colleagues, friends, or family; by making product comparisons; or by using the Internet.

Purchase

Beyond needs and research, *purchases* can also be triggered by factors such as price, purchase options, location, color, size, and so on. The ultimate goal of all advertising efforts is to get the target to take some kind of action—such as calling, writing, coming into the showroom or store for more information, or, best of all scenarios, making a purchase. If the product or service can solve a problem for the target, normal consumer behavior is to either purchase or seek out additional information.

Reflection

Was it worth it? Remember, building brand loyalty is the ultimate goal of IMC, so the product must live up to the consumer's expectations and encourage repurchase. The more expensive the product, the more *reflection* will take place. Buyer's remorse is often an unexpected outcome, known as **cognitive dissonance.** Cognitive dissonance is the guilt or anxiety associated with decisions concerning extravagant or excessive purchases. It is the role of advertising to anticipate and alleviate these fears by addressing them prepurchase in copy or guarantees, and postpurchase via follow-up customer-service calls or surveys.

BUILDING TARGET/PRODUCT RELATIONSHIPS

Building a relationship between the target and a product or service is like building a personal friendship. On the one hand, the target must trust the product to do what it says it will, and the target must consider the product to be reliable.

On the other hand, the target will ask, "What's in this relationship for me?" The answer may be that the product or service will build or sustain personal image, increase self-esteem, address a special interest, reinforce an image of success and wealth, or create a sense of belonging. Whatever it is, it must exist and flourish within the product. There are four possible ways to build a relationship with the target:

1. Prolonged inquiry
2. Minimal inquiry
3. Customary inquiry
4. Repeat purchase, or brand loyalty

Prolonged Inquiry

Prolonged inquiry is usually associated with higher-priced products or those affecting social status. The first step is to acknowledge a need and the second step is to determine a foundation for purchase. Once the target has determined a need, he will exhaust all research options before deciding to purchase.

Minimal Inquiry

Minimal inquiry requires little or no thought or research and usually deals with everyday types of products. Without motivation or personal involvement, the target will usually select the first product she encounters that will fill her need or solve her problem.

Customary Inquiry

Customary inquiries are typical when the target has a history with the product, and thus little thought is given to or required for a repeat purchase.

Repeat Purchase, or Brand Loyalty

The *repeat purchaser*, or brand-loyal customer, knows and has developed a relationship with the product and automatically repurchases it when needed.

Agencies rely on research to assist with creative development and with evaluation. Creative-based research not only helps with message development; it also helps determine the type of individual most likely to use the product or service, and how that consumer views and will use the product or service. Evaluative research helps advertising agencies learn what worked and what needs to be reworked. It will also look at message memorability and level of persuasiveness. Because evaluative research is expensive, it is not employed very often. Success is usually measured by the percentage of sales.

It's important to understand that age, lifestyle, ethnic factors, and ethical issues can often affect how a consumer ultimately makes a decision to buy. An individual's standard of living and the way economic forces affect that standard also affect the success of advertising. Values and beliefs are expressed through the products consumers buy and the services they use. These beliefs are tested by both good and bad economic times.

When studying how consumers buy, the first thing to determine is how they think and what affects their purchasing behavior. Messages that talk directly to the consumer about his or her wants and needs; that address lifestyle; that take into account the state of the economy; and that address the motivations behind buying—such as ego, self-image, peer pressure, or other social motivations—will ultimately have the best chance of success.

CHAPTER THREE

THE MAKING OF AN IMAGE

BRANDING AND POSITIONING

Rachel Kennedy

To establish a favorable and well-defined brand personality with the consumer the (advertiser) must be consistent. You can't use a comic approach today and a scientist in a white jacket tomorrow without diffusing and damaging your brand personality.

—Morris Hite, quoted in Russ Pate, 203.

DEFINING A BRAND, ITS IMAGE, AND ITS WORTH

The AMA defines a *brand* as a "name, term, sign, symbol, or design, or a combination of them intended to identify the goods and services of one seller or group of sellers and to differentiate them from those of the competition."

Quite simply, a brand *is* the product or service. *Branding* is a product's identity and its legacy. By building a strong *brand image* for a product or service, the advertiser gives it a personality, an image, and a single voice or message. This ultimately determines how the consumer thinks about the product or service and how it stands out from the competition. The more unique the persona created, the more memorable the brand will be.

Target perception is only one aspect of a brand's image. Another key characteristic is brand and/or corporate reputation, or the ability to deliver a reliable performance from purchase to purchase. Repetitive results create repeat purchases and build brand loyalty and brand equity.

Repetitive results relate directly to product performance. Over time, the product or service that has repeatedly proved itself to the consumer creates trust and goodwill. If a product is inconsistent or cannot deliver on the promise made in the advertising and promotional efforts, it can result in unfavorable reviews or bad word of mouth—one of the most powerful forms of communication. Think about it: How many people do you talk to in a day, a week, or a month? Consumers trust the unbiased opinions given by friends, colleagues, or professionals over those they hear in advertising claims. Eventually, repetitive negative comments will discourage repeat purchases and affect brand equity.

Another way for a company to increase brand awareness is to become involved in some form of sponsorship, such as by sponsoring a 10K run for charity, a concert, or a sporting event.

BRAND EQUITY: WHAT IS THIS BRAND EQUITY?

Brand equity is a company's or a product's reputation in the marketplace. Over time, a brand must repeatedly deliver reliable results to create trust between the target and the brand. Trust translates into brand loyalty and repeat sales.

Brand equity is our perception of quality based on experience, often even before we buy a product. For example, Campbell's is a brand, even though it is not a specific product. A consumer may buy Campbell's chicken soup or tomato soup—a product—because he believes that Campbell's is a quality brand, and he favors it over, say, a store brand. Consequently, Campbell's has more brand equity in the mind of that consumer than does a grocery-store brand.

Once a product or service becomes so well known that its name is no longer its sole brand identity, other aspects of its package design or logo treatment—such as a typeface, a graphic symbol, or a distinctive use of color—can be just as representative as the brand name. For example, most consumers can conjure up the Coke script, the Nike "swoosh," or the Bayer yellow in their minds without the product in front of them. This is because those brands have equity, or ownership, of their product categories.

But being the recognizable face of a product category can have its drawbacks. For instance, a brand's equity can be threatened when its brand name becomes the noun used to describe all products within a category, such as *kleenex* for any tissue, or *xerox* for any photocopy, or *coke* for any cola. We have all been guilty of using one of the above brand names to represent a generic product. Each of these companies has been almost too successful at building brand equity, setting itself apart from the competition so well that its equity is being eroded away as its brand name becomes the representative for a product category or even a task.

TRADEMARK AND SERVICE MARK PROTECTION

Most companies provide both products and services to the public. To protect and maintain ownership of these products and services and differentiate itself from competing brands, a company will *trademark* a product name and *service mark* all services provided. Very simply, a trademark is designed to protect both a business and its product names; services provided by a company are protected by service marks.

A trademark will normally appear on the product in the form of a tag or label, as opposed to service marks, which often appear in advertising and promotional efforts. A service mark can be made up of letters, words, phrases, or symbols to identify the marketer or manufacturer.

Trademarks and service marks can be either locally or federally registered. Local marks will use "TM" or "SM." Only federally registered products can use a ®.

Trademarks and service marks attempt to keep a product's or a service's name from becoming a part of everyday conversation, which in turn could cause the name to lose its trademark protection. Xerox has been one of the most vocal companies, reminding the public that you can make a Xerox photocopy, but you cannot "xerox" a document; in other words, *xerox* is not another word for *photocopy*.

A company can lose ownership of a trademark if they fail to protect it and are not diligent in policing violators. The following is a list of well-known, once-trademarked names that have lost their trademark protection: aerobics, aspirin, cellophane, cola, corn flakes, escalator, granola, hoagie, kerosene, linoleum, nylon, raisin bran, shredded wheat, super glue, thermos, touch tone, trampoline, yo yo, and zipper.

IMC can be used to identify and turn around this generic use before a product's name becomes commonplace and the company loses its brand identity, its trademark protection, and target loyalty to the brand. This can be done by tackling the problem head-on in public relations announcements or through news or magazine feature articles. Advertising or direct-marketing efforts can be used to create awareness and reinforce not only product differences, but also the relationship with the target.

BRANDS: WHAT'S IN A NAME?

A *brand* is a product's name. Its image is created through advertising—often over a long period of time, becoming part of that brand's reputation. Brands are identifiers: some are easy to acquire, while others we aspire to obtain because of the status they bring or the success they represent.

The more intimate the relationship between the target and a brand, the less likely it is to be affected by competitive promotions.

BRAND AWARENESS: PERCEPTION IS THE BETTER PART OF ADVERTISING

It may seem obvious that before a brand can succeed, the target needs to be *aware* of its existence. But what is not always so obvious is that the target needs to be aware of what the product or service has to offer, how it is different from competing brands, and how it can address the target's specific wants or needs. It is important that the provider of every product or service, whether new, old, or mainstream, knows his own product's attributes and perceived image before making any claims against or comparisons with the competing brands.

Once the target is aware of the brand, the next hoped-for step is that she will develop a favorable opinion of the product or service, based on its reputation (or the corporation's reputation), its advertised image, and/or its ability to fulfill a specific need or want.

BRAND IMAGE: THE MAKING OF A PERSONALITY

A brand's image is its personality and its status, as compared with other brands of the same or similar quality in its category. The target must decide if he likes it or doesn't like it, and whether he cares about what influencers, whose opinions are valued, will think of him when they see him using the product or service.

A brand's image is created and maintained by what we think about a product before or after use. *Brand image* is built in the media and maintained in the mind of the consumer, based on product quality or lack thereof. Brand image is based on consistency. Every time the product name is mentioned, the consumer associates it with an image or with specific qualities.

A brand's personality must be built around the target's needs and wants. It should become a reliable old friend that does not change with each passing fad, but can be trusted to bring home consistent results, purchase after purchase.

Most brands in a given product category are the same; it is easy in this day and age for a company to quickly create a product exactly like a successful competitor's, often at a lower cost. But reputation cannot be recreated. Advertising should build on that. By creating a brand image or personality for a client's product, it can continue to stand apart from the competition. Creative teams should concentrate on making it more distinct through creative ideas, packaging, and logo design; consumers should be able to see, hear, and feel a product before they need it, through the use of distinctive typography, color, and slogans. If a client's product is the one they think of first and the one they trust, they will purchase it because they believe it delivers on its advertised promises.

Image development begins by asking a few questions about the product: Is there

Daniel Sanders

anything holding the brand back, such as limited size or color choices? How much does the target already know about the product, as opposed to competing products? Is there any confusion relating to the product's visual/verbal identity, the purchasing options, or the product's life-cycle stage?

THE VISUAL/VERBAL BRAND

Before a brand can achieve equity or develop or maintain loyalty, a product must first have a consistent brand image that can parallel the target audience member's perceived image of himself. This consistent identity begins with the development of a logo design that appears in all communication efforts and on all packaging. A product's *visual/verbal* identity should not only define its personality and image, but should also represent a solution to the target's problem. Its distinctive look should be one of the factors that make the product or service stand out from the competition.

A brand's identifying symbol or logo design can include a representative type-face, color or colors, and graphic symbol that reflect the brand's personality and/or use. Another, more simple option might be nothing more than a basic black-and-white treatment. A slogan or tagline representing the corporate or campaign philosophy may also accompany the symbol.

When producing multiple pieces for use in multiple media such as public relations, advertising, direct marketing, and sales promotion, it is imperative that the logo design be visible and consistent. Believe it or not, the target may not remember the name of the product but may remember the package, color, slogan, or logo, and look for it when buying. Obviously, the promotional goal is to encourage name recognition, but color or logo recognition will do just as well.

Once the product or service has an individualized visual/verbal identity, image development must also take into account the life-cycle phase the product or service is in: new, mainstream, or reinvention.

New Brand

A *new product* will need to have an image developed for it that matches the target's self-image and reflects her lifestyle. A new product is a blank canvas that will, over time, need to develop brand equity and earn consumer loyalty. In order to create a competitive advantage, a new product must immediately distinguish its product advantages from those of its competition.

Determining which product advantage to promote will depend on the target, what the competition is doing, what needs to be accomplished, and the creative strategy used to influence the target. Considering these options, a product's advantages may be implied; found among its features and benefits; or based on price, status, or elitism. Additional advantages might center on the creation of a fad or trend, or they might be based entirely on emotional or rational needs. Creating brand awareness is critical to the success of a new product launch.

Staying ahead of the competition means paying attention, and adapting to trends and fads that define consumer buying habits. Whoever is first to introduce a product that becomes part of a fad or trend will successfully build equity.

The creation of a fad or development of a trend is what makes a product or service memorable over the long run. If the agency is going to create a fad or trend, it's important to know the difference.

A *trend* can evolve from media and advertising exposure, and is influenced by movies, music, travel, politics, and pop culture.

Fads come and go, leaving little lasting impression on society. Trends develop within the fabric of society and reflect attitudes, values, and beliefs. Trends are set by the lucrative and influential 18-to-39-year-olds, and often define a period of time. Trends come in two sizes, *macro* and *micro*.

Macro trends are big and define the way we now view happiness and satisfaction. Micro trends are the specific details of a macro trend, and may include such things as music, fashion, sports, and so on.

Mainstream Brands

Once a brand has been established, communication efforts must work to consistently *maintain awareness*, reinforce quality and reliability, and continue building the relationship with the target.

Reinvented Brands

Reinvention can occur when a brand is in need of a new or updated image, or as a result of a damaged reputation. A product's reinvention means looking past sins in the eye and eliminating outdated approaches that directly affect image and target perception. Products that are reinvented, no matter the reason, will have to prove themselves over time in order to rebuild lost equity and regain brand loyalty.

A product's life-cycle stage will play an important role in advertising and promotional efforts. An agency can focus a product's creative message on any one of, or a combination of, the following options:

1. Brand image. How does the target audience view the product or service?
2. Word of mouth. What kind of experiences did the target audience have with the brand? Whether good or bad, their opinions carry a lot of weight with others within the targeted group.
3. Positioning. What does the target think about the product or service as compared to the competition?
4. Consumer education. How will the product be used? Is it expensive, professional, or technical?
5. Brand awareness. What does the target audience know about the product or service?

6. Promotional offers. Is there a need to create involvement through coupons, contests, or samples?
7. Creating a reaction. Is there a need to get the target to come into a show-room to try the product, or to visit a website to obtain more information, or to make a purchase?
9. Direct comparison with the competition. Will a point be stronger if a direct comparison of features is made to those of the competition?
10. Use. Is the product or service revolutionary? Is it easy to use?
11. Product introduction. What is the state of the target's knowledge? Is the product new or old? Is it considered a reliable old standard?

The bottom line is, no matter what life-cycle stage a product or service is in, for it to become or stay successful the target must believe the message and relate to the image.

BRAND LOYALTY

Brand loyalty refers to the relationship between the product and the target. Brand loyalty—the target's dependable repurchase of a brand based on favorable and reliable past experiences—is critical to IMC and to brand equity. It is important that all advertising and promotional efforts represent the product as it is, not as an exaggeration of what it is. This is the best way to build and maintain brand loyalty, which in turn leads to brand equity.

Brand loyalty is built on trust and the knowledge that the product will deliver what it promises every time it is purchased or used.

Remember, advertising is developed to accomplish something. The product's position in its life cycle will determine what is accomplished as it relates to brand development, maintenance, or reinvention.

Brand-loyal consumers require less coaxing to repurchase. With the high cost of advertising in today's market, it is (or it should be) every client's goal to build brand loyalty by targeting advertising efforts to the right audience; providing consistency of product; and building a brand image consistent with the product's use and/or personality—after which the goal is to maintain the level of brand loyalty that has been established. The more intimate the relationship between the target and a brand, the less likely the target is to be affected by competitive promotions.

POSITIONING: THE CONSUMER'S VIEW OF THE BRAND

Positioning relates to how the consumer thinks about a product or service and/or rates it against the competition. Positioning requires highlighting the target-relevant benefits of the product's features. Benefits must be tied to uses that will enhance the target's lifestyle or image. The position of a brand is sometimes confused with brand image; a brand's positioning in the mind of the consumer is created via advertising and promotion, whereas brand image is created based on experience.

Positioning is effective only if fully researched. The creative team must *know*—not think they know—how the consumer thinks and feels about the product or service. To be sure, a few questions need to be asked: Who is most likely to use the product or service? What are the benefits to the target of using the product? How does the product stand up against its competition—what makes it unique, and what features are duplicated? What is the perceived value of the product within the marketplace? How will the product be made available to the target? Does it come in different sizes, colors, or price ranges? Is it relevant to the target?

One of the ways to break through the advertising clutter is to find out what makes a client's product or service unique, and then position the product directly against the competition's image. If communication efforts can prove a client's product to be bigger, faster, or longer lasting than the competing brand, it is more likely to be noticed and remembered.

It's important to remember that a client's product is probably not the only product of its kind; it is most probably one of many virtually identical products in the category. To make it stand out from the crowd, the creative team must carve out a niche or position for the product. Today, the majority of products are no longer mass advertised; rather, as discussed earlier, advertising vehicles are more selectively targeted, to eliminate media waste.

A strong position is a direct result of a strong brand. This position is built up over a period of time, based on reliability of performance. Branding gives a product or service an air of exclusivity and a unique identity, differentiating it from its competitors within the product category.

Successful, memorable advertising begins with an established position. Once a product's identity has been established and accepted, consumers remember it and use it as a measurement device for all other competitors within the category. Measurement may be based on quality, convenience, reliability, or service, to name just a few possibilities.

Brand image helps to determine the product's position. This is because positioning relates to who the target audience is; what they currently think about the product; who the competition is, and what the target audience thinks about them; and, finally, what features are relevant to the target audience. Once this is known, the AE and creative team can determine and then communicate positioning strategies.

In his article "How to Position Your Product," Luc Dupont outlines the seven ways to position a product or service:

1. Originality. Being first at anything is a short-lived boast, but if a client's product is, it can be used to set the product up as unique.
2. Low Price. Less expensive does not necessarily mean lesser quality. A low price can be a selling point if the consumer is convinced of the product's value.
3. High Price. More expensive does not necessarily mean higher quality, so the target must be convinced an expensive product is worth the investment.

Some Things Just Come Natural.

All-natural ScienceDiet is the logical choice for your pets.

Robby Cockrell

4. Sex of the Consumer. Not all products are made for both sexes. There are razors especially designed for women and others designed especially for men; fragrances are also gender based, such as colognes for men and perfumes for women.

5. Age of the Consumer. Few products appeal to consumers of all ages, so it is important to consider the age of the target audience. Baggy jeans are for teens; Dockers are for the upwardly mobile professional. A Volkswagen Beetle appeals to a younger audience, whereas a Mercedes reflects status and/or success.

6. Time of Day the Product Should Be Used. Some products are intended for use at specific times of the day, such as a cereal for breakfast, soup for lunch, frozen entrees for dinner, or popcorn as a late-night snack.

7. Distribution Channels. This relates to how the consumer will receive the product. Examples would include ordering through a website or direct-marketing efforts delivered through the mail, versus the need to visit a showroom.

Al Ries and Jack Trout, specialists in positioning and marketing, sum it up this way: "In the communications jungle out there, the only hope to score big is to be selective, to concentrate on narrow targets, [and] practice segmentation. In a word, positioning."

REPOSITIONING: CHANGING THE CONSUMER'S MIND

A product needs to be *repositioned* when there is a need to change the way it is viewed in the mind of the target. Changing perception is much more difficult than working with an existing position or creating a new one. Repositioning should work to define a new or special niche in a consumer's mind. The often-fragile perception of product superiority associated with any competing product can be reversed or eliminated if one's own product can be both innovatively and creatively advertised. This is one place repositioning can play a big role.

WHAT IS INTEGRATED BRAND COMMUNICATION?

Integrated brand communication (IBC) is a direct result of the success of IMC. IMC, if you will recall, concentrates on one organized message that is heard across various media; IBC concentrates on creating the tie that binds between the consumer and the brand. In short, IMC creates a position, while IBC works with what is already there. IBC is about maintaining a brand's existing position: what does the consumer feel about the brand? This feeling becomes the brand and defines the corporation. The feeling then dominates all advertising efforts throughout all media, consistent with IMC efforts.

IMC is one message delivered through multiple and varied media. IBC takes an existing symbol, image, and overall message and makes it *the* message. Creating a more distinctive position further strengthens this image.

Traditionally, a brand's image was built over time based on quality, reliability, and a product's desired features and overall benefits. IBC is the calculated creation of an image for a product rather than the development of an image by the consumer. Because it is more consumer-focused, IBC uses more Internet-based or interactive media choices in order to interact directly with the consumer. Interaction strengthens the brand image.

As we have already learned, a successful IMC campaign means building a strong relationship with consumers. It also means building a strong brand, whose image matches that of the consumer and whose performance is consistent with every purchase.

SPEAKING FOR THE BRAND

Product spokespersons or character representatives speak for the brand. Their use constitutes one of the ways a brand's image can be created. Image for a product or service is much like image for a person: a product has an individual look, feel, and sound (and sometimes a smell), all of which make it recognizable within a crowd of competing products.

Image representatives come in two forms: the *spokesperson* (a real person, often a celebrity or athlete) and the *character representative* (an animated figure). Spokespersons and character representatives can easily move between media vehicles. They are especially successful on television and the Internet, where sight, sound, and motion bring their personalities to life, and where relationships between product and buyer can be developed and nurtured. This type of image and relationship development is known as *experiential marketing*.

If the image representative has a distinctive voice or makes an interesting sound, radio can also be used along with print, broadcast, and the Internet.

It is important that an image representative be distinctive in both looks and voice; that he, she, or it fit the product or service; and that the image representative have a unique personality that motivates consumers to tune in to see what he, she, or it is up to now.

Not all reps live forever. For example, Kellogg's, as discussed earlier, is revamping several of its cereals to make them healthier for children. This puts some well-loved and long-running character representatives, like Toucan Sam and Snap, Crackle, and Pop, at risk of being retired. However, that need not be the case. Images can be updated or "tweaked" to reflect a new direction in the advertising. For example, Kellogg's representative Tony the Tiger, whose only antic, traditionally, was to growl out the slogan "It's great," was repositioned several years ago into a coach and mentor-like figure, who encourages kids to "earn their stripes" by becoming involved in sporting activities.

Other corporate changes to character representatives include McDonald's revamp of Ronald McDonald from a clown-suited friend of children to a track-suited, fitness-friendly representative, who symbolized the company's new commitment to health and health-related concerns.

Changing a product's image representative can be tricky and should be done slowly. Any changes should make sense for the brand and the rep, so as not to damage the brand's existing image.

Engagement is the trend of the day in advertising. *Engagement* refers to the amount of interest consumers have in an ad and their receptivity to the message. Receptivity hinges on the product's success in attaining the right viewers and on its appearance in the right media. Engagement is a direct result of receptivity.

Creative that defines a brand's image needs to adapt to the different environments (e.g., programming environments, locations) in which it is seen.

When developing a brand's image, the creative team must think "memorable" and "long-lasting." A brand that is to capture the heart and mind should assiduously, and tirelessly, defend its importance to the target's life, health, and happiness.

Memorable messages and catchy jingles can extend a product's life beyond that of the advertised message.

It is important for the creative team to understand how the product will be used and the results of the experience. If a tie cannot be found to bind the product to the consumer's needs and lifestyle, the advertising will fail to excite consumer interest.

If the product fails to deliver the intended promise, it will fail the consumer's expectations. Once negativity enters the consumer's consciousness, it will take a great deal of time, initiative, and money to alter the consumer's opinion.

In an online article published November 20, 2006, titled "Consumers Cite Past Experience as the No. 1 Influencer When Buying," *Ad Age* reports, "In a survey by GFK Roper Consulting, 83 percent of adults cited past experience with a brand as the most important factor in their purchase decisions. Quality and price—issues often promoted in advertising—ranked second and third. Personal recommendations came fourth, highlighting the importance of word of mouth."

When advertising promotes a brand's specific features, it's known as **brand advertising**. **Generic advertising**, on the other hand, promotes use. Marketers who sell "like" products such as raisins or oranges sponsor generic advertising.

Modern advertising no longer simply sells you something; its job is also to entertain. Consumers are no longer necessarily a captive audience to an advertisement's message. Because they can often fast-forward through commercials, it is necessary that advertised messages be as entertaining as the programming they are associated with.

Geico has been very successful with their "caveman" spots, promoting their insurance while they entertain viewers with the frustrating urban lives of their caveman spokespersons.

Internet advertising only needs to be relevant to be successful. Television viewers do not elect to watch commercials, considering them an interruption. Internet viewers choose to search for information and make a conscious choice to watch.

A brand is more than a logo and a spokesperson: it is an image that the target buys into as his own. In the words of Walter Landor (a creative icon famous for his design of some of the world's most famous and recognizable brands—such as Kellogg's, Coca-Cola, and Miller Lite), "Products are created in the factory, but brands are created in the mind."

Today, a product is more than a name—it's an icon for an image and a lifestyle.

Brand building is needed to differentiate a product, service, or company from its competitors. If a product or service is not distinct in some way from competing brands, it must have a lower price.

Determining product differentiation is much easier if a product does in fact have unique characteristics when compared with the products of competing brands. This uniqueness is not as common as you might think, and thus the product or service must often rely on invented attributes like service or ambience.

Branding is all about creating and introducing a name for a product or service that creates a unique image in the mind of the consumer.

MARKETING PLANS AND CREATIVE BRIEFS

HOW MARKETERS AND CREATIVES WORK

You wouldn't feed your miniature puppy a bone this big.

Feed him ScienceDiet® Puppy Small Bites, specially made for miniature breed dogs.

Lindsay Frankenfield

There's no secret formula for advertising success, other than to learn everything you can about the product. Most products have some unique characteristic, and the really great advertising comes right out of the product and says something about the product that no one else can say. Or at least no one else is saying.

—Morris Hite, quoted in Russ Pate, 207.

THE ROLE OF THE MARKETING PLAN

The **marketing plan** dissects the overall environment in which the product or service will be used. Before any creative executions can take place, the company must first determine what it is it wants to do—financially, strategically, and competitively.

A marketing plan is a client's business plan; it diagnoses the current market situation by looking at any internal and external factors that could affect a product's success. It is an internal document that outlines the company's strengths and weaknesses, as well as the opportunities and threats affecting the product or service. It also determines marketing *objectives*, or what is to be accomplished; profiles the marketing *strategy*, or how objectives will be met; identifies the target audience; compares current competitive strategies; and determines implementation and evaluation tactics.

Without a marketing plan, the client cannot determine overall operating and business decisions or justify advertising expenditures.

Think of it this way: All advertising begins with a client who has a product or service she needs to promote. In order to do this effectively and expeditiously, the client must first know a few important facts. To begin with, a thorough knowledge of the product or service is important when comparing its attributes to competing products or services. Next, the client needs to determine the target audience most likely to buy the product or use the service, and what product attributes the target likes or dislikes about competing products. Finally, the client must decide what kind of message strategy it will take to set its product apart from the competition.

All the questions and all the answers begin and end with research. Each section of the marketing plan must be carefully researched to determine current trends and attitudes, and both market and target needs. Any problems that need to be addressed or favorable trends that might be exploited will need to be researched further.

What Does a Marketing Plan Do?

Simply put, a marketing plan is a comprehensive look at a business's place within its product category. Its primary functions are to detail the strengths and weaknesses of a business and/or its products, as compared to the competition, and to determine any opportunities or reveal any relevant threats within the marketplace. It also defines marketing or sales objectives and determines the appropriate marketing strategy for accomplishing those objectives; defines both the target to be addressed and the competition; and determines evaluative measures.

Developing a plan that incorporates input from customers is the first step in developing a strong IMC plan. For the plan to be truly integrated, it must ensure that all messages use the same tone of voice and that the messages are reflected in all internal and external communication. So if the client wants to increase sales, profits, and brand equity, he must have a plan that will specifically talk to the right audience, define the product and the competition, and offer a product that is unique and consistently reliable.

A typical marketing plan is comprised of the following seven sections:

1. Situation analysis (SWOT)
2. Marketing objectives
3. Market strategy
4. Target-market analysis
5. Competitive strategies
6. Implementation tactics
7. Evaluation

Situation Analysis

The *situation analysis* looks at current marketing conditions and their possible effect on marketing efforts, and at how factors in the marketplace can affect outcome. It is here that the product or service; the competition; the target audience; and any environmental, economic, legal, or political situations are dissected and analyzed.

Each of these factors can be broken down and examined further by developing the situation analysis, or *SWOT*. A situation analysis looks at a company's strengths (S) and weaknesses (W) as compared to the competition, along with any opportunities (O) and threats (T) to the product or service within the marketplace.

Further studies will compare and contrast current product features with those of the competition, analyze any previous communication efforts, and determine distribution needs.

A thorough look at the target market and any competitor's advertising efforts will help to determine how the situation analysis can be used, if the objectives can be met, or if any modifications will be needed.

Marketing Objectives

From the data developed in the situation analysis, a set of *marketing objectives* will be devised to determine what the company wants to accomplish through its marketing activities. Over the next year, client objectives will concentrate on various financial outcomes such as sales or profit levels.

Marketing Strategies

A *marketing strategy* determines what steps will need to be undertaken to accomplish the stated objectives. It is here that the marketing mix will first be identified.

The **marketing mix**, also known as the "Four P's," is a brand's marketing plan of action. It includes product, price, promotion, and distribution (or place). Many believe today's market environment requires adding a fifth "p": people. Each element will play a vital role in message development.

1. Product. This specifically refers to anything that has to do with the product, including quality, features, packaging, servicing arrangements, and warranties.
2. Price. Any and all price issues are looked at here, including payment terms, cash versus credit options, and any discounts or sales materials.
3. Promotion. This refers to the communication or promotional mix, including public relations, advertising, sales promotion, direct marketing, and Internet marketing. The promotional mix provides a foundation for examining the best promotional options available for reaching the target audience with the right message.
4. Distribution, or place. This pertains to where the product will be available for purchase.
5. People. Knowing whom you're talking to builds relationships with buyers and helps you personalize products to meet individual needs more easily.

The strategy communication efforts employ is critical to accomplishing brand differentiation. Brand positioning creates brand awareness by creating a brand image that is important to the target. Only through research can we know what the *influencers*, or specific factors, are.

Target Market Analysis

The more you know about who will be using your client's product, the better you can target your message directly to them. As previously discussed in chapter 2, this section breaks down the intended target audience, or those people research has determined are most likely to buy the product or use the service, using the following tools: demographics, psychographics, geographics, and behavioristics. Segmentation can also be based on usage patterns, level of loyalty, and specific benefits. There may be times when you will need to divide a larger target audience into smaller market segments or secondary markets to ensure that they will be reached. For example, if your client is in jewelry and your primary market is 18-to-34-year-old women, a good secondary market might be husbands, significant others, parents, or even grandparents. Each would require a creative approach unique to that market segment.

Competitive Strategies

Knowing what the competitors are doing with advertising and product development is the difference between being a leader and a follower within a product category.

Understanding the similarities and differences between a product and its leading competitors is crucial in order for a product to stand out from the competition in the mind of the targeted consumer. Two of the most common types of strategy are positioning and branding.

A *positioning* strategy is one of the best ways to make a brand stand out from competing products. Basically, this relates to how the product is looked at as compared to the competition. In order to favorably position the product in the mind of the consumer, marketers must determine what factors or benefits are important to the target and build their message around that. Another option is to use a *brand strategy*. Branding develops a personality for a product or service that creates a favorable relationship between product value and target need. Building brand loyalty through quality or reliability guarantees repeat purchase by making sure the product is the only purchase option in the mind of the consumer.

Implementation Tactics

Implementation tactics determine whether everything can come off on schedule and in the right order, with the right materials in place, and with the proper people available to carry off the marketing efforts. Also to be discussed and developed here are budgets, as well as the specifics of enacting the marketing mix.

Evaluation

Evaluation takes place before the marketing plan is put into effect and again after implementation, to determine whether results in fact reflect corporate goals and whether objectives were successfully met. Evaluation is critical to a successful IMC program.

THE CREATIVE STRATEGY AND THE MARKETING PLAN

Once the agency understands the corporate goals, it is time for agency executives to begin considering a creative strategy to direct results. A *creative strategy* is a synopsis of the product or service and the target audience. It should describe the key features of the product or service and define the overall benefits to the targeted audience.

The marketing plan should answer the target's main question: "What's in it for me?" There should be enough information in the marketing plan to identify a unique product feature or specific target need, and to start imagining creative direction.

Creative strategies are most often created for existing clients, where the majority of research has already been done. They are usually no more than three to four sentences in length. The creative strategy defines the target to be reached, the key benefit, and the objective of the message.

Defining a Creative Strategy Statement

Creative describes a unique and individual idea. *Strategy* is a plan to execute that creative idea or concept. Employing an IMC creative strategy is all about sending the right visual/verbal message to the right target audience, through the right media, in order to achieve the overall communication objectives.

A creative strategy statement is an integral part of the marketing communication process. Once the objectives set up by the client are known, a creative strategy can be developed that will accomplish them. Effective strategies are the elusive yet essential monsters that define advertising direction. Determining the right one requires research. Agencies are not looking at ideas, describing a creative look, or solidifying media outlets at this point; agencies are looking at solutions to an advertising problem. These solutions assist in the development of a concept or theme that can be consistently executed, both visually and verbally, within multiple media, without losing substance or focus.

Cameron Dicken

A successful creative strategy statement is developed from information found in the client's marketing plan, and is written from the consumer's point of view. It needs to ask, on behalf of the target, "What's in it for me? How will it solve my problem or make my life better?" The answers should ultimately lead to an idea, associated uniquely with the product or service, that will influence the target to act on the message, and that will make the product or service stand out from the competition.

The creative strategy statement will define the IMC campaign's visual/verbal tone and is the foundation for the communication phase of an IMC program. The creative strategy affects every aspect of IMC and will ultimately give the product its image and voice and define seller-to-buyer contact.

Creative Briefs: The Big Influence inside a Small Document

The *creative brief*, also known as a *copy platform, creative work plan, creative plan*, or *copy strategy*, is the next step in the evolution of the creative strategy. A creative brief is used in lieu of a creative strategy statement when more information is needed about a product or service than is currently known. Information found in the marketing plan is used in the creative brief to outline the communications plan of attack.

A small internal document created by the AE, the creative brief should dissect the product or service for the creative team. It should redefine the target audience, introduce the key benefit, describe individual features and consumer benefits, define objectives, address the competition, and outline tactics. It is the encyclopedia the creative team will use to define the IMC message that needs to be communicated. Think of it as a set of building blocks, meticulously laying the foundation for the concept or idea that will become the visual/verbal message.

The creative brief is not a document that speculates or generalizes; it needs to be concise, just detailed enough that the creative team of art directors and copywriters can develop a creative solution for the client's communication problem. A creative brief also ensures that the creative team, the AE, and the client all have a thorough understanding of exactly what objectives communication efforts need to accomplish.

First and foremost, the creative brief is a business plan that provides the guidelines for developing the creative message. It is not a creative outlet: it does not determine copy or define or determine what creative should look like. It is a road map for idea generation and visual/verbal development only.

There is no exact length for a creative brief. The only absolute is that it must contain all the information the creative team needs to inspire ideas and keep them focused on what problems need to be solved.

Overall length, information content, and format vary by agency, but most creative briefs contain some or all of the following:

1. Target-audience profile
2. Communication objectives

3. Product features and benefits
4. Positioning of the product
5. Key consumer benefit
6. Creative strategy
7. Tone
8. Support statement
9. Slogan or tagline
10. Logo

Target Audience Profile

The *target audience* will be briefly redefined here based on the profile developed in the marketing plan.

The goal of advertising is not only to inform, but also to find just the right way to inspire the target to act. When developing a creative direction, it's important that the creative team never lose sight of who the target is. The target audience is the reason communication efforts are being developed. In order to successfully advertise any product, it is important to know how they will react to the message. Just knowing what the target thinks, what he finds important, and how the product or service can fulfill his needs and wants makes creating the right message a lot easier. Copy and layout can strike out by communicating to the masses with a generalized message, or they can hit the ball out of the park with an individualized, consumer-focused message.

Communication Objectives

Communication objectives, or goals, clearly define what the communication efforts need to accomplish. Objectives should pinpoint what the target needs to think about the product or service, what the target should feel when using the product or feel toward the product overall, and what the target should do—such as make a purchase or request additional information.

There is a limit to what can be accomplished with one ad or even a campaign. On the average, no product or service should have more than one to three attainable objectives. Each objective needs to focus on communication-related issues. Communication-based objectives give consumers usable, personalized information (as opposed to marketing-based objectives, which are sales related). Primarily, creative efforts will focus on positioning objectives that inform and educate the consumer about the product or service as compared to the competition. It is important when determining objectives to know the target's level of knowledge about the product or service. A look at the life-cycle stage of the product or service will also be beneficial when determining what needs to be said or shown; what needs to be introduced, maintained, or expanded; and what needs to be overhauled completely. This will affect whether objectives can be accomplished, over the short or long term.

Think of it this way: If there is a new product launch or a brand that is being reinvented, a relationship must be built first on image and then on trust. So the first thing that needs to be accomplished is to position the brand in the mind of the consumer, while working to build brand awareness. Over time, the objective will be to achieve loyalty and, eventually, brand equity. This type of traditionally based or mass-media advertising is known as *brand image advertising*. To be successful, all objectives must translate into results.

Product Features and Benefits

The *features and benefits* section looks at product attributes and attaches them to the target's needs and wants. One mistake young AEs or designers often make is to sell a product's features and not its benefits. A *feature* is a product attribute; a *benefit* answers the question, "What's in it for me?" Let's use a toaster as an example; see table 4.1.

Features are lovely, but have no point. The point that needs to be hammered home is what the feature can offer the consumer. Determining a benefit for each of the product's features helps break down the product information into smaller, more manageable bundles, giving concept development a visual/verbal starting point.

If the product comes in five colors (feature), the creative brief should inform the creative team about the feature by listing all five colors. Research gathered on the target audience might suggest to the creative team that the target is upwardly mobile, and might be someone who has just bought a new home, is on a budget, and will be remodeling; or that the target is trend conscious and likes to keep up with the most current look in decorating. Advertisers might inform the target that one of the toaster's benefits is that it can be purchased in a color to match any decorating scheme; or they might inform her that another benefit, the availability of the toaster in two-, four-, and six-slice models, takes into account variations in family size. These are both examples of talking to the consumer's current needs.

Benefits answer the question, "What's in it for me?" and can focus on the product or the consumer. Features can be elements that are inherent in the product (e.g., ingredients) or implied qualities, such as the status or image of a brand (e.g., Rolex), which can affect the consumer's personal image or lifestyle.

Positioning of the Product

Next, the creative brief should concisely discuss the brands that represent direct competition to the client's brand. It should examine each product's similarities to

Table 4.1.   Product Features and Benefits

Feature	It comes in five different colors: red, green, blue, yellow, and orange.
Benefit	It makes coordination with any kitchen color theme easier.
Feature	It comes in two-, four-, and six-slice models.
Benefit	No matter what size of family you have to feed, there is a toaster size that makes it faster and easier.

the client's brand, along with the differences, and explain how the targeted audience sees each brand. It should then rate the client's brand against its direct competitors based on brand image, positioning, and so on.

This section will help keep the creative team from duplicating what competitors are saying and doing with their promotional efforts. In order to chose a key benefit and determine the best way to make a product stand out from the competition, it is important to know what the competitors are doing creatively.

Key Consumer Benefit

The *key consumer benefit* is the one feature-benefit combination that either is unique to the client's product or can be positioned as big or important. The key benefit will be the point that screams from every ad, either visually or verbally, positioning the product as the one that meets the target's internal and external needs. It will become the one voice of the IMC message and should be chosen because research has determined that it is important to the target audience and will speak directly to their interests and lifestyle, encouraging some sort of desired action.

There are two basic types of key benefits: a **unique selling proposition** (USP) and a *big idea*. The big idea or USP is determined by analyzing the target market and determining which key benefit can accomplish the stated objectives. It will be the tie that binds all advertising and promotional efforts together. Along with the strategy, the USP or big idea will help determine the visual/verbal direction the communication efforts will take.

A UNIQUE BUT BIG SELLING IDEA

Determining whether to use a USP or a big idea depends on what the product or service has to say about itself as compared to the competition, and on whether the target audience thinks its benefits will enhance their lives. If the product or service speaks of individualism or uniqueness, or is the first to introduce a product, benefit, or feature, the best key benefit to use would be a USP. Products that have no outstanding or unique characteristics to differentiate them from the competition will need a big idea. A big idea takes the feature-benefit combination and turns it into a memorable idea that sells.

A USP has a feature-benefit combination that is unique to the client's product or service. USPs are also used in promoting a commonplace feature as unique. Differentiation can come from a creative idea touching a known interest with the target, fulfilling a need, or creating a status symbol.

Although the practice of using a USP is giving way to the use of multiple selling propositions (MSPs) and permission marketing, it is good to first focus on one main point before branching out to meet or interpret individual target needs and wants.

An MSP is better suited than a USP for use in an IMC campaign, since multiple messages based on the same feature-benefit combination can be used to reach the target in the same media. USPs concentrate on running a single ad multiple times, which is sure to bore or cause the target to tune out the oversaturated message.

MSPs, on the other hand, concentrate on the rotation of several ads, over the same amount of time. The rotation of multiple ads is better suited to reaching today's active, inattentive, factionalized, competitor-savvy, and advertising-avoidant consumer.

THE BIG IDEA

A big idea is a creative solution that sets the product off from the competition, while at the same time solving the client's advertising problem. This does not mean the competition does not have the identical feature, only that they are not pushing it in their advertising. Big ideas that are consumer focused or based on lifestyle will have more longevity than product-oriented ideas. This is because concepts based on lifestyle are more difficult for the competition to duplicate. When using a big idea, creativity is the key to success.

Finding inspiration for a big idea is a little more difficult than determining a USP. The big idea most often has to create something unique and interesting out of nothing in order to attract attention and create a relationship with the target. By focusing on the consumer and his lifestyle, even a generic product feature can alter

Daniel Sanders

a target's existing view of a product. The key is to shape it into an unusual, different, or interesting benefit that will catch the target's attention.

A product or service will never stand out among the competition or build brand loyalty if the USP or big idea has a "me too" message or "been there seen that" creative. A product must have an identity and offer personalized benefits that the target can relate to, and a creative approach that offers the target a reason to try the product.

John O'Toole, a member of the Advertising Hall of Fame, sums up the big idea this way: "While strategy requires deduction, a big idea requires inspiration. The big idea in advertising is almost invariably expressed through a combination of art and copy."

Advertising objectives determine what needs to be accomplished through advertising efforts—such as building awareness or changing an attitude; the advertising strategy determines how goals will be accomplished.

Creative Strategy

The *creative strategy* is the foundation for the creative direction or concept. Strategy tells the creative team how they will talk to the target and accomplish the stated objectives, and informs them regarding the best way to feature the key benefit. The strategy's main objective is to discuss how advertising and promotional efforts will position the brand, and how the brand will compete against other products in the same category. The client's product must be made to step up and away from the competition in a way that is important to the target. If research, media, and creative efforts reflect the strategy, a successful outcome is within reach.

The strategy employed by communication efforts is critical to accomplishing brand differentiation. Brand positioning engenders brand awareness by creating a brand image that is important to the target.

There are several things that need to be decided before choosing a strategy direction. The first is the approach that will be used to determine how the product or service will be positioned; the second is the kind of appeal that will be used to reach the target; and the third is the execution technique or tone that will be used to make the appeal.

Many factors can affect the creative strategy. One of the most important is the life-cycle stage of the product or service. Many communication obstacles can be overcome and opportunities exploited by considering and using this information. For example, during a product launch, building brand awareness is one of the most important steps; as interest in the brand grows, building awareness plays less of a role.

The creative team uses the creative strategy section to determine the approach and appeal combination that will be used to determine the look and overall tone the creative message will take. The approach chosen can focus on the product, the consumer, or the objectives, while the choice of appeal relates to whether the product or service will fulfill an emotional or rational need. Every concept will be built around the choice of approach or approaches, appeal or appeals, and tone or execution technique.

The strategic approach that will be used will depend on the product or service, the target audience, the key benefit, the overall objectives, and the appeal and execution package employed.

An ad's job is to persuade. Whether it is successful or not depends on the type of appeal used. There are two types of appeals: emotional and rational. Consumer response depends upon whether the product fills an emotional or rational need. Many advertising efforts will employ both appeals.

Emotional needs include lifestyle enhancers such as cars, iPods, jewelry, and the latest fashion trends. Emotional appeals target image and are used on status-related products. These ads appeal to the target's need to fit in, to be a trendsetter, or to stand out from the crowd.

Rational needs are life sustaining, like food and basic clothing needs. Rational appeals are information based and use facts, charts, or expert opinions to back up claims. These ads are meant to educate the consumer on the product's use, quality, and value.

Appeals are used to attract consumer attention and influence the perception of need for a product. The focus is most often placed on the consumer's need for, or use of, the product, and/or on how it will affect the consumer's lifestyle. Message content reflects on the features and benefits of a product or service. Often emotional appeals will work better on brands that have little or no differentiation from competing brands, since communication efforts are more creative and memorable and build image based on the target's psychological or social needs.

It is important that *strategy* not be confused with *tactics*. Tom Altstie and Jean Grow, in their book *Advertising Strategy: Creative Tactics from the Outside/In*, describe the difference between strategy and tactics with a military analogy: "Strategies deal with achieving objectives, like capturing a city. Tactics are the means used to achieve strategies, such as using a combination of close air support, flanking maneuvers from infantry, frontal assaults by tanks, and constant artillery bombardment."

Tone

An extension of the creative strategy section, the *tone* or *execution technique* defines the personality and overall voice or style the advertising message needs to portray. The only rule is that it should reflect the key consumer benefit.

Once the approach and the appeal have been solidified, the next step is to determine how the information will be delivered. The *execution style* (or *execution technique*) refers to the development of the visual and verbal tone—what the ad will look like and sound like—or the overall way the ad will be presented to the target.

The tone will basically describe a product's personality and the attitude, mood, or spirit of the ad or campaign, as presented in the key benefit and strategy sections. This personality can be either stated or conveyed visually in the advertised message.

The visual/verbal tone used to address the target audience has to be very effective: if the target audience does not connect with the product, there is a good chance that they will not be buying it. By now the creative team should be able to determine how that connection can be developed and how the target will respond to humor, facts, or testimonials. If the product or service is newsworthy, can it teach the target something, or will consumers be more interested in a demonstration? Whatever tone is taken, it should work toward creating or supporting the brand's image, promoting the key benefit, and advancing the strategy. The technique chosen should be the tie that binds the approach and appeal together.

Support Statement

The *support statement* highlights one feature-benefit combination that can be used to directly support or advance the key benefit. Consider the toaster example used earlier, with regard to color and kitchen decor. If this becomes the key benefit, then the support statement for the two-, four-, or six-slice toaster could address how much counter space is required for its use or how its stylish design will complement any contemporary decorating scheme.

Slogan or Tagline

The *slogan* and the *tagline* (terms that are often used interchangeably) are associated with the logo and appear either above it or below it. A slogan expresses a company or corporate philosophy, and a tagline defines the campaign or ad philosophy.

Logo

The *logo* is the product or corporate symbol. It could be a simple graphic, a line of text, simple initials, or a combination of graphics and text.

When all is said and done, the job of the creative brief is to summarize facts, features and benefits, and strategic goals for the creative team. No creative direction should be offered within the brief, but the facts found within the brief will help define creative direction. The next step is conceptual development, or the "idea stage." How will the information presented be used to meet the stated objectives? What will be said, how will it be said, how will it be shown, and how will it be laid out on the page? The creative brief is a blueprint; it is the creative team's job to build the house and organize the details.

PICKING THE RIGHT MESSAGE

Its important to remember that there are many companies that sell a diverse selection of products. This diversification is used to give them a competitive advantage over companies who produce just one product or service. However, companies today cannot be all things to all people, so corporations work to become global leaders in a few categories, concentrating advertising efforts on their leading brands and eliminating weaker ones, thus saving money in the long run.

Marketing strategies that concentrate on creating need or demand for a product can build equity. But before they can do that, marketers and agencies alike need to know what consumers want and don't want, and what message and media vehicles will reach the target audience, create interest, and fulfill their wants. How the message is delivered will assist with building awareness and brand image.

CHAPTER FIVE

MEDIA

Size Does Matter.
That's why Science Diet has developed a new formula
especially for the needs of large breed dogs.

Cameron Dicken

The buying of time or space is not the taking out of a hunting license on someone else's private preserve but is the renting of a stage on which we may perform.

—Goward Gossage, quoted in Randall Rothenberg, 188.

DEVELOPING THE MESSAGE FOR THE TARGET

"Innovative," "creative," and "unique" no longer describe just the advertised message. Today, these words express media's new role in the art and science of the advertising process. Media placement in today's highly competitive market, with its multiple media options, requires a very detailed and strategic message-delivery system. No longer playing an insignificant role in the advertising strategic process, the media buyers and planners who make up an agency's media department work beside the creative team to determine the best media vehicle(s) for delivering the creative message to the targeted consumer.

Because an integrated media plan launches the creative idea and/or maintains brand awareness through appropriate media placement, it is important that the creative and media teams look at the different media types/classes and vehicles available, to determine which ones will best reach the target, with the most appropriate message, at the best place and time.

More than ever before, consumers have a choice as to which media they will pay attention to and which they will ignore, making innovative, creative media choices invaluable.

The term *media*, as it is used in this text, incorporates all media vehicles that have a flat enough surface to display a logo or that can otherwise deliver a message to the public. These include newspapers, magazines, radio, television, billboards, transit vehicles, coffee mugs, ball caps, and calendars. It encompasses stickers on fruit, posters, banner ads and Web pop-ups. It extends to the backs of tickets, grocery receipts, flyers, shelf cards, text messages, and e-mails, and to product placement in movies and on television.

The diverse media mix available to media planners and buyers includes **traditional, nontraditional**, and new or **alternative media**. *Traditional* advertising includes print (newspapers and magazines), broadcast (radio and television), and outdoor. *Nontraditional* forms of advertising include direct marketing and public relations. *Alternative media* refers to such vehicles as the Internet, mobile marketing, and guerrilla marketing.

Traditional, or mass-media, vehicles no longer get the lion's share of marketing dollars, as marketers now seek relationships with individual consumers. Often traditional media vehicles are not employed at all, with spending diverted to nontraditional and/or alternative media, the categories whose vehicles are more consumer-focused.

It is important to remember that before the introduction of IMC, advertising was all about reaching and selling to the masses. Traditional mass-media vehicles are considered to be one-way vehicles, consisting of a monologue that talks *at* the consumer. IMC has changed all that, and today advertising is all about building a relationship with the individual consumer by employing media vehicles that talk *to* the consumer, creating a critical dialogue between buyer and seller.

Media vehicles used in an IMC campaign must keep the creative message in mind, ensuring that the tone of voice, message, and overall appearance remain constant from vehicle to vehicle, so that a cohesive message and image are delivered. Seamless media coordination is researched, designed, and organized by the media planner.

THE ART AND SCIENCE OF MEDIA PLANNING

Media Planners

Planners are responsible for research, developing the media plan, and determining the media mix. *Media planning* focuses on what media vehicles should be used, in order to give the IMC campaign the strongest tone of voice; when ads should run; where ads should be placed (i.e., local, regional, national, or international venues); what the message is; and how often the message must be seen by the target to be remembered.

Media planning is critical in making a product stand out from competing products by linking the right message to the right target audience in the right place. Understanding the media options allows a media planner to look at each media vehicle and determine which most closely match the target's lifestyle, values, and beliefs, so that the correct vehicles can be employed.

A typical IMC advertising campaign will employ many different types of media, depending on what needs to be accomplished. For example, television may be used for building brand awareness, while direct response or print may be employed to reinforce brand loyalty, deliver detailed copy points, and/or direct the consumer to the Web for more information or ordering. Choices will also depend on the brand's image, the overall message, and the purpose of the advertising.

Planners have hundreds of media vehicles to choose from, which can be combined in even more diverse ways. Today, navigating the media maze is more difficult than ever before. Where there used to be only three network television stations, there are now hundreds of TV stations, segregated into network, spot, cable, satellite, and syndicated options. A handful of general-interest magazines have exploded into hundreds of special-interest and business or trade publications, not to mention those who publish local, regional, and national editions. Radio, once limited to AM stations, eventually added FM and now offers digital and satellite options.

But relying strictly on traditional media vehicles to deliver a product's message is fast becoming a thing of the past. Knowing when, where, why, and how to employ traditional, alternative, and/or guerrilla tactics, and in what combination, is the art of media planning.

Successful convergence between traditional and alternative media options requires innovative thinking. Alternative media options such as advertorials or serial novels deliver variety to traditional media outlets. For example, *advertorials* (often found in magazine advertising and newspaper advertising) use an editorial format to deliver public-service information; to express an opinion about an economic, political, or social issue; or as a lobbying device for legislative changes. Advertising that blends seamlessly with editorial content is less likely to be viewed as an intrusion. However, these ads often mimic the look of editorial content so closely that some magazines and newspapers consider them misleading and will not print them without an accompanying disclaimer, such as a tag that says "advertisement."

Another innovative media tactic used by marketers, the *serial novel*, is a form of advertising that uses an ongoing, slice-of-life dramatization. This tactic has been employed, for example, by the luxury carmaker Lexis. Rather than rely on traditional advertising efforts alone, Lexis decided to engage their target audience by incorporating an entertainment component into their existing advertising efforts. Using their consumer magazine, the *Lexis Quarterly*, the company presented a series of feature stories that seamlessly integrated the product into the plot. This entertainment form of advertising is also known as *branded entertainment*, or, according to an article appearing online in the *Wall Street Journal* on January 17, 2007 ("YouTube Executive Walks a Tightrope"), as "fictomercials" or "literatisements."

Other examples of entertainment-based advertising include **webisodes**, or Internet-hosted video segments used to promote a product or TV show, preview a music video, or deliver other promotional content; and *advergaming*, or ads that are incorporated into video games. Product placement in video games, movies, or television programs requires imperceptible brand integration. If it doesn't fit in the story line, it's intrusive and/or unbelievable. When it does work, it can end up receiving a lot of publicity and word-of-mouth attention.

When new media techniques are successfully merged with traditional vehicles, it is known as *media convergence*.

Whatever forms of media are employed, planners must be sure to chose the right vehicle or combination of vehicles to avoid negatively affecting a brand's image. Improperly placing a product in a medium that does not reflect its image can both damage a brand's equity within its product category and negatively affect brand loyalty. The correct choice is critical to obtaining both media and message exposure. For example, putting a coupon in a high-end jewelry ad would negatively affect the store image in the mind of the consumer, perhaps causing her to change where she shops for jewelry.

Overall content and editorial policy can also affect the choice of media vehicle(s) employed. For example, placing an ad for barbecue grills in a dog magazine, even though the target audience is the same, would be ineffectual. When looking through a dog magazine, the target is not thinking about family dinners or picnics; so it is important that media planners use vehicles such as *Better Homes and Gardens*, whose readers might be persuaded to consider the purchase of barbecue grills at the time they view the ad.

Planners must also be able to accurately decipher what the intended purpose of the advertising is. For example, is it a new-product launch, reminder advertising, or advertising used to reinvent a product? Understanding an ad's function helps determine what happens first, second, and third. Media choices for a new-product launch might be television first and sales promotion second, followed by a lighter concentration of television and radio.

Creating and managing brand contact is another area of concern to media planners. *Brand contact* takes place when a target has any form of planned or unplanned contact with a product or service. *Planned contact* includes any advertised message initiated by a marketer in any media vehicle. An *unplanned message* might be transmitted through word of mouth via conversations with friends in chat rooms, or via viral e-mail sharing or blogs. To consumers, unplanned messages are considered more reliable than those coming from marketers or advertising.

Unplanned media events offer media planners an excellent opportunity to build upon this often-free form of exposure. Anything that initiates media involvement is a great opportunity for free advertising.

Media planners are also responsible for where an ad will appear locally, nationally, or internationally; and when it will run, or where it will be placed, in any one medium. In radio, for example, the planners might choose drive times, or they might sponsor weather or traffic reports. Television programming is chosen on the basis of viewership. In magazine advertising, placement on the front or back covers or in the center spread is highly coveted; but though this guarantees exposure, it also increases costs.

In business, cost is always a factor. It is up to the media planner to determine the number of vehicles that will be used, the length of the campaign, the best vehicle(s) for reaching the largest percentage of the targeted audience, and the number of times an ad must be seen in order to be remembered. A well-designed *media plan* can accomplish all of this within a set budget and within a predetermined timeline. After media choices are determined, it is up to the media buyer to purchase the selected media options.

Developing the Media Plan

The media planner is responsible for designing and implementing the *media plan*. Like the marketing plan and creative brief discussed in earlier chapters, the media plan is the road map for determining the best use of media, time, and space. A media plan consists of five very distinct parts: target-audience profile; media objectives; media strategy; media tactics; and evaluation.

The target-audience profile dissects the target's lifestyle and product usage. Media objectives detail what media needs to accomplish. Media strategy spells out how the media objectives will be accomplished. Media tactics outline what will need to be done to accomplish the strategy, and evaluation will look at the effectiveness of the media plan.

Today, most media plans are developed at the same time as the creative brief. This is mainly because of the large number of media options available, budget considerations, and the fact that certain audiences are extremely difficult to reach—

requiring that messages be designed based on the media vehicle. However, there are still instances where creative is done before a media plan is developed.

Target Audience Profile

The *target audience* a media planner works with is the same one used in the marketing plan and creative brief. After the target audience has been broken down into demographic, psychographic, geographic, and behavioristic profiles, planners must next determine the target's overall product usage. Product usage is made up of brand usage and category usage. *Product usage* measures a consumer's level of product use, determining whether she is a heavy user, medium user, light user, or nonuser. *Brand usage* looks at the specific brand-name products the target uses, whereas *category usage* looks at generic product categories such as paper towels or cleaning products.

Media Objectives

Media objectives are also determined based on the marketing plan and later the creative brief. Media objectives outline what media needs to accomplish in order to expose the target audience to the message. Most media plans will state objectives in terms of reach and frequency. Additionally, media objectives often talk about how much money is available for media purchase, and about communication goals.

Communication goals determine the number of consumers within the target audience that media efforts will reach, the number of times it will reach them, the target's overall interaction with the advertised message, and the amount of exposure required to sustain memorability and accomplish media objectives.

It is the job of the media planner to determine which media vehicle will be used in any IMC campaign. In order to determine media needs, media planners have to consider several factors before making a decision, such as (1) *reach*, or the number of people who will ultimately be exposed to the message; (2) *frequency*, or the number of times the target needs to be exposed to a message before it's remembered or purchase takes place; and (3) overall cost.

REACH

All media objectives deal with some combination of reach and frequency. For advertising to be successful it must *reach* the appropriate target audience. Media people define reach as the number of different consumers or households who are exposed at least once to a media schedule, within a specified amount of time. It is important to understand that reach is determined based on the target's opportunity to see a vehicle (e.g., a magazine or TV program), not an ad within the vehicle. Each media vehicle used will measure exposure differently.

Broadcast vehicles, for example, measure the percentage of the target audience reached (or number of individuals who viewed a specific program) using rating points, while print uses circulation numbers, based on the number of copies sold.

Austin Daniel

The goals are (1) to have as many people see the ads as possible, and/or (2) to achieve the highest frequency possible, resulting in the largest number of ads viewed and the highest volume of sales.

Reach is made up of three parts: (1) the size of the audience; (2) the growth of the audience over a set period of time; and (3) the number of times consumers have been exposed to the media schedule.

A planner can successfully attain a desired level of reach in one of two ways: by repetitively using the same medium, or by combining multiple media vehicles (i.e., employing a *diverse media mix*).

Choosing a media vehicle whose audience most closely matches that of the product's target audience is critical in effectively determining reach.

FREQUENCY

Reach deals with the number of times the consumer is exposed to the advertising schedule. *Frequency* is all about how many times the target repeatedly sees the message.

Frequency is defined as the number of times an individual or household has an opportunity to see (or is exposed to) a message. The more times the consumer sees the message, the better it will be remembered and the more likely it is to be acted upon.

Since consumers are likely to remember their exposure to a media vehicle before they remember the ads within the vehicle, the message must be not only memorable, but also placed within a vehicle the target is likely to be exposed to repeatedly. Complicated messages for, say, expensive products, will require multiple exposures before the message will be understood, remembered, and acted upon. On the other hand, ads that are scheduled to run during peak sales periods will not require as high a frequency, which saves the client money.

Media objectives also define *message weight*, or the number of media vehicles that will be used within a media schedule. Very simply, message weight is a projection of the overall number of possible exposure opportunities a set of ads or an entire campaign will have in any particular market. There are two ways message weight can be conveyed: gross impressions and gross rating points.

Exposure by a single individual to a single ad is known as an **impression**. An advertising impression is defined by the number of exposures, and is often recorded in terms of numbers of individuals or households.

Once a planner knows the audience size of a particular medium, he can multiply audience size by the number of times an ad runs or is viewed. The resulting figure, the number of **gross impressions**, represents the quantity of possible exposures available from that medium.

To manage the often-large number of gross impressions, each medium is rated. Very basically, a rating is determined by the overall percentage of households exposed to any one advertising vehicle.

Here's how it works: A single rating point is the equivalent of 1 percent of any one demographic group. For a TV program to have a rating of 20 basically means that 20 percent of homes with television sets were watching that particular program.

When we combine the ratings of multiple media vehicles, the message weight of the overall advertising schedule can be defined in terms of **gross rating points**. *Gross rating points* are a way to measure the amount of total exposure to a message a household receives, without worrying about duplication or repeat exposure.

CONTINUITY

Continuity is a timing pattern within a campaign and refers to the length of time a campaign will run, or be seen by the target. It is unlikely a media planner will plan for all media efforts to run at the same time or even evenly throughout the year. Since many products are seasonal, efforts will be heavier during peak use and lighter during seasonal drops. Alternatively, a new product launch will require an initially heavy introduction period of perhaps a month. Once brand awareness has been achieved, exposure may be cut in half for the next four to six months; this reduced level will be sufficient for maintaining continuity. Since media buys affect budget, media planners need to know when to stop advertising, when to maintain advertising, and when to alternate advertising, and they must schedule in accordance with the product's heavy and light usage periods.

A typical media schedule for a seasonal product like a lawn mower might call for advertising to run for a month before the season begins. The schedule might then skip a month or two, after which additional flights might run during the height of the season, and again at the close of the season. A heavy flight schedule would be used to introduce the product, and different reminder ads would be used in alternation throughout the season.

It's important to note that in today's crowded media environment, not all media vehicles need to be purchased: some just need to be planned for. As discussed earlier, word-of-mouth options as well as public-relations events are excellent "vehicles" for planners to employ to reach the target.

Strategy

In order for the creative message and the choice of media vehicle(s) employed to complement the brand's image and creative execution, it is important that media planners be a part of preliminary discussions about *strategy*.

Strategy looks at the scope of media required to accomplish the objectives. For example, it examines whether media will need to be bought at the local, regional, national, or international level. Media planners concentrate on three major areas: (1) what markets to advertise in; (2) the best times of the year to advertise; and (3) what media vehicles to use.

Strategy is the bridge that connects the brand message with the target. Strategies should somehow create a memorable experience between the product and the buyer. Strategy also addresses audience size, price, and the complexity of the message.

The mutual planning between creative and media allows for selection of the best media vehicle(s) to deliver the message. Since creative messages come in many different forms, media planners must understand what type of visual/verbal message the product or service will need, and then choose the right media mix to enhance awareness, reach the target, and promote the message.

Message delivery can be emotional or rational, simple or complex. A simple, emotional appeal can often get its point across using a featured visual and few words, making billboards and transit vehicles great media options. An emotional appeal can enhance and maintain its emotional message when media exposure appears at regular intervals. Rational, complex appeals, on the other hand, often require a great deal of copy to explain features and benefits, and media vehicles such as magazines and direct response will allow the target to spend time with the message. The product's life-cycle stage also affects media selection. A mature product, for example, will not require as much copy, as high a frequency, or as much exposure in order to be remembered as will a reinvented product or a new product launch.

Because media is responsible for the strategic placement of creative's voice, it is important not only that media planners and buyers understand each media vehicle's pros and cons, but also that account management and creative understand each vehicle's unique characteristics, so that the agency can develop appropriate strategies and creative executions which get the most out of each vehicle's use.

Media Mix

Those vehicles that will successfully accomplish the objectives make up the *media mix*. Being able to choose the right media mix is as important as being able to develop the right message. Reaching the target in a creative way is critical.

When a product or service employs more than one media vehicle, it is referred to as a **mixed media approach**. This is a great way for an IMC campaign to not only create a relationship with the intended target, but to deliver the correct message at the right time.

When a media planner sits down and decides on the most appropriate media mix for a campaign, she will consider two specific points: which vehicles to use, and how much to use each vehicle.

Most decisions will include a mix of traditional (one-way) media and interactive (two-way) media. Media mixes can be broken down into two separate strategy formats: concentrated and broad.

An advertiser with a complex message should consider using a **concentrated mix**, since the greater frequency will allow a consumer to digest the message. These types of messages are easier to understand in print, rather than through a thirty-second TV or radio spot; in print, the message can be read slowly, reread if necessary, or saved for a later time.

A concentrated media mix uses fewer media and less money. It allows for higher frequency within fewer media categories. This approach is great for highly competitive product categories, where there is little difference between products. The more concentrated the media mix, the higher the chance that an ad will stand out and be remembered.

Concentrated media strategies can affect a product's share of voice. *Share of voice* refers to a brand's dominance within a product category, and its total spending compared to that of competing products. If the client's budget is limited, a concentrated strategy works great, basically because fewer media need fewer messages. These types of strategies are a calculated risk. If a message or media buy misses its mark, then advertising efforts will be unsuccessful.

Media plans that employ a concentrated media mix strategy improve frequency and decrease reach. The more media used, the greater the reach. The best media vehicles when employing a concentrated mix are magazines and newspapers, since they are subscription based and viewed repetitively, making it easier to build relationships with heavy users.

Since fewer media are used, concentrated media mixes cost less to produce. For example, if you use three different media vehicles, each vehicle will require a different message. For simple messages such as reminder or maintenance messages, an advertiser should consider a broad mix to increase reach.

A *broad media approach* works best for an IMC campaign because it uses multiple media vehicles to disperse the message and reach the target. This is a great approach when the target is diversified and hard to reach. The repetitiveness of this approach in multiple media make it much more likely the ad will be seen and remembered by the intended audience.

Additionally, a broad media mix allows for several media vehicles to carry the message at one time. For example, TV might be used for building awareness; sales promotion might be used to promote trial; newspapers might be employed to announce a sale; and the Internet might be used for encouraging additional research, providing coupons, or enabling the purchase.

The decision to use a concentrated or broad media mix strategy will also depend on the creative message.

The choice of vehicles that will make up the media mix will be based on how many opportunities the consumer will have to interact with the brand, both traditionally and nontraditionally.

Scheduling

Once planners have determined the media mix, they next need to determine the best time to advertise. *Scheduling* determines insertion dates, commercial lengths, and promotional activities for a product or service. It is not unusual for products to receive a heavy dose of advertising during seasonal highs and lows. To achieve continuity throughout a campaign, planners will use one of three scheduling tactics: continuous scheduling, flighting, or pulsing.

Which to use is determined by three factors: (1) consumer timing, or purchasing cycle for the product; (2) the consumer purchasing schedule; and (3) seasonality.

The first factor has to do with the amount of time a consumer requires between a purchase decision and the actual product purchase. When a consumer is very interested in a product like perfume, jewelry, or a sports car, it's known as *high involvement*. These type of purchases do not often take place on a whim. Often a lot of thought and research precedes purchase, because price is normally an important factor in the purchasing decision. Because of this, it is important that advertising efforts appear during this decision-making process, rather than at the time of purchase. When consumers give little thought to the purchase of products like toothpaste or toilet-bowl cleaner, it's known as *low involvement*, which requires a more intrusive media approach.

Ads for products with low involvement work great in home-decorating or parenting magazines, or paired with programs like *Oprah*. High-involvement products might be promoted by means of product placement, sponsorships, or ads in business or high-end fashion magazines.

Low-involvement products are usually advertised in mass-media vehicles, since there is little commonality among members of the target audience—everyone needs toothpaste and toilet-bowl cleaners. A high-involvement product corresponds to a target audience whose members have a high level of common traits, so a more personalized medium like direct mail works well.

The types of media chosen should reflect both the product's and the target's image. A successful choice of vehicle with respect to target-audience profile will

Black and Decker:
A name your grandfather trusted.

1917 Screwdriver.

A name your father trusts, and a name you'll trust to pass on to your son.

2006 Screwdriver.

Black and Decker stands behind your tools.

A tradition trusted since 1917

BLACK AND DECKER®.

Amandalynn Thomas

eliminate *media waste*, or messages viewed or heard by people unlikely to use the product or interact with the vehicle.

The second factor affecting scheduling is the amount of time a consumer takes between purchases. Everyday products like bread, cereal, and shampoo will require a continuous weekly schedule, to reinforce and to remind consumers about purchase options. Products that are repurchased less frequently, like cleaning supplies, require less advertising throughout the year.

The third factor is seasonality. Most specialty products have their own season for use, such as lawn mowers in the spring and summer, sweaters in the fall and winter, and hot chocolate in the winter. Some products, like Cadbury chocolate eggs, come out once a year and then disappear. Seasonal products will best be served by using a flighting schedule, whereas everyday products like toothpaste and paper towels will fare better with a continuous schedule.

CONTINUOUS SCHEDULING

An advertising message that runs on a repetitive basis, with little variation over the life of the campaign, is running on a *continuous schedule*.

One of the best ways to build continuity for products that consumers purchase or use on a regular basis is for media planners to use continuous scheduling. With a continuous schedule, the pattern of the media schedule does not need to change much over the life of the campaign. Continuous scheduling is used most often for frequently purchased products and by brands with big budgets and consistent sales. It is a great way to build or maintain product awareness.

FLIGHTING

When heavy periods of advertising alternate with periods of no advertising, it's known as *flighting*. This type of alternating schedule is great for seasonal products like swimsuits and snow blowers.

PULSING

A *pulsing* schedule combines continuity and flighting. An advertiser using a pulsing approach will schedule advertising throughout the year, with heavier advertising periods during seasonal peaks.

Tactics

Tactics detail the types of media vehicles employed, such as broadcast, print, sponsorship, mobile marketing, and out-of-home, or any advertising seen outside the home, to name just a few.

The media planner is in charge of developing the media objectives and media strategy. Initiating media tactics is usually the job of the media buyer. Tactics determine how the media strategy will be carried out.

Media planners determine the best media values in three ways: cost per thousand (CPM), cost per point (CPP), and cost per response (CPR).

In order to determine the overall cost of exposing 1,000 members of the target audience to an ad, buyers will calculate media costs in terms of CPM.

CPM is what a media vehicle charges to deliver a message to 1,000 members of its targeted audience. The lower the CPM, the more efficient the choice of vehicle is—assuming that both are a "nice fit" with the target.

CPP is used almost exclusively for buying broadcast media. It's how broadcasters measure audience delivery within a specific market or region for a specific broadcast medium. It is best to compare a vehicle's CPP with that of vehicles in the same medium (e.g., radio to radio), because the strengths and weaknesses of each medium vary.

For advertising to be successful, the target must act upon the message in some measurable way, such as by making a purchase or visiting a store. Thus, the best way to compare any media vehicle's value is on the basis of cost per response CPR.

Once the media plan has been developed and the planner has determined the best media vehicle(s) for the product, its image, its concept, and its visual/verbal voice, the media plan must be put into action. Executing the media plan is the job of the media buyer. It is her job to negotiate and ultimately buy the media packages best suited to accomplishing the media plan.

Execution of the media plan begins with the media buy. It is the media buyer's job to negotiate the best media deals with various media representatives, in order to accomplish the objectives laid out in the media plan. Successful media buys are based not on pure cost, but on the return on the media investment as it affects the target audience.

Media buyers will rely on qualitative and quantitative research data to compare vehicles. *Quantitative* properties can be measured, and include such things as audience and vehicle duplication, cost, and geographic coverage. *Qualitative* properties amount to mere judgment calls and include such things as vehicle image, printing issues, and editorial content.

For media buyers who want to reach a large audience of male consumers, the Super Bowl is worth its weight in advertising dollars—thirty seconds of airtime costs a mere $2.6 million. To reach a large audience of women, the Oscars are a great place to start, at only $1.7 million dollars per thirty-second spot.

Media buyers negotiate prices and often negotiate integrated media packages to save money. Larger media companies often bundle their diverse media options together in what are known as *value-added programs.*

Value-added programs allow media buyers to diversify their buys and save their clients money at the same time. Most large media companies own more than one media vehicle, so many will offer value-added programs that include multiple buys from their large assortment of media options, such as TV and radio stations and/or newspaper and magazine options. Value-added packages could also include direct mail, sales promotions, and even public-relations opportunities.

For each individual medium, buyers must know print sizes and specifications (for print vehicles), broadcast options (for TV and radio—for example, the cost of a fifteen- or thirty-second spot), and the insertion deadlines that must be met in order for print to run or broadcast to air at a specific time.

How is media space purchased? Print and out-of-home vehicles sell space in terms of inches or feet; broadcast vehicles sell fifteen-, thirty-, and/or sixty-second time slots; and Internet-based vehicles and other interactive media vehicles sell by size and/or access.

A good media buyer knows the market and the media options, and is a good negotiator and closer, who will make sure ads run when they where scheduled to run.

Evaluation

Evaluation is quite simply a detailed look at the effectiveness of the decisions made.

Evaluative measures concerning the media plan can be conducted by either the agency or an independent source. There are several ways a media plan can be evaluated, such as target feedback, observation, and tracking. To gain target feedback ads might include Web addresses, toll-free numbers, coupons, or reply cards. Responses will be added up and evaluated. Observation allows media buyers to participate in a little undercover work by observing the target in the place where the product is purchased. Tracking is used by media buyers to evaluate the effectiveness of online ads, sales promotion tactics, and coupon distribution, to name just a few examples.

Media effectiveness basically means the client saw a return on his or her investment (ROI). Usually ROI is determined based on sales. Many things beyond message and media can affect a marketer's ROI, such as economic or political factors and competitive issues and prices.

GEOGRAPHIC PLACEMENT

Once a planner has designed the media plan, he next must decide where the advertising will be placed. He must do this before final scheduling can be completed. Planners can chose from one of four geographic levels: international, national, regional, and local.

Internationally placed advertising and national buys can employ multiple and diverse vehicles. The most common buys will include traditional vehicles such as magazines, television, and out-of-home.

A media buyer has three options when the scope of a company's advertising efforts will be national: (1) advertise in all markets across the United States; (2) employ a *spot*, or regional, approach where advertising is placed only in specific markets; or (3) employ a combined approach, where advertising runs in all markets but is heavier in specific markets (e.g., those markets where sales are weak or where there is a need to support cooperative advertising efforts).

National distribution is usually an option for products all consumers need, like laundry detergent or toothpaste. The choice of a national approach is best if sales are good across all markets. Many products, however, have their targeted audiences in specific regions of the country like the Southeast, making a spot or regional approach more effective. Spot approaches are also great for eliminating advertising waste, or advertising in places where the target is unlikely to see the message. A choice to use combined is sometimes made when a product or service is struggling in certain areas of the country. In order to reach this inattentive audience, advertising efforts will need to run more often in these markets; whereas, in areas where the product or service is successful, only a light maintenance schedule will be required.

Advertising efforts by local companies can be combined with those of national or even other local sponsors in what is known as cooperative or *"co-op" advertising*. *Co-op advertising* most often features national products in local advertising. In return for the exposure, national advertisers will pay part of the advertising costs.

Most commonly, local advertising efforts are for products that are sold in only one location in one city or town. Advertising can be localized to include current or upcoming events. These types of ads often feature some kind of sale or promotion to get local audiences into local businesses quickly.

DECIPHERING THE DIFFERENT MEDIA CATEGORIES

Very simply, media options can be divided into three different categories: mass media (traditional), direct response (nontraditional and/or niche), and sales promotion (promotional).

If advertising efforts need to maintain or reinforce brand image, create awareness, or encourage trial and repeat purchase, then mass-media advertising, typically reaching large numbers of people, is the best choice. If the goal is to build a relationship with the target, then a direct-response vehicle such as direct mail or the Internet is a good idea. Promotional vehicles are great as support vehicles for building awareness and promoting trial. If encouraging trial is the overall objective, then the best sales-promotion vehicles might involve the use of point-of-purchase options such as coupons, trial offers, or sampling that will ultimately boost sales.

It is important that the media planner know each media vehicle's pros and cons, and how each will interfere with or promote the advertised message. Ultimately, media choice will not sell the product—it is still the message that sells the product, changes attitudes, alters behavior, and enhances or defines values—but good media decisions can sure help the message along.

MEDIA DEVELOPMENT BEGINS BY KNOWING THE COMPETITION

Knowing what the competition is up to is as critical to the media planner as it is to the marketer and creative team. Unless the product has a matching budget or the product is truly unique, it is best to use different media vehicles from those used by competing products, in order to ensure that the product will stand out and reflect a unique product image.

On the other hand, choosing media vehicles used by competing products is a good idea if the target is the same or similar to that of the competition, or if the competitor has a weak image or media package. Overall, the more closely a product competes with other products in its category, the more advertising the target will need to see, and the greater the cost will be to the marketer, for the product to stand out from competing products and be remembered.

Media planners must always keep the creative message and overall concept in mind when choosing media vehicles. It is critical that planners match message personality to media image. For example, to understand how a new product, or a change to a reinvented product, works or performs, creative efforts might require that the product be demonstrated. In this case television, sales promotion, or the Internet would be a better choice than any print vehicle.

GATHERING RESEARCH FOR MEDIA ANALYSIS

Media research looks at the target and media options. Data includes a detailed look at both the size and overall characteristics that comprise the target audience, as well as the media use associated with the target. When media planners want demographic and psychographic profiles, or any information on product and media usage, they turn to research provided by companies such as Mediamark Research, Inc. (MRI) and Simmons Market Research Bureau (SMRB). MRI research originates from a consumer sample of 25,000 individuals who are interviewed on a yearly basis. SMRB provides existing databases on a multitude of diverse product categories. SMRB also provides both demographic and psychographic target profiles, as well as information regarding the media options that will best reach that target.

Planners can also use data that is available from individual media vehicles. Major media vehicles profile their target audiences in much the same way as agencies do, using demographics, psychographics, observation, and product usage. These profiles can also help planners pair product image with media image.

Just like marketing and general advertising research, media employs primary and secondary media vehicles. The primary medium is chosen because the media buyer knows the target will be exposed to the medium and thus the message.

One or two secondary media choices are used when (1) a large section of the target audience will not be exposed to the primary media vehicle, or (2) media needs to get the target to do something the primary medium cannot accomplish. For example, a television ad may refer the target to a website for ordering or to acquire more information.

PART TWO

THE CREATIVE PROCESS

CHAPTER SIX

CREATIVE

DETERMINING THE PRODUCT'S OR SERVICE'S VISUAL/VERBAL TONE OF VOICE

Lindsay Frankenfield

I regard a great ad as the most beautiful thing in the world.

—Leo Burnet, quoted in *100 Leo's*, 94.

THE MANY STAGES OF DESIGN

Once the media have been determined, creative can be developed. It can then be designed to fit various sizes and allow for various image combinations.

There is no document that outlines the creative concept development stage. The documents we have looked at—the marketing plan, creative brief, and media plan—concentrate on marketing assessments, an overall communication profile, and media placement.

Creative—along with its interpretation and its ultimate ability to produce a sale—is the driving force behind any integrated marketing campaign. Creative today must embrace multiculturalism, and craft a message that not only titillates but also educates and informs. If creative efforts fail, it is because the marketing plan failed. The fate of an ad or a campaign is sealed during the development of the creative brief.

Everything creative—copy and layout—begins in the creative brief. Before any brainstorming takes place, any copy is written, or any concept is laid out, the creative team needs to thoroughly study the creative brief and understand the media options.

The creative brief lays an informational foundation for the creative team to build upon. It outlines what the IMC creative efforts need to accomplish, and it is the rationale behind creative direction. The creative team will use the knowledge about the target to define the audience they are talking to. Objectives will determine what the creative efforts will need to accomplish, and the strategy and positioning will help determine how the message will be delivered and the image and position needed to stand out from the competition. The key benefit will become the voice of the IMC promotion and must dominate all creative executions, both visually and verbally.

All creative efforts must be written and designed specifically for the target audience, in a *vernacular*, or language, they can understand, about problems or situations they can relate to; and they must appear in a medium that target audience members frequently encounter.

There is a lot of bad advertising out there, with no direction, no strong brand identity, and no defined target audience. This kind of advertising usually carries what I call a "been there, done that" creative label. This means the idea has been used before—sometimes many, many times. How many times do consumers have to see creative teams animate the Statue of Liberty—or, worse yet, make the Mona Lisa smile—for yet another product?

When you've seen something once, it's interesting; when you've seen it two or three times, it's boring. Once consumers are bored, they stop paying attention to the message.

Today's consumer is bombarded with hundreds of advertising messages each day. A good creative team recognizes this and looks for an innovative way to make their product stand out among the clutter. Geico did this with the "gecko" and "cavemen" campaigns, and Aflac did it with the "duck" campaign.

THE SOCCER GAME OF IDEA TEAMWORK

Once the creative team has decided on a creative direction, the next step is determining a visual/verbal solution that will bring the idea to life. Jump-starting the imaginative process requires an understanding of what advertising efforts need to accomplish, who needs to be reached, and how those people will be reached. Once the creative team has reviewed and digested the research, it is time to imagine a solution. Coming up with that extraordinary idea is not as easy as most people think it is.

The search for a great idea requires an active imagination and an ego that recognizes that that imagination is fallible, and that not every idea is a good idea. However, believing your idea is the best idea is the only way to approach the creative process. Fortunately—or unfortunately, depending on how you look at it—there are always other people around to deny or confirm brilliance. An idea needs to bounce around in your head, and once you've got it under control, it needs to be bounced off a colleague before it can be molded into a good idea. This may seem a little like a soccer match, with the ball hitting everyone in the head a few times. You need a partner to play the idea game; this is why creatives often work in teams.

The creative team, as defined in chapter 1, includes an art director and one or more copywriters. It could also include a media planner and/or an AE. This team is responsible for developing the idea, writing ad copy, and designing ads that bring the product or service to life for the consumer. The creative team then takes these ideas and designs them to each media vehicle's strengths and limitations. When copywriters and art directors work together, visual and verbal communication are joined into a powerful problem-solving combination.

WHO ARE THE CREATIVES?

Creative, as used in this text, is a broad term related to the conceptual process. A *creative* is a person who is involved in *creative* activity, especially, in this context, activity involving the creation of advertisements. The creative team is comprised of some very eclectic and imaginative personalities. One is thinking how to tell the product's or service's story, while the other plots what it will look like.

When these two diverse minds sit down together with the creative brief in what is known as a brainstorming, or idea generation session, interesting, imaginative, strange and downright stupid things begin to happen. These sessions are used to generate multiple ideas that will solve the client's advertising problem. Hundreds of good and bad ideas are presented for discussion; most will be discarded, but many will be worked on and developed further.

Everyone associated with a creative team must be open minded and well versed in economics, social behaviors, current issues, politics, movies, music, and the classics. They should be able to use anything from historical references to present-day slang to sell or represent a product or service. These brainstorming sessions are critical to getting boring "been there, done that" ideas out of the creatives' heads, after which they can get down to the new, the unusual, and, eventually, the successful ideas. New ideas set a product apart from its competitors and can be the catalyst to building lasting brand images and, ultimately, an essential position in the minds of the consumer.

The key to a good brainstorming session is to never be afraid to look and feel stupid by coming up with a really, really bad idea. It's humbling but it's necessary, in order to ignite the ideas of others in the session: one really bad thought voiced aloud can spark another—hopefully better—idea in someone else.

Stale advertising begins and ends with stale ideas. The typical young creative believes her first idea is her best idea; but it's only her best idea because it's her *only* idea. Once creatives successfully test the waters and stretch their legs a bit, they are often surprised where they end up.

The qualities necessary in order for someone to be a successful copywriter or art director include the following:

1. An ability to see what is not there. If a product comes in six colors, what does that represent: A canvas? An oil spill? A sunset?

2. Continued motion through ideas. A creative solution is often elusive and must be chased down through the clutter of one's own mind. Staring off into space, acting something out, or borrowing actions from the guy on the subway might evoke new ideas.

3. Knowledge of the profession. What is old can be made new again, but it should not be copied if it is already associated with another product. Using nostalgia in a message can make a point; copying a competitor can be confusing and is often disastrous.

4. Media expertise. Creatives need to watch TV; go to mainstream and independent movies; read books, newspapers, or magazines and learn about current and historical events; watch for fads and trends; watch the fashion wheel of fortune; and listen to the radio. Knowing and interpreting what's going on in society helps them set new trends rather than having to follow them.

5. A habit of observing the human species. We're interesting and we're unique, and we can relate to each other's mannerisms, body language, style (or lack thereof), eye movements, and hand gestures. Creatives might study how different personalities and age groups move, eat, sit, stare, and read.

6. Knowledge of the product or service. If unfamiliar with the product, a member of the creative team needs to pick one up and try it. If unfamiliar with competing products, he needs to use them and compare. A product can only be sold if the creative team first understands it. Knowledge is power; it empowers the message and should be able to ignite action and interest in the target audience.

7. The understanding that advertising is a business. Creative is based on a business plan. It must be "on strategy" and meet the stated objectives, and it must be on budget. Creatives never get to do what they want. They must learn to accept that great ideas are not hindered by limitations, but challenged by them.

8. Excellence. Copywriters should be able to weave an interesting story out of boring facts. Designers must be able to envision the product or service in a way no one else would or could, and be able to execute it flawlessly. Clients pay out large sums of money for the expertise advertising brings to the table. Because of this the competition is fierce, the life span short, and the stress high.

9. The ability to cry a little but laugh a lot. The creative process is a tough one. The chances of anyone liking any idea in its original form are slim to none. Changes are a fact of life; rejection of ideas is right up there with death and taxes. When an idea does take form and fly, it's worth all the pain and frustration.

It's important for clients and AEs alike to understand that creative doesn't happen in a vacuum. It takes long hours and a lot of reworking before an idea can be presented, first internally to the team and then eventually to the client. Because the creative work takes place toward the end of the advertising process, time is limited. Brilliance may have from as little as a few hours to as much as several weeks to

Helen Benson

show itself. Any creative team member must be able to turn on the creative juices at a moment's notice and for long hours at a time. He must be willing to fight for what he believes in, but he must also be able to let go of those ideas that just don't measure up, so that he can live to fight another day. Stress should be considered a creative catalyst, not a paralyzing force.

THE CREATIVE CONCEPT

Creatives have a wide-eyed view of the world that marketers or others in advertising don't have. They see the world as a distorted mistake that a bit of quark, grit, drive, and competitive difference can't find an excuse for.

Frustration and exhilaration are the endpoints of the range of emotions any creative can experience in any given day for any given product.

Art directors begin the creative process by staring off into space, clearing their minds of all prejudices or preconceived notions about the product or service. Somewhere between here (mind) and there (space), a good idea wants to be picked up and developed. The creative team needs to anticipate response to the product or service by asking themselves all the important questions, or those questions that the target might ask about the product or service. This series of questions begins with *who*, *what*, *when*, *where*, *why*, and *how*.

The *creative concept* is an idea that imaginatively solves the client's advertising problem. Before a great idea can be isolated, many mediocre ones will be pursued. Conceptual development, or brainstorming, is a process that starts when the creative team members kick their imaginations into overdrive and expose the "unthought of."

BRAINSTORMING

Brainstorming is the imagination at work. In the process, good ideas, partial ideas, and bad ideas are considered, developed further, or thrown out.

Brainstorming is still done the old-fashioned way—from gray cells to mouth or paper. Brainstorming sessions usually involve a creative team of copywriters and art directors, but a session could also be a solitary one, in which the art director or copywriter allows his thoughts to mature. Nothing is set in stone, apart from the product's features, so as not to limit the number of ideas the session may generate.

There is no set way that creatives brainstorm ideas; the main goal is to discuss the creative brief and imagine a way to solve a problem. Within the key benefit lies the product's inherent drama. What makes it tick? What aspects are interesting or unusual? How will it benefit the target audience? Brainstorming isolates that benefit and places it within various scenarios that have meaning to the target audience. The result should cause them to think. People don't pay attention to abstract ideas; they pay attention to concrete images, and they want to know "What's in it for me?"— how the product or service can solve their personal problems or needs.

A traditional brainstorming session may begin with a copywriter throwing out a headline to promote the key benefit while the art director, with drawing pad and marker in hand, quickly roughs out a visual that supports the headline. On the average, a creative team can come up with anywhere from 50 to 100 ideas per session. Of course, not all of these ideas will be brilliant. Some ideas are weak, some too complicated, and others just plain stupid—but each one inspires another direction, or even the possible combination of ideas.

WHAT MAKES A CREATIVE IDEA GOOD?

That's a good question. The short answer is that if you've seen it done before, it's no longer creative. It's that "been there, done that" thing again. Once an idea becomes mainstream, it won't hold the target's interest the way a new and innovative approach will.

A good idea is recognizable when it comes along, basically, because it doesn't stink as much as the rest. It's also dead-on strategy, it features the key benefit, and it meets the goals laid out in the objectives.

Ideas can come from anywhere. A member of the creative team might witness something relevant on the street, or overhear a devastatingly good conversation on the bus or at a coffee shop. Cocktail conversation is often enlightening, and nothing can compete with basic personal experiences or a good discussion about the product itself. The creative team can talk about it; think about it; question it; position it; brand it; place it in a relevant setting (or even an irrelevant one); let it stand alone; compare it to the competition; show results, "before and after" style; twist it or bend it . . . but they need to make it their own. When enlightenment finally does come—and it always does—they need to pounce on it.

The next step is to search for quality in the quantity. Ideas with potential will eventually be reworked and narrowed down to anywhere from three to five concepts that are presented to the client and then prepared for printing.

THE VISUAL ELEMENTS THAT BRING THE CREATIVE IDEA TO LIFE

Putting Ideas on Paper: The Stages of Design

In this section, we'll look at four stages of the design process: concept, thumbnails, roughs, and super comprehensives.

Concept

The first stage in the design process is brainstorming, or concept development. *Concept* refers to any thoughts and ideas on how to creatively solve the client's advertising problem. Concept sets the tone and direction for a single ad or a combination of ads. This is where bad ideas come to die, and good ideas get a second look and perhaps an overhaul and face-lift. It's also where dreams begin to see the light of day. Here, the creative team hammers out sometimes hundreds of ideas, only 10 percent of which will bear further development.

Thumbnails

Thumbnails, or *thumbs,* are an internal design tool and are rarely if ever seen by the client. Their creation constitutes the second stage in the design process. *Thumbnails* are small, proportionate drawings (usually measuring around the size of a business card) that are used to place concept ideas on paper.

Roughs

Roughs, or *layouts,* which represent the third stage in the design process, are chosen from the best thumbnail ideas. *Roughs* are often quickly drawn ideas, used to represent how the final ad will look. Roughs are often presented to the client, especially if she is an established client. Roughs are done full size (i.e., in the size of the final piece), and are done in either black and white or, if relevant, color. All type—such as headlines, subheads, and slogans—should be accurately reproduced in position on the rough, and in the representative typeface and weight. Any visuals appearing on a rough must be tight enough for the client to understand what is going on or what is being shown.

Super Comprehensives

The fourth and final stage in the design process—though not technically a part of the design process—involves the production of super comprehensives, or *super comps,* which are created from the final roughs. They are generated on the computer with all headlines, subheads, photographs, and/or illustrations, a logo, and—for the first time—completed body copy in place, simulating exactly how the finished design will look and read.

Katelan Crawford

Visuals, Options and Decisions

The visual chosen for any creative piece is important. It should take into consideration the media to be used as well as the product or service to be advertised. The visual the target eventually sees is a representation of the client's product or service. Designers can decide how to present that image—perhaps through the realism of photography, or perhaps with the artistic expression of an illustration or graphic design. A simpler effect can be achieved with black-and-white line art; or perhaps budget constraints will call for clip art or stock art. Whatever image becomes the visual voice of the client's product, it should support the strategy, headline, and concept, and it should reflect both the target's and the product's image.

Visuals speak to all cultures better than even the longest copy can. An ad's visual options are diverse. There are five possible visual options that the art director might consider using: photography, line art, illustration, clip or stock art, and graphic images. We will also look at logos as representing image. The choice ultimately depends on budget, media, and image.

The Image of Photographs

Believability is one reason to use photographs. Unfortunately, photography can be expensive, especially color photography. The decision to include a photograph instead of an illustration or line art depends on the concept being used, the image of the product or service, and the medium.

The visual realism offered by photographs allows readers to see patterns, textures, quality, and color as if the product were sitting before them. The range of visual variety offers designers the options of showcasing the product alone or in use, of placing it in a relevant setting, and of comparing it to a similar product. Size is also a visual variable; images can be enlarged to dominate the page or reduced in order to show multiple views or options.

WHAT'S IN A PHOTOGRAPH?

There is no better way to create a mood or conjure up emotions than with photographs, especially those with people in them. Although photographs take time to set up and shoot, consumers prefer them in ads promoting services such as banking and investing, or those featuring food products. Photographs can more easily show the product being used, and they allow consumers to envision themselves using the product or service.

THE "POP" OF BLACK-AND-WHITE PHOTOGRAPHS

Why use *black-and-white photos* when color is available? One reason is price. It is much less expensive to use a black-and-white photograph than a color photograph. Another reason is that a black-and-white photograph stands out against a lot of color. This independence in appearance attracts readers' attention.

SPOT COLOR

An excellent alternative to a full-color photograph is a black-and-white photo featuring one element in color. This is an example of *spot color*. This is an excellent way to highlight the product, by making it stand out in stark contrast to the rest of the photograph. Spot color can give a visual the illusion of three-dimensionality. By adding a spot of color to the photograph, the designer can control eye flow, drawing the viewer's eye directly to the product.

The use of photographs, especially color photographs, requires a large budget. However, color photography at any level, even just spot color, is often worth the price. It brings an ad alive and helps to create consumer interest and involvement.

Line Art

Black-and-white line art consists of a drawing that has no tonal qualities. A drawing is a great choice when an ad is spotlighting a product with small details, such as a lace tablecloth or a delicate china pattern. Drawings simplify a design and create a strong black-and-white contrast on the page.

Illustration

Illustrations, unlike line art, have tonal qualities, so they are more like photographs. But, unlike photographic images, illustrations are created rather than captured. With illustrations, advertisers can take a more analytical approach, by presenting charts and graphs; or a lighter approach, by creating characters to represent the product.

Illustrations can create a mood or express a point of view as easily as a photograph does. Depending on the style and color usage, they can represent a laid-back or upbeat approach.

Clip or Stock Art

Using either clip art or stock art is a great option when money is tight. *Clip art* refers to existing line art drawings. *Stock art* refers to existing photographs. Both clip art and stock art are available in many varieties for purchase and use. These terms are often used interchangeably. The only problem with using clip or stock art is it is not original art, or art created especially for advertising the product or service. However, the designer can ensure a unique appearance by combining photos together or cropping out unwanted areas.

The Energy in Graphics

Graphic design uses a combination of visuals and type to colorfully, symbolically, and uniquely represent an idea or concept. Graphics have great potential when color is an option. If the client's product is youthful or modern, the use of graphics can lend a more expressive or upbeat approach. Graphic design looks at life and at situations abstractly. Bright colors, often chosen for their symbolic meanings, are combined with both geometric and organic shapes to create modern and bold designs, or an alternative view of life. When set off by a lot of white space, this design style screams "new," "bold," or "eclectic," especially if other advertising surrounding it uses a more traditional approach.

The Logo as a Symbol

A discussion about visual/verbal relationships would be incomplete without a discussion of logos. A *logo* is the symbol—and ultimately the image—of a company or product, and it should be prominently displayed on any creative piece. A logo can consist of nothing more than the company or product name represented typographically; it can also be a graphic symbol, or a combination of type and graphic. A logo needs to close every ad, ensuring it is the last thing the viewer sees.

Spokespersons and Character Representatives

When creative has something to say visually, the creative team might consider using or creating a visual personality in the form of a spokesperson or cartoon/animated character representative.

Spokespersons

The *spokesperson* for a product is important. He or she must be likable, and have an appearance that fits the campaign's overall visual/verbal concept. To determine an appropriate spokesperson, the creative team needs to ask, "Who does this product remind me of?" Remember, it's the product's personality that sets it off from the competition, especially if there are no major differences between brands in the same category.

There are three basic types of spokespersons:

- Celebrities
- Specialists and CEOs
- Common Man

Josh Cantrell

CELEBRITIES

A *celebrity*'s popularity with younger target audiences can be transferred to a product, and this popularity can actually build a product's brand equity. It is important that the celebrity's professional image be tied to the product's key benefit. This image translates to the product, so any character flaws that arise in a celebrity over time will reflect upon the product.

Celebrities' lives on and off the screen, courts, or fields can threaten endorsement deals. Marketers know a spokesperson's antics can reflect badly on their products; as a result, they are currently looking for ways to avoid "endorsing" celebrity endorsements. Some alternatives include product placement in movies and television programming, and arena advertising.

SPECIALISTS AND CEOS

If something needs to be proved, use a *specialist* in the field—such as a doctor, scientist, or engineer. If the ultimate goal is to develop a philosophy, create a friendship, or instill trust, the use of a *CEO* or owner of a small company or business is the way to go.

COMMON MAN

The *common man* can be someone who uses the product and can talk about his or her experiences, or a paid actor representing the common man based on feedback from real consumers.

WHAT ABOUT POLITICIANS?

A discussion on spokespersons would not be complete without adding another group of possibles to the list: *politicians*. The voice of a former mayor, governor, or U.S. senator or representative—or even a former president—can be very persuasive.

Character Representatives

A *character representative* begins in the creative team's imagination, much like a live spokesperson does. In this case, the imagination is specifically that of the art director. The choice of whether to use a live person or to create a character spokesman such as the Energizer Bunny or Jolly Green Giant will have a lot to do with concept and a little to do with budget.

There are times when a live actor who fits the client's direction or the art director's conceived personality for the product simply cannot be found. When it can't be found, it needs to be created. In addition, budget can affect whether a spokesperson will be local talent or a celebrity. But at any level, live talent is more expensive to maintain than a character on a page.

Color's Representational Role

The Mood of Color

Effective color choices can be used as design elements. Certain colors evoke specific emotions and can be used to set a mood or attract the eye. In the unfortunate event of the target's forgetting the product name, often the use of unique color combinations on packaging can help with recall when the target is determining which product to purchase.

The Meaning of Color

Color can make us feel warm, cold, stressed, or lethargic. We know the sun should be yellow and the sky blue. The elegance, reassurance, or casualness of a color comes from our life experiences; we see life in colors and use them to describe events, emotions, the passage of time, or life and death.

Elements That Make Up an Ad: What Goes Where?

There is no right or wrong answer to the question of what goes where in an ad. An ad can be nothing more than a visual, or it can be extremely copy heavy. As long as it is informative, advances the product's image, and creates interest in the mind of the target, it's on the right track.

An ad can be made up of some or all of the following five elements: headline, subhead(s), visual(s), body copy, and logo. Not every element needs to be present in every ad; however, order is somewhat predetermined.

The order in which elements appear depends on the concept being emphasized. If the headline presents a great consumer benefit or is extremely important to the ad's direction, then it must go first, at the top of the design. If the visual says more than words can, then it should be placed at the top of the design. This thought process will also help determine which element should be the dominant element on the page.

Controlling the order of what the target sees and reads aids him in understanding the advertised message.

Type Is a Personality Thing

The **typeface** used in an ad is as important as the message itself. Understanding the visual message of type is critical to building or maintaining a brand's image.

The choice of typeface should reflect the personality of the product or company. Type is not a whimsical or temporary choice. Like layout style, once a typeface is chosen, it should appear in every ad—no matter what the media vehicle. The typeface should become a representative device for that product or service. Type is an art form of shapes, curves, circles, and lines. Giving the product or service, and thus the client, ownership of these elements is an extension of the conceptual process. An ad's typeface should also reflect the target audience. Bigger type and less formal layouts work well when attracting younger consumers; whereas cleaner, more structured layouts work well in attracting older consumers.

Type Styles and Identifiers

There are two distinct varieties of *type styles*, serif and sans serif. A *serif* typeface has *feet*, or delicate appendages that protrude from the edges of the letters, as in the type you're now reading. These appendages can appear at the top and/or bottom of a letterform. *Sans-serif* type has no appendages.

Type is categorized by a typeface name, like Helvetica or Times Roman. Typeface refers to type of a specific, uniform design. A typeface is part of a larger *type family*, which includes all the sizes and styles of that typeface. A **font** consists of a complete character set in one typeface—i.e., all upper- and lowercase letters, numbers, and punctuation.

The Language of Type

Different type designs reflect different images, moods, or even genders. Serif typefaces, because of their delicate lines, have a more feminine appeal. Sans-serif typefaces boast straight, unadorned lines that give them a more masculine appearance. Sometimes the same typeface can express either masculine or feminine appeal, depending on the weight, or thickness or thinness, of the typeface's body. For example, Helvetica, a sans-serif typeface, comes in so many weights that Helvetica Light—a stately, tall, and thin typeface—bears little resemblance to the bulky, stout-looking Helvetica Ultra Bold. Serif typefaces such as Goudy—a round, elegant, yet squat typeface—can represent both masculine and feminine products. The best place to begin when determining which typeface and style to use is to match likely candidates to the creative strategy, the product's personality, or the tone of the ad, and experiment from there.

Readability, Legibility, and Design

One of the greatest challenges to advertisers is convincing people they need advertising. The fact is, very few people will admit to wanting to see advertising. So it's important to make sure, when readers are glancing at a newspaper or flipping through a magazine or driving by an outdoor board, that the advertiser's message is clear enough to be quickly read (readability) and understood (legibility). A designer's goal is to get the reader to stop and spend time with an ad by reading it from start to finish.

Readability is achieved when a viewer can read an ad at a glance. *Legibility* refers to whether, in that short look, she understood the message. A type faux pas like using all caps, reverse text, italics, or a decorative face will affect readability and legibility because the format is unfamiliar, requiring the target to read more slowly in order to concentrate on the message. Begrudgingly, consumers will admit to needing advertising; but they will not take the time to sit and decipher an unclear, illegible message.

Type size, placement, and spacing also directly affect readability and legibility. Understanding the role of what is said will affect the delivery of the message. Large text should be used to catch the reader's eye; medium-sized text will whet his appetite; small text will sell the product or promote the service; and the smallest text will tell the reader what he needs to know about where and how to shop.

Type as a Graphic Element

If you look at type—*really* look—you will see its beauty beyond content. Its form alone is a graphic device. Each typeface portrays a personality, an individualism that takes shape via content. The very individuality of the letterforms creates a uniform message with character and flair. Whether it's childish, traditional, expensive looking, or "shabby chic," each typeface awaits the shape and expression given it by the designer.

A typeface's personality should match the image projected by the product or service and that of the target audience. However type is manipulated—whether the face is altered by condensing or expanding it; or by increasing or decreasing letter spacing, word spacing, or line spacing, or type size or line length—readability and legibility should take precedence over design.

THE VERBAL ELEMENTS THAT BRING THE CREATIVE IDEA TO LIFE

The Different Parts of Copy

Once the key consumer benefit has been determined, copywriters give it both entertainment and informational value. Headlines promote it, subheads defend it, and body copy develops and highlights its many virtues. Copy is the product's tone of voice. If a copywriter can't write copy that visually and verbally tells the product's story, then he can't solve the target's problem and successfully compete against the competition. Let's take a quick look at how copy is developed.

Copywriting the Idea

Writing *copy* is one of the first steps taken when moving from business thinking to actual creative brainstorming (and toward eventual execution). In a perfect world, the copy would be written first, and it would be the inspiration for an ad's design. However, advertising is not a perfect world. It is most likely that copywriting and design will be happening at the same time. Because of this, it is critical that the copywriter and the art director be on the same page creatively.

A copywriter deals with both the imagination and development processes of brainstorming and writing headlines, subheads, body copy, slogans, and/or taglines. Copywriters must use what they learned during the brainstorming process to produce copy that attracts the target audience and motivates them to not only read the entire ad, but to act on what they have read.

Every piece of copy, no matter what medium it appears in, must relate to and complement the visual message, attract the target's attention, build a relationship with the target, and inspire the target to act.

Successful, memorable advertising is a consequence of a little luck, some good interpretive powers, a few great ideas, and the target audience's ultimate capacity to reflect, digest, and connect to the visual/verbal message.

The Components of Copy

The copy's voice is the direct result of the creative brief. Once a creative direction or concept has been decided upon, the copywriter must determine what needs to be said, how much copy it will take to say it, the tone and style appropriate to project the concept, and how to adapt the copy to a particular media vehicle. Copy for print can be broken down into four main copy areas: headlines, subheads, body copy, and slogans and taglines. The headline, subhead, and body copy all need to function as a unit to build, present, and explain a single message.

Headlines That Steal the Show

A *headline* is the largest piece of copy on the page and is most often the first piece of copy the viewer will notice. A headline's job is to stop attention, stand out on a crowded page, and be unforgettable, by either shouting out the key benefit or supporting the visual. Whether it is a single phrase or one or more complete sentences, a headline must answer the target's question, "What's in it for me?" This not only helps to differentiate the product or service from the competition but also becomes an excellent tool for creating brand awareness or defining a brand's identity for the target.

A headline needs to seduce. It should create enough interest to make the target stay with the ad instead of turning the page. An advertised sales message is not a chosen read; it's what I refer to as an *enticed read*. The target audience is enticed into the ad because the headline is informative, instructional, thought provoking, imaginative, or even suggestive. It lets the target know how the product or service can improve her daily life.

If the headline can communicate both visually and verbally, it may not even need body copy: "Tear. Wipe. Done. Cleaning Is So Labor Intensive." It doesn't get more visual/verbal than that.

Writing effective headlines requires writing and rewriting until just the right statement is made to the target audience about the key benefit, in just the right tone.

The key is to be original; to achieve this, all the "been there, done that" ideas must be exhausted, so that the headline can assume the product's identity.

A visual headline may work with one word, whereas a fact-based headline may require more than one sentence. Five to seven words are typically required to promote a consumer benefit. Length also depends on the media vehicle. When working with limited space, such as on a transit sign, poster, or billboard, the key benefit is about all there is room for.

A Subhead's Response

There are two basic types of subheads: overline and underline.

An *overline subhead* is used as a teaser or attention-getter and appears above the headline. If the headline seems to be too long or will have to be reduced in size to accommodate everything that needs to be said, an overline subhead works great as an announcement device.

An *underline subhead* appears below the headline and explains in more detail what the headline is saying; elaborates on the statement or comment made; or answers the question posed in the headline. Ideally, the main underline subhead should not be another phrase, but one or two complete sentences. Remember, the headline's job is to stop attention; once it's captured, the subhead should whet the reader's appetite, enticing her into the body copy.

Additional subheads can be used to clarify or explain in further detail what the headline is saying, or to break up long blocks of text. Subheads appearing in the body copy should read like bullet listings and need not be complete sentences. A consumer should be able to quickly glance through the subheads and know where the copy is going. Each subhead should relate to the content of the copy below it. Multiple subheads can break long blocks of detailed copy into easily digestible bits of information, while adding visual interest.

Body Copy That Informs

The smaller paragraphs of text in an ad are known as *body copy*. The message within the body copy constitutes the nuts and bolts, and heart and soul, of the concept.

The body copy's story begins in the headline. It must speak in the same tone of voice as the headline, explaining and backing up any claims made. If the headline asks a question, the body copy will answer it; if the headline is humorous, the copy will have a humorous tone. Copy continues the headline's story by educating the target on the facts, features and benefits, and by presenting any additional positive points associated with the product or service.

Body copy is essentially broken down into three areas: an opening paragraph, the interior paragraph or paragraphs, and a closing paragraph. The opening paragraph needs to finish the thought that was introduced in the headline and further developed in the subhead. If the target has proceeded this far, those two sections must have captured his attention.

The interior, or *body*, of the copy is where the actual selling will take place.

This is where supporting features or benefits, which will enhance the key benefit and overall lifestyle of the target, will be presented.

The closing paragraph needs to ask the target to do something: come into the store, pick up the phone, or go online for more information. Advertising is about making sales; copywriters cannot be afraid to tell consumers what they need to do.

It is very easy to bore the target audience by droning on with a continuous list of the product's features and benefits. Copy needs to entertain them by creating a story, something that is fun or interesting to read and flows toward a climax. That climax is whatever you want the target to do. Advertising copy should be developed in the same way the storyline for a novel would be. A novel has a plot (concept); that plot is advanced by events (features/benefits); and those events affect the characters (target).

As a general rule, body copy should use short sentences and simple words. It should not offend or use slang. A time element should be woven into the copy to get the target moving toward the desired action. One way to do this is to offer some kind of guarantee, removing any perceived risks associated with purchase (especially if done over the Internet, or through a catalog or direct mail).

The following list promotes copy that will reach out to the target audience:

1. When writing, craft copy that talks to just one member of the target audience, in his own vernacular. A conversational tone allows the copy to speak to the target or ask questions of the readers. It's impossible and inappropriate to address the message to a group. Copy should always talk in the second person, using "you" instead of "they," and it should avoid saying things like "people" or "they will," opting instead for constructions like "*you* will." This personalizes the message for the target and allows him to relate the message to his own lifestyle.

2. Appeal to the target's rational and emotional sides. In other words, present information factually and then tie the facts to how the product or service will make the target feel.

3. Write copy that pushes the benefits of the product or service based on its features. The client's product is not special because of its features; its competition either already has them or will have them in a couple of months. Carving out a niche that features the product's benefits or solutions ahead of the competition will make consumers identify certain features or benefits with the product, which is a great way to attract the consumer away from competitors.

4. If the copy is long, break it up into multiple short paragraphs and subheads. If the message is broken up into short paragraphs of no more than three to four sentences each, the target is more likely to read it.

5. In the opening paragraph, continue the discussion of the key benefit first introduced in the headline and further explained in the subhead. Copywriters should think about what it takes to keep the target reading; the copy must grab her attention and be important to her.

6. Keep copy simple, and stay on target. Even the most dynamic body copy will not succeed if it is off target.
7. Avoid abbreviations and technical jargon, unless you are writing copy for a particular profession.
8. Avoid exclamation points at all times. If it needs an exclamation point, the *point* obviously did not get made.
9. Get to the point and avoid exaggerated claims. Bragging or puffery is great, but only if copy can back it up with facts. It is the facts that make a product claim believable and inspire the target to act.
10. Close the sale. Every ad should close by asking the target to do something. If a purchase is the intended outcome, copy should include a toll-free number, information about where to purchase, and/or a Web address; if motivating the target to seek more information is the goal, then phone, website, and/or physical address details should be supplied for that purpose.

Copy Length

The *length* of body copy depends on how familiar the target is with the product and whether the advertising or promotional efforts are to change or maintain the position in the mind of the consumer.

Copy length is also affected by:

1. The medium. Reminder advertising, such as a billboard, requires little more than a headline or statement to promote the key benefit. Direct mail, on the other hand, requires long copy in order to explain the key benefit and move the target to action. Magazines need time to develop the key consumer benefit and define an image; broadcast gives the key benefit a voice; and newspaper advertising encourages trial.
2. The target audience. Better-educated older targets will wade through longer copy in order to find out more about a product or service. Younger readers will respond better to large, colorful visuals and spend less time on copy points.
3. The product or service. If the product or service falls into the rational category, more information will be needed to set the product apart from the competition. Products or services falling into the emotional category have few, if any, distinctive features (as compared with those of the competition) that will need to be explained in any detail. So products such as clothing, perfumes, liquor, snacks, jewelry, beauty products, or soft drinks will traditionally use less copy, and focus more on the visual to tell the story.

Longer copy is best when used for:
   a. New product introductions
   b. Technical copy
   c. Repositioning or reinventing the brand image

    d. Expensive products
    e. Rational products

Shorter copy is best when used for:
    a. Mainstream products
    b. Emotional products
    c. Reminder advertising
    d. Inexpensive products

Too much copy can keep the target from getting involved with the copy. This concern can be addressed by inserting multiple subheads, or visuals demonstrating copy points, within the copy, to break it up into smaller, more readable chunks. Too little copy, on the other hand, may result in a failure to separate the product from the competition, or to strengthen or build the product's image.

Crafting the Copy's Tone

As we have already learned, every concept has an individual approach and appeal that define its personality or image. How these are expressed depends on the execution technique, or *tone of voice*, employed to communicate the key benefit. It is important that the copywriter ask him- or herself what kind of image the product or service should project. Can that image be developed with a sexual tone? Through an emotional tone? By means of a humorous tone? Is it newsworthy, or should a specific feature be promoted? Does the target need a reminder approach? A teaser approach? Or will a demonstration, or an instructional tone, do the trick? Whichever tone is used to express the key benefit, it should work toward building up the brand's image and successfully promoting the key benefit.

The Detail of Copy

Detail copy is the small copy placed near the logo or the bottom of the ad to inform the target about locations, phone or fax numbers, and/or Web addresses. Other items to include might be store hours, parking information, or the roster of credit cards accepted; or information about layaway options or gift certificates. Not all of these will be applicable to all ads.

SUMMING UP A PHILOSOPHY OR CONCEPT IN A FEW WORDS

Slogans

A *slogan* represents the company's philosophy or a product's image. It is usually placed either above or below the logo. The two are a unit and should always be used together. A slogan is usually three to seven words in length and can either be a phrase or a complete sentence.

The slogan must aid in positioning the product. It must say what the target needs to know about the company or product. Good slogans have longevity and add to a product's brand image, thus building brand equity.

The slogan's relationship to the image of the product or service helps make the product or service memorable. The slogan should make an association through visual/verbal cues. Consider how a product works or when the product is used: Some kind of word association, pun, or rhyming scheme may be memorable and representative. By using visual/verbal cues, the slogan represents a product's image and message.

Taglines

A *tagline* is not the same as a *slogan*, although the two labels are often interchanged. A tagline generally represents a current strategy or concept. Taglines do not have the longevity associated with slogans, and they often change to match the product's life-cycle stage or current campaign efforts.

SELLING THE CLIENT ON THE CREATIVE IDEA

I would be remiss to close this discussion of copy and layout without discussing what happens next. Once copy and layout are done, the entire concept will have to be sold to the client.

Ideas are usually pitched to the client by the AE in charge of the account. There may or may not be a member of the creative team present. The AE may present anywhere from three to five ideas for the client to consider. A new product pitch will be done with super comps that feature the headline, subhead(s), visuals, and body copy, to promote the concept. Pitches to existing clients may be a little less formal, using roughs. Roughs will show only headlines, subheads, and visuals, with the body copy not yet written and depicted with lines.

The creative team must first be sure the AE understands the idea, where it came from, and how it relates to the client's communication goals. It's helpful if the creative team can back the idea up with research. It is especially important they be able to back up how the idea addresses the objectives, reaches the target, and reflects the key benefit; and that they understand how the product will be positioned in the marketplace, and the brand image they are trying to build.

In the end, advertising efforts that attract attention, are memorable, and initiate action will accomplish the stated objectives and successfully answer the consumer's question, "What's in it for me?"

Once an ad is accepted, the client needs to sign off on it. Then it can be sent into production, prepared for printing, or inserted into a publication.

CHAPTER SEVEN

DIGITAL PREPRESS

PUTTING THE PIECES IN PLACE

Tradition and Variety for every occasion.

Our Cheese, Pastries, Nuts and Meats are guaranteed to please.

SWISS COLONY

Michele Lawson

Advertising is the life of trade.

—Calvin Coolidge, quoted in John P. Bradley,
Leo F. Daniels, and Thomas C. Jones, 13.

This chapter will deal mainly with print production. The discussion on production for radio and television will be covered in chapters 12 and 13.

THE CONSTRUCTION OF THE VISUAL/VERBAL MESSAGE

Digital prepress, or *production*, has little to do with designing and everything to do with the construction of ads. After the client has approved the rough or super comp, copywriters will send the production department a digital file of the completed copy, and art directors will begin the production process by setting up photo shoots, choosing paper stock and color, determining type sizes and styles, and choosing the appropriate visuals that will develop or maintain the product's image. Production artists will develop an electronic *mechanical*, also known as *production art*. Here the ad's visual and copy elements will be placed on the page to match the original rough or super comp. When all elements have been gathered and organized into position, the ad is ready to go first to the client for changes or approval, and then on to the printer or publication.

IS IT OKAY?

The approval process is always tough on creatives. Once the ad has been designed, it must go to the client for approval before any photo shoots occur or the preparation for printing begins. Clients complete the approval process by signing off on concept, copy, and overall appearance of ads. If everything is good to go, which it never is, the client will sign off on the idea, and preparation for printing can begin.

The odds of winning the lottery are about as good as those of an ad's being approved without additional changes. Some changes are small; others are major and require a great deal of work to accomplish. Unfortunately, what never changes is the printing or publication deadline. All changes must be made immediately, no matter how big or small; the revised ad is then resubmitted to the client before going to the printer. Jobs are lost if deadlines are missed either for printing or for insertion into magazines or newspapers. A lot of money is at stake. Missing a deadline is like throwing money down the drain. Occasionally, but rarely, missed deadlines are the client's fault. Once the ad is at the printer, plates will be generated and any necessary prepress proofs will be prepared. Before printing begins, the production manager must sign off on the final press proof. He or she will look for such things as image quality and placement, special colors, type quality/accuracy, and overall project completeness. The next step is to place the preordered paper and inks on the press and begin printing.

A Brief History of Traditional to Technology-Driven Production Techniques

The addition of the computer has made everything faster and more efficient, as well as less expensive. Presentation techniques have also evolved from hand-drawn sketches to super comps, and storyboard drawings have matured into professionally finished slides and *animatics* (computer-generated, filmed, or taped approximations of the final commercial).

Today, in design, copywriting, and production, if it doesn't happen on the computer, it doesn't happen. Mechanical preparation that used to be done by hand and took hours and sometimes days of tedious attention can now be done quickly and efficiently by computer. Although most creative teams still brainstorm the old fashioned way, design and production use technology to stay ahead of the deadline.

Thanks to technology, copywriters can produce or edit copy quickly, with little effort. Ads that once required customized copy (for different markets) used to require separate copy for each market. Today, the computer allows the copywriter to easily update and/or personalize copy for multiple markets quickly and easily using a copy-and-paste function.

Art directors and production artists have benefited the most from the introduction of the computer. Art directors, who used to have to order type from typesetters and then wait for it, can now design letterforms, and tweak line spacing or letter spacing, from their own offices. Visuals from photo shoots, once sized, cropped, and developed in darkrooms, can now be quickly reproduced and edited digitally or recreated by a scanner and a few keystrokes.

Technology now oversees production and printing. The checks and balances that were once a major part of traditional printing—as mechanicals went from negatives to plates, and several prepress and press proofs were required to check color, photographs, and type—are all electronic now. Today, mechanicals often go directly from a computer file to plates, eliminating steps and minimizing prepress needs. As a result, the amount of time it takes to create a mechanical is dramatically cut, allowing time for the art director and production artist to test out alternative design options for little or no extra cost.

The minimization of skills once required to design and produce a mechanical makes it important to point out that owning a computer and design software does not make everyone an art director. Without creative ideas and an understanding of design and type principles and media and production knowledge, the computer enthusiast lacks the skills to develop innovative visual/verbal messages.

Jeffery Parnau, in his book *Desktop Publishing: The Awful Truth*, sums it up this way, "Professional designers and writers have always been able to work with or without sophisticated tools. Certain desktop publishing equipment and software make the professional's job easier, but do not make the professional. Design is in the head. Creativity is in the soul."

THE PEOPLE BEHIND AD PREPARATION

Supervising the production department is a *print production manager*, or *mechanical director*. With the help of the *traffic manager*, this individual will keep projects moving through the agency. Production managers are also responsible for assigning each project to a production artist, and for supervising press runs. It is imperative that production managers keep up with technological changes, especially those affecting digital, multimedia, or interactive options and those related to the graphic software used by the creative team, freelance sources, and production artists.

The job of a *production artist* is to reproduce the rough or super comp exactly as it was designed. She will gather its various components, including all copy, visuals, and type, and place them into position on a computer-generated mechanical layout. Once the mechanical is complete, it is described as *finished art*, meaning that it is ready to go to the printer, where film and/or plates will be produced. Additionally, the printer will assemble all components needed to prepare the finished art, such as paper, inks, type, and photographs. All visual/verbal images will then be reproduced onto lightweight metal plates, in preparation for printing. These plates will then be placed on a large, four-color printing press, and a press run will begin.

THE COST OF DOING PRODUCTION

Design is all about the final mechanical. No matter how good a design looks on marker paper or a computer screen, if it doesn't meet printing specifications or stay within budget, a good idea will look bad fast.

It takes a lot of people to make a good idea a reality: writers, designers, illustrators, graphic designers, photographers, stylists, printers, production managers, production artists, and retouchers, to name just a few.

Production is a very expensive and highly specialized part of the final development process. Rolls of paper, inks, color separations, and pre- and postpress proofs are just a few of the items that contribute to overall cost. So it is important that AEs be educated enough to know why certain decisions are made, to understand overall outcomes, and—probably most important—to understand where the client's money is going. Overall costs are affected by the size of the design, the number of pages and number of colors, the type of visuals, and the type of paper and ink. Special cuts such as die cuts also impact cost, as do the number of folds and the size of the pressrun. It is equally important for an art director to understand production, in order to design within a set budget.

PREPRODUCTION

Once the client has approved the roughs or super comps, they are submitted to the production department to be prepared for printing. Before production on the mechanical begins, the traffic manager will assign the project a number and create a "job jacket" to hold all the information and relevant pieces associated with the job. By the time a project hits the production department, the project is close to a publication or production date—so organization is critical. The traffic manager will assign enough time to complete the original project and accommodate any changes that may be required.

At the same time, the production manager will meet with the art director to determine color, paper, visuals, and the type of printing process needed to complete the job.

Typography

The final look of printed type is affected by the kind of paper stock used, the color of the paper stock, and the style of the type. Delicate serif faces can all but disappear if printed on dark, textured paper stocks.

Readability and legibility can be adversely affected by several design faux pas, as previously discussed in chapter 6. These include the use of all caps, the use of reverse or italicized copy, and the use of decorative faces.

Line and Letter Spacing

The amount of space appearing between letterforms or between lines of text also affects readability and legibility. On the computer, line spacing—the amount of white space appearing between lines of text—is known as *leading*. Text that is too close together can be hard to read, while text that is too far apart can make an ad look more like a greeting card. Also affecting readability and legibility is the spacing between letterforms, known as *kerning*. To kern is to reduce or increase the amount of white space between letterforms.

Generations of Type

Type quality is affected by the numerous stages leading up to and including printing. When a project is released to the printer, this is generation 1, or its "teen years." The printer will then create a printing plate from the file, creating generation 2, or "middle age." Once the ad is printed, you have generation 3, or the "retirement years." With each generation, the quality of the type deteriorates more—as it ages, it begins to fall apart.

Choosing a serif typeface, whose letterforms go from thick to thin, is risky on uncoated or textured paper stocks: the thin areas can "fall out" during printing. Once parts of the type disappear, readability and legibility are severely affected.

Representing the Product or Service Visually and Colorfully

As discussed in the previous chapter, the choice of visuals for an ad—such as photographs, illustrations, line art, or graphics—is important. Choices should take into consideration the characteristics of the media that will be used, the paper on which the ad will be printed, and the product or service that is to be advertised. The visual the target eventually sees is a representation of the client's product or service. And because it will become the visual voice of the client's product, it is important that it be able to hold detail during printing.

Cropping

All visuals need to be sized, no matter what type of image is used. *Cropping* is the removal of any unnecessary parts of a visual, allowing the designer to dispose of information that is not necessary to the design. For a viewer to understand what is going on or being shown in a visual, it's often enough to include just part of an image and very little of its background. By using only what is needed in a visual to impart the ad's message, the designer allows the viewer to zoom in on emotions or important details.

Adding a Dash of Color

SPOT COLOR

As previously discussed, using a black-and-white photograph that features the product with a spot of color can be an excellent way to highlight it. This use of *spot color* will make the product stand out, in stark contrast to the rest of the photograph. Overall cost depends on the kind of color added to the photograph. Options include using a four-color spot and using a color off the PMS palette.

DUOTONES

Most often used in newspapers and on the Web, a *duotone* gives a black-and-white photograph a second color. If using a design with a black-and-white photograph, the designer may want a "tonal" look that spot color cannot achieve. By adding an additional color, the art director can give the ad a bit more eye appeal.

The Different Paper Stocks for Printing

The paper an ad is printed on directly affects the readability and legibility of type, and the fine details and color variations within visuals. Paper stocks are either uncoated or coated. Uncoated paper can be inexpensive. Its rough texture is not a great medium for reproducing fine details, due to the fact that when ink hits the surface of an uncoated paper stock, it will spread out to a large enough degree to blur these fine details.

Setting the appropriate mood is made a little easier by the clay-coated paper stocks on which higher-end projects are printed. The clay-coated surface allows the ink to sit on top of the paper rather than soaking in, as it does with uncoated paper stocks. Coated paper stocks have a shiny surface, as opposed to the softer appearance of uncoated stocks. The results show patterns that are more detailed, food that looks tastier, and fashions that are more colorful.

The Photo Shoot

At a *photo shoot*, the photographer, the art director, the AE, and often the client all get together to photograph the product. Photo shoots are expensive. You are paying for time, equipment, and the reputation of the photographer. Depending on the product and the number of photographs needed, a photo shoot can take anywhere from a couple of hours to a couple of days.

If the shot requires working with food, the assistance of a good food stylist will be needed. These are the people who painstakingly work at making apples look shinier, hamburgers juicier, and vegetables fresher.

Photo shoots are most commonly done after the client has approved layouts. In preparing the shoot, the photographer, with the art director's assistance, arranges and rearranges the products in groups, as shown on the rough or super comp. In order to match the grouping to the rough, props are often required. It is not uncommon to use such things as bricks, duct tape, string, wire, and assorted rags and towels to get a desired result; none of these items will show in the final photographs.

Lighting is also very important during a photo shoot. Noting where highlights should appear, and where shadows need to be added or removed, is important. These things need to be looked at and considered during the shoot. Even though some lighting issues can be corrected on the computer, the client will have to pay for any extra time it takes for the photographer to retouch or edit the photograph(s).

Reproduction Issues

Once the photo shoot and any photo retouching are completed, it is time to think about getting the photograph(s) sized and cropped (if this has not already been done) and ready for printing. This can be done by scanning, by using traditional photographic techniques, or by transmission of digital photos via e-mail (smaller images) or by file transfer protocol (FTP; larger images).

RESOLUTION: THE SQUARE-TO-DOT PROCESS

Resolution determines the amount of detail that will appear in the printed image. It is determined during the scanning of photographs into the computer or by the photographer at the time the image is photographed. Additionally, resolution refers to the number of pixels per inch (ppi). The higher the resolution, the more detail will be apparent in the image. Pixels are an array of small, colored or gray-tinted squares that create the photo's image and color variations on the computer screen.

Finally, resolution can also affect how long it takes a photograph to reproduce on the computer screen or how long it takes to produce quick, in-house proofs. Because of this, a designer or production artist may choose to work in a lower

Lindsay Frankenfield

resolution during the design and/or approval stages. However, as the piece goes through prepress, all images will be converted to a higher resolution, typically 300 dots per inch (dpi).

RESOLUTION VERSUS LINE SCREEN

Professional printers do not work in pixels; they work in dot patterns called *line screens*. In printing, resolution is determined by the size of the line screen that is used to reproduce the ad in the printed piece. The line screen, accordingly, is what is used to reproduce photographs and illustrations.

Line screens come in various sizes—anywhere from 55 to 300 lines per inch—and are comprised of thousands of lines of dots. These numbers refer to the size of the dot. The higher the line screen number, the smaller the dot and the greater the quality and overall amount of detail visible within an image. The smaller the line screen number, on the other hand, the larger and farther apart the dots will be; their spacing has to do with the need to accommodate *bleed*, or the spreading of ink, on uncoated paper stocks. A line screen replaces pixels when reproducing an image through printing.

The smaller the dot, the better the reproduction on coated paper stocks. The line screen number informs us not only about dot size but also about the quality of the paper on which the ad is printed. A line screen of 85 means the paper stock is of a higher quality than one that uses a line screen of 65. Higher-quality newsprint, for example, is usually whiter in color and produces less gain or spread, allowing for the use of a larger-number line screen, producing a smaller dot pattern.

Resolution, as determined by pixels, must be able to convert to the proper line screen. For example, suppose you are working on a newspaper ad that will run in the local paper, which uses a line screen of 65. This number tells you that the dots are relatively large; you can see them with the naked eye, and they are spaced far enough apart so that when printed on newsprint, each dot can spread out toward neighboring dots without overlapping. These dots are noticeable in newspaper photographs. If the wrong line screen is used, it is obvious: the bleed overlap makes for a muddy-looking photograph.

A black-and-white photograph that already has a dot pattern is called a *halftone* photograph. No black-and-white photograph is printed without first being converted into a black-and-white halftone.

The tough part is that resolution, as used during the computer process, does not match the line screens used in printing. Art directors and printers recommend a resolution of 150 dpi for ads in newspapers that use a line screen of 65 to 85. A resolution of 300 dpi is recommended for ads in magazines that use a line screen of 150.

When working with a photograph, a designer must determine a resolution compatible with the line screen used by the publication. Desktop-publishing software is used to process and assemble all elements of the ad, basically reproducing the rough on screen. Currently, the most common software used includes Photoshop (for editing photographs) and Illustrator (for designing headlines, logotype, and illustrations). Copy is most commonly written in Word, and the mechanical is usually produced in either InDesign or Quark. There are many other software options, but these are the most common programs.

PREPARING PHOTOGRAPHS TO PRINT

All photographs are placed, sized, and cropped in position within the layout. They appear on the screen as low-resolution versions of the original photograph. At the printer, a halftone or color photograph, an illustration, or a graphic replaces the low-resolution image. Why the need for low-resolution images? To keep file sizes small enough to send as an e-mail attachment, if needed, and/or to aid in rapid processing of working files.

The most common type of photograph used in high-end printing is referred to as a *four-color process photograph*. All printed photographs must have a dot pattern or line screen in order to be reproduced. When printing in black and white, the dot pattern is made up of black, white, and gray tones; in four-color photography, the dots are composed of concentrated percentages of cyan (C), magenta (M), yellow (Y), and black (K)—known collectively as *CMYK*. Combinations of these four colors create all colors found in a color photograph.

To get a color photograph ready for printing, a *four-color separation* is prepared; it is made up of four separate plates, one for each CMYK color. Tens of thousands of four-color dots are used to recreate a color photograph.

Photographs are turned into four-color separations by professional color separators. However, Photoshop can do it for you. But, as with photo retouching, four-color separations are best left to the experts.

The differences between the computer and professional printing can be daunting. The pixel-versus-dot issue is bad enough; but the way the computer monitor shows color is different as well. The computer does not display a full-color photograph in terms of CMYK, but in red, green, and blue—or *RGB*. Like our own eyes, the computer combines colors together differently in order to create multiple colors and tones. Before any photograph can be placed in a desktop publishing program or sent off to a printer, it must first be converted to CMYK in a program such as Photoshop. This conversion takes place after any and all photo manipulation is complete.

Resolution, along with paper choices, will determine the quality of the final printed piece.

PICKING COLORS BEYOND CMYK

Color choices can be based on the CMYK system, or they can be chosen from an assortment of *Pantone Matching System* (PMS) colors. PMS colors are a series of colored chips that have each been assigned a number; they are separated according to whether they are "coated" or "uncoated" colors. A PMS chip book can be found in any art department. PMS choices accompany an ad to the printer. Choice of coated or uncoated is determined by the paper stock that will be used when printing. It is important to choose the right (coated or uncoated) label, because a PMS color will change in intensity depending on paper saturation levels. Colors on uncoated papers will be richer than those on coated stocks. So a designer must choose accordingly, making sure color matches are consistent from piece to piece, no matter the paper stock.

The addition of a PMS color is expensive. If you think about each color as being a tube of paint, each additional color beyond the four process colors must be purchased separately. CMYK can reproduce all colors very closely, but not exactly. If the art director wants an exact navy blue, he or she will have to order an additional tube of paint, creating a five-color print job. PMS colors are used to add an additional, specific color beyond those found in four-color photographs. They are often used as graphic accents or in logos.

FOUR-COLOR PRINTING

Printing cost is very much affected by the number of colors incorporated into an ad. Depending on the budget, ads can be created in one, two, three, or four colors. A one-color ad is usually a simple black-and-white ad, black being the single "color." (White is not a "color" in printing, since the white will come from the white of the paper.) A two-color ad is usually black plus one PMS color, and a three-color ad will most likely be black plus any two PMS colors. Black is usually one of the color choices, because type is easier to read in black. A four-color ad uses what is known as a *four-color process*; this is used when photographs, illustrations, or graphics are present, and it requires a color separation.

Because of the need to reproduce the infinite colors in any one color photograph, each of the four process colors are transparent, so they can overlap to varying degrees and thus create new colors. Black is used for type, depth, and shadows in a photograph.

PRODUCTION

Putting the Pieces in Place

How does printing work? Each production artist will work closely with an art director to match the computer-generated mechanical to the rough or super comp. Print-production techniques that lack precision can take a great idea and turn it into a mediocre idea. Poor photographic quality, dropped or unreadable typefaces, or poor color saturation can destroy a product's image as quickly as the wrong strategy or wrong choice of media vehicle.

A mechanical is the final design stage; any mistakes that happen at this stage will show up in the final printed ad, so a discriminating eye is critical. The production artist will assemble type, color, and visuals to match the original design as closely as possible. The print production manager will work closely with the printer, making sure the proper printing process, paper, and inks are used to avoid anything that will affect the quality of the visuals and copy.

Print production is more than just placing elements on an electronic page; it's about the details that give an ad personality, structure, and balance. Preparation of computer-generated mechanicals begins by determining and inputting size and adding any guides. Second, all photographs have to be cropped, and/or matched to the sizing shown on the rough or super comp. Production artists will have to consult the *SRDS*, or *Standard Rate and Data System*, for line screen and bleed information before sizing and determining resolution. If a photo is not yet available and is to be added later, production artists will use a closely related or lower-resolution photo to temporarily fill the space. This will be labeled *FPO* ("for position only"). The production artist will take the copy supplied electronically by the copywriter and place it in position, noting any changes (such as prices or addresses) that may be required for different versions. The third step is the addition of any visuals, such as photographs, illustrations, graphics, or logos. Any tweaking of type or visuals—like adjusting the kerning, leading, or sizing of type, or resizing or cropping an image—is done after all elements are in place. Both the art director and the production artist must spend a lot of time obsessing about details. Often, an ad will not be finished until photographs and illustrations have been sized, resized, and moved left or right mere fractions of an inch. Type may require manipulation, with a bit of kerning here and a little reduction in leading there. Color use can entail obsessive searches for the perfect highlights, contrast, and color combinations.

Art directors will use what's known as a soft proofing system to view results on the computer screen. *Soft proofs* are used for quick looks at the project and not for detailed or final color correction, since results are affected by the calibration of the monitor.

Finally, a hard copy of the final mechanical will have to be approved by the production artist, the production manager, the art director, the AE assigned to the project, and the client.

File formats for photographs are chosen during the assembly stage. Most photographs coming from Photoshop into Quark or InDesign should be saved as *TIFF* (tagged information file format) files. Anything coming from Illustrator should be saved as an *EPS* (encapsulated PostScript) file. The production stage is much more complicated and diverse than indicated in this discussion, but the choice of TIFF and/or EPS formats will satisfy most print needs.

Collect for Output

Before sending any job to the printer, a couple of things will need to be considered. The first question is, how should the ad be sent to the printer? A small file such as an individual image can be e-mailed or sent as a *PDF* (portable document format). A file too large to e-mail, such as a brochure or something with oversized images or a large number of images, can be sent on a CD, DVD, Jaz drive, or FireWire drive. Final, high-resolution files can be uploaded to a printer's FTP site, where the printer can then access them. However they are sent, each will need to have an accompanying hard copy (laser printed) or a separate PDF file that has all specs and color information for the ad marked on it, to help the printer with specific details and assist with any questions or concerns he may have.

Next, the production artist has to make sure all the pieces are attached to the ad. Just because photographs or fonts are viewable on the computer screen doesn't mean the printer will be able to see them.

All photographs need to be collected. In the desktop software used there is an option called "Collect for Output" in Quark, or "Preflight" in InDesign. This function will let the production artist know if there are any missing fonts or photographs.

All fonts used in the ad should be sent along to the printer. Everything can be salvaged if all existing work is sent with the ad. Each component needs to be saved in a different file folder, to make it easier for the printer to locate specific items. The labeling of file folders should be kept simple, either by numbering them or by labeling them according to the enclosed contents; see table 7.1. Folders can be kept separate or placed into one holding folder.

Once each of the above steps has been completed, the files can be sent to the printer.

Troubleshooting

When you are using the Collect for Output or Preflight function, two kinds of error messages concerning visuals or text may pop up. The first pertains to missing or modified pictures, and the second to missing or modified fonts.

A prompt saying that there are missing or modified pictures or fonts usually means some change has taken place to the type or the photograph within the desktop publishing software.

If a piece can't be printed in-house, or there is trouble bringing a photograph into the desktop publishing program, several things could have happened: (1) a photograph did not get saved as a TIFF; (2) layers in Photoshop were not flattened; (3) there was a drop shadow added; or (4) a bold or italic style was applied to a typeface that does not support that feature (or whose bold or italic version is not installed on the computer).

Getting an Ad Printed

The term *printer* as used in this section refers to two different aspects of the production process. First there is the human printer, who is in charge of producing plates,

Table 7.1. File Folders

File Folder 1	The completed ad
File Folder 2	All photographs
File Folder 3	The font file
File Folder 4	Any work done in Illustrator

assembling final photographs, and running the press, to name just a few of her jobs. Then there is the actual printing machine. Now, I am not talking about the small printer that sits on your desk. I am talking about professional printers. These things are huge; some models could fill up a large classroom. These printers have the capacity to print in both black and white and color, and they can produce a large volume at one time.

Human printers are also responsible for making sure the right colors and paper are used and, as mentioned above, for producing the *printing plates*—each a thin metal sheet, flexible enough to wrap around a large printing drum. The ad's images are etched into the plate, which is used in the printing process. The plate works like a big rubber stamp, reproducing the ad by transferring ink to paper.

Printers' Marks

A mechanical needs to lead the printer through each of its components, laying out a detailed visual and verbal map of what is taking place on the page. Printers' marks such as crop marks, bleed marks, and registration marks are necessary for cutting, printing, and the alignment of colors and photographs during the printing process.

Crop marks, or *trim marks*, can take many forms, but most commonly they consist of one horizontal and one vertical line placed at each of the ad's corners, about a quarter inch out and a half inch long. If you were to place a ruler between marks, you would get the *trim size* or ad size.

Bleed is considered to be present when any visual or graphic extends beyond the trim marks or edges of the page, and it will be marked accordingly. Bleed is expensive, because a larger sheet of paper will be needed when printing; so before incorporating it into the design, art directors need to be sure the client's budget will support it.

Unlike crop and bleed marks, registration marks are added to the mechanical by the printer. They are usually centered and placed on either side of the ad. They can take many forms; but they usually consist of a plus sign enclosed within a circle. The printer uses these marks to align multiple images or plates while printing.

Printing

Production managers, art directors, and sometimes the AE and client will attend a press run. Depending on the number of copies needed, a press run can take up to several days. The first several hours are critical. Preliminary copies will be checked for color registration, screen mixes, and alignment. Photographs will be checked for clarity and placement, and to make sure they haven't been flopped and that no photo has acquired a blemish or scratch.

The number of colors used in the design will determine the number of plates required. A printing press will run one color at a time. A two-color job will require two plates and a four-color job will take four to get exact color reproduction.

There are two types of printing presses: sheet fed and web fed. Sheet-fed paper is precut to size, while web-fed paper is one continuous roll of paper that is cut after printing.

Sheet-fed presses can print both front and back, and are normally used for smaller press runs (50,000 or less). Individual sheets of paper are used, by contrast with the continuous rolls of paper used in web-fed jobs.

Web presses are used for projects requiring a large number of copies, such as newspapers, magazines, books, or brochures. Faster than most sheet-fed presses, web presses are great for high-speed, high-volume runs. A web press can also fold, cut, or punch a project during printing, removing an often-expensive second step.

The production manager will choose the best printing process for the ad based on the paper being used, the size of the press run (i.e., the number of copies being printed), and the quality required. The most common printing options include letterpress, offset lithography, rotogravure, flexography, silk-screen printing, and digital.

A *letterpress* is basically a metal or plastic sheet, or *plate*, with a raised printing surface, much like a rubber stamp. It is also used for numbering pieces like tickets, and for special effects like embossing, die cuts, and perforations. Because any of these tasks can be accomplished on the press rather than as a separate step, it can save the client money.

The most commonly selected print process used by advertising agencies is *offset lithography*. Offset plates are produced photographically, are smooth, and are chemically treated in order to transfer the image. The ink used is oil based and adheres only to certain parts (the image area) of the plates. Offset lithography is the most common choice for posters and brochures.

A *rotogravure plate* has the image etched into it. The etched image fills up with ink, which is then transferred to the paper. This technique is usually used for large, long-running print jobs requiring web-fed paper. Rotogravure plates are used mostly for publications, packaging, catalogs, and promotional materials.

Billboards and unusual shapes like packaging or ball caps use *flexography*, a process that uses a rubber surface flexible enough to bend around irregular shapes. Flexography is also great for projects that use uncoated stocks, like newspapers and telephone books.

Silk-screen printing is great for posters and point-of-purchase materials. Silkscreen uses a frame with a printing surface of nylon, silk, or stainless steel. A stencil of the desired image is affixed to the screen. The area around the stencil is the printable area. A squeegee is used to press the ink through the screen, in order to transfer the image.

With *digital printing*, or *variable imaging presses*, computer files are connected directly to the printing press. This type of printing eliminates the need for most prepress operations, such as stripping and color separations. Its low cost and quick turnaround, along with its ability to produce small, often personalized print jobs (under a couple of thousand) in black and white or color, make it a popular printing process. Digital printing uses PostScript computer technology to translate pixels into dots for output. This is known as "ripping," or *raster image processing*.

Printing is expensive and requires someone with a keen eye to catch errors or printing inconsistencies. Any mistakes can cost the agency and/or the client hundreds of thousands of dollars; the cost of a mistake can sometimes even be someone's job.

Once the print run has been completed, any postproduction work will be done—such as folding, cutting, binding, or shipping.

Prepress, Press, and Postproduction Issues

Prepress happens when the elements that make up a mechanical, including computer files, are readied for the printing process, and proofs are pulled for editing, correction, and final approval. There are several types of proofs pulled during this stage. Let's take a quick look at a few of the most popular.

Press Proofs

Before a press run actually begins, there will be several starts and stops to adjust alignment of colors. *Press sheets* will be pulled before the printing process picks up speed. A production manager will use a press sheet to check paper and ink compatibility, *traps* (the overlapping areas of colors that butt up against each other), and *bleeds* (the extension of color or images beyond an ad's final size); and to look for improperly sized or flopped images, uneven ink coverage or color reproduction, and blemishes. The most common kinds of press proofs are bluelines and digital proofs.

BLUELINES

Bluelines are normally used on larger press runs and consist of a blue printout of the original design when it's ready for printing. Before printing begins, the production manager will check the bluelines for any problems, such as flopped or scarred photographs, typographical errors, incorrect registration, incorrect placement of elements, or problems with color saturation or trapping.

DIGITAL PROOFS

One of the least expensive color prepress proofing options is *digital proofing* (also known as *ink jet proofing*), which provides some of the best photo reproduction available for the price. Digital proofs come directly from a computer file, and are usually sent as hard copies to a publication. Digital proofs show color and give mechanical specifications and directions to the printer. A digital proof is a quick and inexpensive, if less accurate, way to check color contrasts and trapping.

When proofing, production managers will look for any spelling or grammatical errors, incorrect or flopped photographs, and smudges or dropped text. Page numbering will be checked, and any names and numbers will be double- and triple-checked, along with color consistency and trapping.

EPSON PROOFS

Another frequently used proofing system relies on *Epson proofs*, which are also created directly from computer files. These continuous-tone proofs (i.e., proofs printed out in CMYK) show low-resolution photographs, traps, and overprints, and are great for replicating various sheet- or web-fed printing processes. Epson proofs are terrific for printing large pieces such as posters.

What to Look for in a Proof

Colors that butt up against each other will need to be trapped. **Trapping** is implemented when two different colors touch each other in a design. The goal of trapping is to ensure that the darkest color will slightly overlap the lighter color, in order to keep any white space from appearing between the colors. Without trapping, this white space might result if plates or paper are misaligned, or *out of register*. This is a very serious business, because it can affect how the ad looks in print. When production does not produce exact results it can affect not only brand image, but brand equity as well.

To avoid any problems with trapping, dark type will usually be set on top of a lighter colored background. But when type is light enough in color to be affected by the color underneath, the background color must be knocked out to create a white hole the exact shape and size of the overprinted image. Trapping is best left to the experts, but it can be done in any desktop publishing software. Printers cannot always handle all the postproduction work, and they may turn specialized jobs such as die cutting or embossing over to others. Bindery work may include such things as stapling, saddle stitching, and spiral binding.

Specialized Services

Some of the specialized services beyond printing include die cutting, embossing or debossing, foil stamping, tip-ins, and thermography.

Die cuts are created using a sharp-edged stamp that cuts out shapes, such as the offset diagonal cuts that might hold a business card in a brochure.

Embossing uses pressure to create a raised surface; *debossing* uses pressure to create a depressed image.

Foil stamping molds a thin metallic sheeting to an image.

Tip-ins are provided to publications by the advertising agency to be bound or glued into a publication. The most common examples of this are perfume samples that release a scent when pulled apart.

Thermography, used most often for logos, is a raised, colored, rubber coating that is added to a design.

Binding It All Together

There are many different ways to bind multiple pages together after printing. The most common binding types include saddle stitch, perfect, side stitch, and spiral.

Saddle stitching is a relatively inexpensive and common binding method used in most small magazines. In this method, one or more staples are placed through the magazine's centerfold to hold the pieces together.

Perfect binding is for larger documents (50+ pages). The cover is wrapped around the pages and glued at the spine. Unlike with saddle stitching, the size of the spine allows copy to appear on the wraparound cover. The downside is that a *spread ad* (an ad that comprises two pages) has to cross the gutter of the magazine or document. The *gutter* is the area that will be pulled into the binding. It is vital to ensure that nothing of importance falls into that gutter—so designers must leave at least a quarter inch of space on either side of the gutter, oftentimes losing valuable design space. During printing production managers must be sure the two halves of a spread ad line up, so the design's symmetry is not compromised.

Side stitching entails stapling the pages together from the side, as opposed to stapling on the fold.

Use of a spiral binding involves drilling holes in the piece and employing flexible plastic or wire coils to bind it from the side. Although not the best-looking form of binding, it does allow for the document to open up flat.

In the chapters that follow, we will look at how the pros and cons of different media, and the similarities and differences among them, affect IMC's voice; a product's brand image, positioning, and equity; and consumer brand loyalty.

MEDIA USE

HOW IMC USES DIVERSE MEDIA
VEHICLES TO SPEAK AND REACH
THE TARGET AUDIENCE

PART THREE

CHAPTER EIGHT

PUBLIC RELATIONS

Theresa La Guardia

Publicity is the life of this culture—in so far as without publicity capitalism could not survive—and at the same time publicity is its dream.

—John Berger, 154.

WHAT IS PUBLIC RELATIONS?

Public relations is a mostly nonpaid form of communication that builds relationships with both internal and external audiences through communication efforts that reinforce, defend, or rebuild a corporation's or product's image. The term *external audiences* refers to "the public," or the target of a company or organization. *Internal audiences* are referred to as the *stakeholders*, that is, those who have a stake or a vested interest in the company's success and reputation.

MARKETING PUBLIC RELATIONS

When IMC uses public relations to promote a brand, it's known as *marketing public relations* (MPR). MPR uses nonpaid media vehicles in either print or broadcast to inform the public about a product, service, or corporation.

MPR deals with the "selling" of a corporate or brand image to a specifically defined target audience. Traditional corporate public relations deals with many different publics, both internal, such as shareholders and employees, and external, such as consumers and organizations. This traditional public relations, which is different from MPR, is most often utilized as a promotional or informational outlet. Public relations in the past has been relegated to a support role, responding more to what the client wanted than what the advertising message required. This disconnect has often generated unplanned, mistimed, incompatible messages that confuse the target and erode a brand's identity. In MPR, timing is controlled, and all communication efforts coming from public-relations representatives use the same tone of voice and appearance as other IMC messages. It is not unusual for public relations to be called upon from time to time to create or promote media events, in order to strengthen or maintain interest in a product or service. Because they have access to the press, an ability to reach the target, and credible reputations, public-relations staff are able to grease the way for the rest of the promotional mix, both internally and externally.

Tactics used in MPR might include:

- Print news releases
- Media kits
- Video news releases (VNRs)
- News conferences
- Celebrity spokesperson interviews or personal appearances
- Sponsored events

Reinforcement

Public relations comes into the IMC process with experience in creating opportunities for two-way communication between the company and the target—making it a vital player in determining and managing the relationship between buyer and seller. Because of this, public relations is excellent at initiating communication efforts through interactive exchanges between the consumer and customer service representatives or technical assistance reps. This dissemination of information gives symmetrical information to all interested parties, bridging the gap between word-of-mouth gossip and fact.

Defensive MPR

Ideally, public-relations practitioners will find themselves in an offensive position when introducing or maintaining image; but if any kind of negative publicity does arise, they will need to take a defensive position. A company's reputation directly affects the ability to create or maintain a product's or a service's brand equity and brand loyalty. In a crisis or negative situation, the way in which the corporation's view or position is handled can eliminate any lingering negative effects concerning the corporation, product, or service.

Rebuilding

If the public is not given the satisfaction of hearing from the corporation or organization, word of mouth takes over and affects equity and loyalty. When corporate ethics result in a scandal, it can be very expensive to win back confidence and brand-loyal consumers. Continual informative messages countering opinions, hearsay, or investigative inquiries are critical to a product's or service's continued success. Initiating or beefing up an old-fashioned "open door" policy is a key first step to reentering the marketplace and the community and to winning back public acceptance.

In an article appearing in the *Public Relations Journal,* Joan Aho Ryan and George H. Lemmond sum up the need for product publicity this way: "Cynical consumers, zapping commercials and ignoring print ads, are more receptive to the editorial message. The third party endorsement allows advertisers to sell a new product while enveloping the commercial message in a creative environment." That is the essence of MPR.

THE ROLE OF PUBLIC RELATIONS IN IMC

Public relations is a form of action. Its job is to inform what a corporation or organization is doing locally, nationally, or internationally, and how that affects its product or service and/or relationship with the target. This action provides usable information to the public. Externally, its most traditional action-oriented tactics include the creation of news articles; of televised events; of interviews with company spokespersons, executives, or CEOs; of news releases for local or national newspapers, radio stations, or TV stations; and of news conferences.

Communication inside a corporation is just as important as the message sent to the consumer. Devices such as newsletters deliver information on company events, insurance, investments, promotions, and retirements. Additionally, the public-relations department may act as a go-between for the corporation and the media, setting up interviews, writing speeches, and arranging sponsorships in order to arouse public interest or attract attention.

Additional responsibilities include planning any necessary restructuring for internal adjustments to new company policies or philosophies associated with an IMC message; the development of corporate or community sponsorships; and the development of celebrity endorsements and arranging for celebrity appearances at events.

When used as a marketing tool, public relations can launch products, build or enhance images, and inform consumers—for very little money. Costs associated with public relations come most often in the form of salaries and the costs of developing printed materials.

A public-relations representative's ability to build relationships and interact with consumers creates an interactive dialogue that makes the customer a part of the product's success and future development. An ongoing relationship with the press gives public-relations media options not available with any of the other communication approaches. This ability to garner media coverage through events, news releases, press conferences, and interviews makes public relations especially suited to:

- Launching a new product or service
- Positioning or repositioning a product or service
- Generating "buzz" about a product or service
- Affecting and reaching specific target groups
- Handling scandal or negative publicity for a product, service, or corporation
- Building or maintaining the image of a product, service, or brand

New Products

With a *new product launch*, public relations can create excitement or anticipation with facts rather than through creative executions. Because of its relationship with the press, public relations is considered more reliable than straight advertising.

Positioning

The way a brand is *positioned* or *repositioned* will have everything to do with the target and the parent company or corporation. If the product is positioned as "safe" and the corporation that manufactures that product is currently under investigation by a federal agency for safety violations, the product's position will be hurt by corporate actions. Once the consumer loses faith in a product or service, both brand loyalty and brand equity are affected. As with rebuilding consumer confidence, it can be very expensive and time consuming to rebuild a product's image. If the consumer dislikes or is distrustful of the corporation, extensive media coverage can enhance these feelings of distrust, successfully dooming any communication efforts.

Generating Buzz

Public relations is a great source for creating a "buzz," or hype, for a new product launch. Perfectly timed "leaks" to the press can create a perceived need for a product or service before it even hits the market. Because the information is coming from a credible source, the news media, a product can hit the market ahead of its competitors based on little information and a lot of excitement. However, the product or service must deliver on what it has promised or implied to reinforce credibility and trust. Public-relations representatives have many options available to them, for use in creating and building brand awareness, that have nothing to do with the use of traditional advertising methods. Consider the following options, when "buzz" is needed:

- Sponsorships. A *sponsorship* is when a corporation or brand commits its name and money to an event, such as a golf tournament, concert, or charity event.
- Talk shows. If public relations can get a talk-show host like Oprah or David Letterman to talk about a product he or she uses and likes or a company that sponsored an event he or she was involved in, the host's popularity and credibility will transfer to the product or service.
- Product placement in movies or television programs. If you remember the Reese's Pieces trail in the movie *ET*, you understand the importance of product placement. A product's success is usually associated with a character; but it can, if repeated often enough, become associated with a movie or television show. The sheer number of loyal TV viewers, or moviegoers for popular features, can boost sales and create or reinvent a brand's image.
- Celebrity endorsements. A celebrity endorsement can represent a product based on the celebrity's success or reputation.
- On-the-spot promotions. In an *on-the-spot promotion*, a corporation takes the product to the people in order for them to try the product or see it in use. These types of events are often set up on busy street corners, in malls, or anywhere a large number of people will be available to participate.
- Inadvertent celebrity spokespersons. An *inadvertent celebrity spokesperson* emerges by accident when a spokesperson's persona is so well liked by the target that he or she becomes something of a celebrity. Often these individuals

appear on talk shows and in the news, creating a nonpaid form of advertising for the product or service.

Reaching Specific Targets

The ability to create a dialogue with both internal and external audiences allows public relations to coordinate messages between its "publics" and it stakeholders. Public relations works from the inside out to reach the target audience members with a product they trust, from a credible source, that has earned a reputation based on its repeat performance and quality.

Handling Scandal

A brand cannot survive if the corporation is under fire or its publics or stakeholders are unhappy or disgruntled. Positive relationships, built from the inside out, are as important to the brand as the message. Public-relations representatives orchestrate much of a corporation's image. How the media, consumer agencies, government agencies, community members, and employee-affairs staff view the corporation is determined by public relations.

Building or Maintaining Image

Any negative publicity is damaging to a brand's image. Corporations who take no corrective action often face intense scrutiny from the media, forcing a corporation to face up to, and act upon, all allegations. Corporations who respond immediately to damaging allegations can kill the momentum of any kind of investigation quickly, often with little or no damage to image or equity.

Public relations brings a reputation built on trust and credibility, with both the media and the target, to the IMC promotional mix. As long-time purveyors of consumer-focused information, public-relations representatives are used to building and retaining a rapport between a corporation, brand, or service and its publics and stakeholders.

How Public Relations Builds a Relationship between the Product and the Target Audience

The emergence of public relations from a supportive role to its role as an essential member of the promotional mix is the result of its compatibility with IMC tactics, such as relationship building, tone-of-voice control, database use, brand management, and two-way communication.

Relationship Building

IMC concentrates on tightly defining a specific target audience. Products and messages are developed with this target audience and their specific needs in mind. Public relations can take this definition a step further by including internal stakeholders in the planning and execution of the IMC message. By segmenting these various targets into smaller, more manageable groups, a key benefit can be adapted to address each consumer's or stakeholder's needs and wants more specifically.

Consumer-focused marketing, or *relationship marketing*, has always been a priority for public relations. The move from traditional sales-based advertising to relationship marketing (the building of long-term relationships with the target or stakeholders) has been instrumental in increasing the capacity for building brand loyalty and creating dialogues between buyers and sellers.

Tone-of-Voice Control

IMC focuses on messages that are all delivered with one *tone of voice* and one image. Public relations will make sure that the key benefit, the strategy, and the visual/verbal message are reflected in all communication, both internal and external. This consistent and repetitive use helps maintain that voice and image, not only through the press, but also through contact with customer service representatives, operators, sales personnel, delivery drivers, and consumers. This coordination of ideals and attitude is as important to brand loyalty as to a brand's image.

Database Use

IMC employs *databases* to personally reach individuals within the target audience. Public relations will use a database as an informational and educational resource, for developing a relationship by interacting one-on-one with the target.

Brand Management

IMC focuses on creating and maintaining the image of a product, service, brand, or corporation, and on developing brand-loyal consumers. Disgruntled employees, negative word of mouth, government investigations, and recalls can affect a brand's image. The job of public relations is to *manage* the image from the inside out before these phenomena can affect a target's attitude or mindset toward a product or service.

Two-Way Communication

IMC focuses on ways to develop an interactive dialogue between the buyer and the seller. Public relations is the first to understand that what happens inside a company affects the product and the consumer. Interactive opportunities allow the consumer to be an internal stakeholder by offering feedback on products and/or customer or technical services.

PROS AND CONS ASSOCIATED WITH PUBLIC RELATIONS

When deciding whether public relations is right for an IMC campaign, it may be helpful to look at some of the pros and cons associated with it.

The more notable pros associated with public relations include:

1. Its ability to elevate a corporate or brand image. Public relations positively impacts what the target thinks about a product or service, or about the corporation that produces the product, by maintaining its positive position in the consumer's mind. It accomplishes this through customer service contact, and the proper and swift handling of any negative publicity.
2. A well-developed interactive relationship with the target. Public relations can reach, and talk directly to, members of the target group or groups, and bring a product or service directly to them. These things are accomplished through such mechanisms as news conferences, sponsored events, infomercials, or public service announcements.
3. Its ability to provide additional communication outlets. Able to communicate at length with both internal and external targets, public relations can tailor a message to an external target individual or, on a larger scale, to internal groups such as union workers.
4. Its low cost. Public relations can get the message out through free media sources such as newspapers, magazine feature articles, and broadcast news sources.
5. Its credibility. Public relations is great at presenting believable technical or scientific evidence through credible news sources. Both print and broadcast news departments choose to report on studies presented through public-relations sources. This is because of public relations' association with the press, and because these studies can be, and most often are, backed up by primary research.

The more notable cons associated with public relations use include:

1. The short "shelf life" of news items. Nothing presented in newspapers or through broadcast channels lasts longer than twenty-four hours.
2. The difficulty of modifying behavior. In order to build loyalty and equity, the target needs to be repeatedly reminded about the product and its benefits. Public relations cannot get this done without the help of other promotional approaches.
3. An inability to measure results. Determining if the objectives were success-

ful requires a way to measure results—such as how many units were sold, or the number of people who attended an event or saw a news conference. Since public relations rarely asks the target to do something like purchase, and is often paired with other mass-media or promotional vehicles that do, there is no immediate way to tell if the message got to the intended audience.

PUBLIC RELATIONS AND ADVERTISING

The tension between advertising and public relations has always been related to timing. The question of who should lead and who should follow should be answered according to the objectives outlined in the creative brief. If the objective is to build brand awareness or maintain a brand's image, then advertising is the best communications approach and should lead the way, via print or broadcast. If the objective is to build or rebuild a brand's image or create buzz, then public relations is a great leadoff vehicle.

Before using advertising as a defensive response, marketers need to let public relations lead the way in rebuilding trust and confidence through education, before concentrating on sales initiatives.

Elements of a rebuilding strategy include:

- Integrity and openness in top management
- Increased emphasis on quality-control issues
- A sharing of business decisions with the public
- Active solicitation of public input
- A policy of addressing issues quickly and publicly
- A stepping up of community involvement or exploring of new avenues of community service
- The provision of a public-relations person at the executive level, who can build an offensive plan of action (as opposed to a low-level individual taking a reactive or defensive approach to issues that are arising)

Any time a product or service has news value or is reinventing its image, or a company is launching a new product or making claims that need to be substantiated to give them credibility, public relations should lead with news articles, press conferences, or even exclusive press events.

What makes public relations and advertising a good communications and media mix?

1. Advertising addresses consumers in the form of a *monologue*, or one-way communication. Public relations turns the interaction into a *dialogue*, or two-way communication.
2. Advertising and marketing concentrate on one product for one consumer group. Public relations concentrates on building relationships with many groups to accomplish varied objectives on many diverse levels.

3. Public relations and advertising make an excellent team for creating brand awareness, building brand equity, and maintaining brand loyalty.

GETTING THE MESSAGE OUT

Before implementing the public-relations portion of an IMC campaign, several decisions must be made, such as:

1. What tools (e.g., news releases, news conferences, brochures) need to be used?
2. What public-relations tactics and approaches will be used to highlight the key benefit and execute the strategy, as they've been determined by the creative brief?
3. What media will be used to deliver the message, and when will the message be delivered?

Public relations and advertising are promotional allies: both try to get the right message out to the right people. Each uses slightly different techniques to achieve the same results; the only major difference is that one is often free and the other is not.

DEVELOPING THE PROMOTIONAL MIX USING PUBLIC RELATIONS

The strategy behind using public relations has everything to do with the key benefit, the target audience to be reached, the message, and the promotional mix that will accomplish the stated objectives.

When you talk about strategy, the first thing that needs to be determined is who will be at the planning table. What roles will advertising, public relations, sales promotion, and/or direct marketing play? Or will some other, less-traditional form of promotion be used to reach the target? The answers will depend on what the IMC campaign needs to accomplish and the best way to reach the target.

Planning involves looking at the target; the objectives that need to be met; the strategy that will be employed to accomplish the objectives; the timing; and the kind of media-vehicle combination that can be used to strategically accomplish the objectives.

IMC planning is not just about message development, but also about the development of a holistic message for change throughout an organization. Change must take place everywhere for an IMC campaign to be successful. Strategically, IMC must execute an internal plan that reflects the external message. This inside-out examination of the various internal and external target groups helps coordinate communication between these very specialized groups. Whether talking to the consumer, the media, retailers, or any other definable target, IMC personnel must give each

Black and Decker:
A name your
grandfather
trusted.

A name your father
trusts, and a name
you'll trust to pass
on to your son.

Black and Decker stands behind your tools.

A tradition trusted since 1917.

BLACK AND DECKER©

Amandalynn Thomas

audience the message behind the key benefit in their own language and with the specific benefit clearly defined. The ability to define each group and its needs is inherent to public relations and invaluable when defining the best member of the promotional mix to meet those needs.

Public relations is in a perfect position to manage word of mouth, maintain customer service, manage brand issues, and oversee any unplanned events such as media inquiries or recalls, all of which affect image and strategy.

Credibility and a virtually no-cost way of doing business make public relations a critical mouthpiece for getting and keeping the word out about a product, service, or corporation, through various media vehicles. IMC's public-relations message can be delivered through press relations, sponsored events, and internal and external communication. Reacting to both internal and external feedback can make the message stronger.

For public relations to hold its own at the planning table, its practitioners will have to see the product or service through the eyes of the marketer and understand that sales and customer relations are intertwined. It is critical that public relations be able to speak the language of marketers, initiate the strategy, and understand the diversity of the promotional mix. This will require adopting an attitude of planned action based on research, as opposed to reacting to events and information from corporate executives.

Today, public relations practitioners need to be more than media liaisons, relationship managers, and designated watchdogs for a brand's image; they need to be strategic market planners.

On the downside, public relations does not have the power the other communication approaches do to effectively remind the target of the message. Because of this, it is difficult to change consumer attitudes using public relations alone. Being able to evaluate the effectiveness of each of the communication efforts is a priority for any IMC campaign. The implementation of an IMC campaign requires each member of the promotional mix to understand what marketers need and want to accomplish; to be able to define how public relations can strategically be used to accomplish objectives; and to be able to determine the estimated ROI.

When public relations is attached to marketing and sales, in order to receive its share of the marketing budget it must be able to show measurable and quantifiable results associated with its efforts. *ROI* very simply refers to the amount of profit left after advertising and other costs have been deducted. Many believe public relations, as a member of the marketing team, cannot show a measurable ROI unless it is the sole member of the marketing team, as might be found in business-to-business marketing. Others believe it is measurable, based simply on the amount of media placement predicted during planning as opposed to the actual placement earned. The question that has to be answered is, do certain media outlets carry more weight than others? The answer is yes. Just like the other members of the promotional mix, the final media mix should be determined based on whether the target is exposed to the media vehicle, in order to see the article or hear the interview.

THE CREATIVE VOICE OF PUBLIC RELATIONS

There are many ways in which public relations talks to its publics and stakeholders. Most creative executed by public relations consists of large, copy-heavy pieces such as annual reports, educational materials, infomercials, press-conference copy, or public service announcements. The choice of vehicle does not depend on length but rather on who is being spoken to, the promotional mix employed, the message to be communicated, and the desired outcome. Let's take a look here at some of the more commonly used message vehicles: news releases, fact sheets, media advisories, pitch letters, press kits, newsletters, brochures, and publicity.

News Releases

A *news release* contains the latest news and information about the product or service in the form of a finished news article. A news release is sent unsolicited to an editor and, if published, will be a form of nonpaid advertising.

The ultimate goal for all news releases is to be noticed. An editor may receive hundreds of releases on any given day. News releases need to be both well-written and newsworthy enough for editors from print or broadcast media to consider them for publication or broadcast. Writing should be clear, concise, and factual. A news release is a business document, and any creative writing should be left to the advertising creative team; news releases are meant to inform, not entertain.

Fact Sheets

A *fact sheet* is basically an outline of the news release. It highlights the strategic information gained from addressing the six basic questions: who, what, when, where, why, and how. It thus, in essence, creates a "cheat sheet" for the media.

Media Advisories

A *media advisory*, or *media alert*, is sent to the media to entice them into providing coverage. It briefly lists the specifics about an event, as well as information about interviews, news conferences, or photo opportunities.

Pitch Letters

The purpose of a *pitch letter* is also to drum up media coverage. The difference between a pitch letter and a news release is that pitch letters are just that—letters. A pitch letter is addressed to a specific editor and should be creatively written; its role is to get attention. This is a good time to get some feedback from the advertising creative team, to make sure the letter is written in the same tone of voice that is used in other communication pieces in the IMC campaign.

Press Kits

Press kits are most often used to promote special events or announce new product launches. The purpose of a press kit is to inform and educate the media, as well as drum up a little media coverage.

The press kit consists of a large pocketed folder, usually attractively designed. Again, the appearance should match that of the other advertising and promotional pieces that make up the IMC campaign. Inside the folder is a news release, a fact sheet, *backgrounders* (i.e., background articles), black-and-white publicity photographs, and maybe even a promotional item or two. Press kits tell the story of the event.

Newsletters

Newsletters are an informal way to reach the target. They educate, entertain, and inform. Newsletters are most commonly distributed to employees or stakeholders of a corporation, or to volunteers and supporters of nonprofit or specialty organizations. Although newsletters are often informal in style and appearance, every newsletter should continue the tone and appearance of the IMC campaign with which it is associated.

Brochures

Brochures are informational documents that the public wants to read and will spend time reading. They are frequently technical in nature, explaining detailed procedures, so the writing style must get to the point, avoiding any hype or jargon and aiming instead for clarity.

As a part of the IMC campaign, brochures should maintain the corporate or product image delivered in the advertising and other promotional efforts. Color and good-quality images make a brochure an attractive communication device.

As style pieces in an IMC campaign, brochures are attractive and informative. Best of all, the target is interested in, and will spend time reading, the brochure.

Publicity

Publicity is the strategic use of public relations. It is through the use of publicity that a product is made newsworthy to the media. Articles placed in the newspaper, if possible in the section most likely to be read by the target, provide the target with information about the product. Other media options include magazine feature stories, radio or television talk shows, and even advertising during programming.

If the publicist can successfully get an editor to pick up a news release, he can expect to receive one of the following types of coverage:

- A new article created around the news release
- Inclusion of the product or service in an existing article (one that is currently being researched and/or written)

CHAPTER NINE

Print Advertising: Newspapers

Say Goodbye to Warhol, Say Hello to Warthog.

The Knoxville Zoo has unique creations just for you.

Own a piece of the zoo.

Make a donation to the Knoxville Zoo by purchasing artwork created by animals at the zoo.

KNOXVILLE ZOO TENNESSEE

Instinctive Creativity

Heather Burke

Advertisements contain the only truths to be relied on in a newspaper.

—Thomas Jefferson, quoted in H. L. Mencken, 17.

Newspapers have been providing information to the public for centuries. Julius Caesar was responsible for ordering one of Rome's earliest newspapers, known as the *Acta Diurna*, to be made public more than 2,000 years ago. In its earliest forms, the newspaper was primarily a text-based medium. Then, in the fifteenth century, handwritten newsletters began concentrating as much on design as the written word. Today's modern look began in the early 1800s, when visuals in the form of illustrations were first introduced in England.

UNDERSTANDING ADVERTISING

Considered a mass medium because it can reach large numbers of consumers, advertising is most often considered a media option for new product launches or more homogenized and inexpensive products such as ketchup, toilet tissue, and cleaning products, to name just a few. Mass-advertised products appeal to large numbers of indistinct consumers and can be purchased across the United States.

Probably the best-known member of the promotional mix, the term "advertising" is often used to describe all forms of marketing-based communication. Although that is not technically incorrect, *advertising* actually refers to the media mix that makes up mass-media advertising, including print (newspaper and magazine) and broadcast (radio and television). Each of these mass-media vehicles will be examined separately over the next several chapters. Let's begin the discussion with a look at newspaper advertising.

WHAT IS NEWSPAPER ADVERTISING?

Newspaper advertising, also known as *retail advertising*, must accomplish two things. The first is to sell a product or service, and the second is to entice the reader into a response. This is a tough job. The reader has to wade through an enormous amount of written information before noticing the client's ad amid the maze of an indistinguishable gray expanse that characteristically makes up an average newspaper page.

Newspaper advertising engages the reader by using bold headlines; juicy, "got-to-buy-it" sales; new and improved claims; and coupons. Action-oriented statements, such as "Buy Now," "50% Off," or "While Quantities Last," are commonly used attention-getters in retail advertising. No matter what claim or approach is being used, it is important for the creative team to figure out how to make the client's ad stand out.

In today's fast-paced, interactive, sight-, sound-, and motion-based media world, newspapers do not have the status they once had with media buyers and marketers. But on paper, newspaper advertising offers it all, reaching readers from all age groups, incomes, educational levels, and ethnic groups.

Advertising appearing in newspapers falls into two distinct categories: local (including classified and display) and national.

Local, or Retail, Advertising

The term *local advertising* has two meanings: The first is that the advertising is of a local nature and tells readers where in their area they can find the product. The second meaning is that the advertising was initiated locally.

Classified Advertising

Classified advertising is done in-house by local newspapers, and it deals with consumer buying and selling. Categories feature garage sales, auctions, job opportunities, and real estate opportunities, to name just a few.

Display Ads

Display ads can be either local or national. The name refers to the complete list of components appearing within an ad, such as any visuals, type, or logos.

National, or Brand-Name Advertising

National advertising features brand-name products that can be found at local establishments or acquired through toll-free phone numbers or Internet access. Carried in newspapers throughout the country, national advertising requires few modifications from city to city, aside from its customization with regard to maps and addresses.

NEWSPAPER'S ROLE IN IMC

Newspaper Delivers the News about Advertising

Newspaper advertising reaches a lot of people, is effective, offers flexible deadlines, and is relatively inexpensive. Since ads normally arrive at the newspaper complete, an ad submitted as little as twenty-four hours in advance—or later—may still be able to make a particular edition.

Newspapers are not only read for news value, but for the news of advertising: it's where people look for information about sales. Advertising makes up more than 60 percent of newspaper content, with the majority of advertising dollars being spent by local advertisers. There are three national newspapers: the *Christian Sci-*

ence Monitor, the *Wall Street Journal,* and *USA Today*; but most newspapers are printed and distributed locally, and, depending on the size of the market, are printed monthly, weekly, or daily.

Advertising should inspire the consumer to feel a want and/or a need for the product or service being advertised right now. Price and product description play a prominent role in doing this. Retail advertising's only job is to make a sale. One way to accomplish this is by instilling a sense of urgency, through such devices as limited-time offers, limited quantities, two-for-one offers, special sale hours, preferred customer sales, and coupons.

Newspaper Is All About the Sale

Newspapers are where consumers go for sales. Everybody loves a sale. They are abundant in retail, and they promote predictable themes. The key is to decide how the client's sale will be unique, and then grab the reader—preferably by the throat.

Sales should not seem routine. The personality of the sale should reflect that of the product or store. Sales create traffic within a store, and traffic promotes additional purchases. Most sales events are associated with holidays, special events, and overstocks; but why limit the message to that? Sales should be creative events. Why not have a sale called "It's Tuesday—Let's Shop till We Drop Together"? Two of the most important sales devices used in newspaper advertising are coupons and freestanding inserts (FSIs).

Coupons

Coupons are the IMC bridge between newspaper advertising and sales promotion. Coupons offer the target an incentive to buy.

All consumers like to get a break, and coupons are a way to offer something in return for their patronage or their loyalty, or as an introduction to the product or service. A coupon is an effective, temporary sales device. It should be easy to remove from the ad, it should clearly point out the offer, and it should be easy to redeem. Incentives often include two-for-one offers or discount deals.

Freestanding Inserts

One of the more attractively designed coupons is known as a *freestanding insert.* FSIs are one-page, full-color ads that are inserted into the newspaper. Printed on a coated or treated paper stock, these inserts can be double-sided and usually feature coupons or announce a special sale or promotion. Sizes vary, but FSIs are most often 8 1/2 × 11 inches. These nationally distributed inserts are also known as *supplemental advertising.*

How Newspaper Builds a Relationship between the Product and the Target Audience

One thing newspaper *isn't* is consumer focused. It does not build a relationship with the target, and it isn't interactive in any significant way. So why use it at all in an IMC campaign?

The answer lies in its relationship with the other members of the promotional mix and the advertising media mix. Newspaper advertising is a great follow-up to news releases, press conferences, or interviews, helping to raise awareness or build an image for an existing product or a new product launch. Other options, supporting public relations, might include the promotion of a corporate cause—for example, by asking the target to bring in a canned good or donate clothing in exchange for free movie passes or a free entrée.

By including a coupon, newspaper advertising can work with sales promotion, promoting "try me" offers. T-shirts, cups, toy characters, or even watches promoting a current movie might be given out in fast-food restaurants when the consumer gives the correct password, or repeats a slogan printed in the newspaper.

Newspaper advertising can refer the target to an Internet site in order to request additional information; or it can feature a toll-free number to call, in order to speak to a customer service representative or place an order.

The Pros and Cons Associated with Newspaper Advertising

When deciding whether newspaper is right for an IMC campaign, it may be helpful to look at some of the pros and cons associated with it.

The more notable pros associated with newspaper advertising include:

1. Timeline. Newspapers have very late deadlines. This allows for the placement of last-minute ads and the opportunity to make changes to existing ads, up until twenty-four hours prior to printing (or even later).
2. Sizes. Because of the low cost of newspaper advertising, ads can be sized up or down to accommodate both budget and information needs.
3. Believability. Advertising takes on more credibility because it appears alongside editorial material. (The difference between this and public relations is that public relations *is* the editorial material.)
4. Loyal readers. Consumers buy a newspaper because they want to read the news of the day and the sales of the week.
5. Cost. The uncoated paper stock, or *newsprint*, that newspaper is printed on is inexpensive. It can be bought in large quantities and used to make a low-priced product which is read and then discarded. Because of this, newspaper space can be purchased fairly inexpensively. It can reach a mass audience on a daily basis, making it a very attractive medium.
6. Geographic concentration. Newspaper ads are seen only by those in the same geographic location as the product or service, minimizing media waste.

We have so many selections,
there might not be room on your bun.

The Original. Large size. $5.99 at Schlotzsky's.

Lindsay Frankenfield

7. Frequency. How many times an ad can be viewed is affected by how often the newspaper is printed. A newspaper can be published weekly, most often in smaller markets, or daily, in larger ones. An ad appearing in a daily for one week is six times more likely to be seen than one appearing just one time in a weekly.
8. Coupons. The use of coupons in newspaper advertising creates an interactive opportunity by giving the target more than information. Coupons must be torn from the ad and carried to the product location to be redeemed.

The more notable cons associated with newspaper advertising include:

1. Its mass-media nature. It is difficult to ensure that an ad will reach the intended target. Newspaper advertising is the least targetable of all media vehicles.
2. Creative disadvantages. The worst problem is the paper stock. The uncoated, inexpensive newsprint causes the ink to bleed, affecting type quality and

causing poor photo reproduction. The fact that the majority of advertisements lack color can also affect both visual and verbal stimulation.

3. Clutter. The gray page of a newspaper has a lot going on. An ad can be missed if it is not designed to stand up and stand out.

4. Its short life span. Newspapers and the advertising within them are old news within twenty-four hours.

5. Declining readership. Readership by younger adults is steadily declining, as they instead rely on news television such as CNN or Fox News.

6. Limited viewing. Special sections, such as the sports and financial pages and the comics, allow readers to bypass the rest of the newspaper.

7. Passivity. Newspaper advertising does not involve the reader in the message.

8. Price-based advertising. Newspaper advertising announces sales. Unfortunately, there is nothing classy or image-oriented about pushing price.

DEVELOPING THE PROMOTIONAL MIX USING NEWSPAPER ADVERTISING

Understanding the capabilities and limitations of print advertising, as opposed to other media options such as broadcast, out-of-home, or direct mail, is crucial for the success of an IMC strategy. Not all ideas can transfer between media. Knowing this in advance will save the identity of the campaign and ensure that the message will reach the target. Strategically, the key benefit must be able to be delivered both visually and verbally in the media outlets most used by the target.

Mass-media advertising alone does not build a relationship with individual consumers or create dialogue; it works to inform and build awareness. Newspaper advertising cannot guarantee that the target will see the message. It is possible, however, by placing the ad in a newspaper section of particular interest to the target to increase the odds that the target will be exposed to the message.

Like all other components of the media mix, advertising selection depends on the target and the overall objectives. If the target is 18-to-25-year-olds, newspaper advertising would be a poor choice, since few in this age group read the paper on a regular basis, and few, if any, read the paper from cover to cover. Objectives that might benefit from newspaper advertising include creating brand awareness, maintaining or retaining brand loyalty, building or maintaining brand image, creating sales or generating interest, announcing product changes or additions, and increasing store traffic. Newspaper advertising features the same key benefit, layout style, approach, tone of voice, and images as other pieces within the IMC campaign.

THE CREATIVE VOICE OF NEWSPAPER ADVERTISING

It is up to the client to decide whether to use an advertising agency or the corporation's own in-house art department to fulfill its communication needs. In-house design is most often used for small jobs that need to be done right away or that don't happen on a regular basis. Most clients working with IMC have large advertising budgets and choose to use the expertise found in an advertising agency to develop and retain a consistent visual/verbal message.

Creating a successful newspaper ad requires that the designer put him- or herself in the consumer's place. What catches the consumer's eye, and what does he need to know? How would he use the product? Where can he find it? Why can't he live without it? The answers can be found through meticulous message construction and the use of a few simple layout techniques.

Advertising is basically a relationship between words and imagery. The creative team should seek to create a match between what is said and what is shown. The key elements of print advertising are divided between copy and art. As previously discussed, the copy, or verbal elements, include headlines, subheads, body copy, slogans/taglines, and logos. Art or visual elements include illustrations, photography, charts/graphs, logos, and graphic design, as well as type style and the overall

Robby Cockrell

layout. A product's or service's logo can be both visual and verbal if designed with both type and graphics.

Design for newspaper advertising isn't difficult but does take organization, and a good design plan needs specific tactics. There must be a strong concept developed from the strategy and a headline that informs the target about the key consumer benefit. The ad must feature the product and promote its price or availability. Each layout should develop or maintain a visual/verbal identity that reflects both the brand and the target and is consistent with the other visual/verbal messages in the IMC campaign. Every ad should have strong black-and-white contrasts when applicable, feature a dominant element, and promote price or availability. Body copy should develop the key consumer benefit and include a call to action. Type should be easy to read and be brand-image specific. Retail ads often have a lot to say and show in a small space. Controlling clutter and chaos is the designer's ultimate goal. The ad should flow easily from element to element and close with the logo, slogan or tag-line, and detail copy to make shopping easier. The simple, inexpensive, yet informative nature of newspaper advertising makes it one of the leading advertising vehicles.

SIZE SPECIFICATIONS

Newspaper space is measured from side to side in *column inches*, a system of measurement based on the width of a column of typeset copy plus the gutter. Width in a standard paper is measured in 2 1/16-inch (i.e., one-column) increments, from 2 1/6 inches to 13 inches. The depth of an ad is measured in 1/4-inch increments, up to 21 inches in a standard paper. While the newspaper works within predetermined widths, the depth of an ad is determined by design and budget constraints. Table 9.1 shows choices for column widths.

A full-page ad in a standard paper measures 13 inches (i.e., six columns) wide by 21 inches deep, for a size of 126 column inches.

CO-OP ADVERTISING

Co-op, or *cooperative advertising*, means that two individual but compatible clients have paired up to share the cost of the advertising and to encourage consumers to

Table 9.1. Column Widths

1 column	2 1/16 inches
2 column	4 1/4 inches
3 column	6 7/16 inches
4 column	8 5/8 inches
5 column	10 13/16 inches
6 column	13 inches

use their products together. It is not unusual, however, for there to be more than two members of the advertising media or promotional mix participating in co-op opportunities. There are two types of co-op advertising: vertical and horizontal. *Vertical cooperatives* are where one sponsor pays more and plays a larger or more prominent role in the ad. *Horizontal cooperatives* have budgets that are equally distributed, giving each sponsor equal exposure.

These highly successful partnerships might, for instance, team an airline with a hotel chain, to promote air-and-hotel packages to a destination accessed by both. Other co-op ventures might include name-brand coffees served at national restaurant chains, or even computers that feature "Intel Inside."

Evaluating Decisions Made

Evaluating results is critical to determining the success of any IMC campaign. Success or failure is defined by whether the objectives were met or not. Advertising will rely on other media within the promotional mix to determine if brand awareness and increased sales were achieved. These are the two most important objectives associated with both print and broadcast advertising.

Buying Newspaper

When buying newspaper space, buyers will need to make several decisions, such as whether the ad will use black-and-white or color photographs, and whether a certain section (e.g., a business or lifestyle section), also known as a *preferred position*, will be required. If the buyer has no preference involving placement, the ad will be placed at the newspaper's discretion; this is known as *run of press*. Another factor buyers need to consider is that a preferred position can often carry a higher price tag than run-of-press positioning.

Unlike broadcast, with limited ad space, newspaper has almost unlimited availability. The only exception would be in the case of special-request positioning such as the bottom half of page 2, where only one such position exists. It is important to note that depending on the product and the target, special-request positioning could affect overall reach.

Newspaper advertising is an important member of the media mix because it is believable, simple to design, inexpensive to place, and informative. Although it is not highly targetable, loyal readers seek out newspaper advertising for "unbelievably low" price points, "to-die-for" sales, limited-time offers, and coupons. Using it as part of the media mix in any IMC campaign can localize a national product, create traffic within a store, or announce a new product launch.

PRINT ADVERTISING: MAGAZINES

Everyone has different tastes.

Fortunately, ScienceDiet® has a wide selection of foods for your puppy's distinctive tastes.

Lindsay Frankenfield

177

Advertising nourishes the consuming power of men. It sets up before a man the goal of a better home, better clothing, better food for himself and his family. It spurs individual exertion and greater production.

—Sir Winston Churchill, quoted in David Ogilvy, *Confessions*, 133.

WHAT IS MAGAZINE ADVERTISING?

Magazine advertising concentrates on the creation of an image or mood through visual and verbal relationships. In order to entice the reader, magazine ads need to create a conceptual environment that the reader can both relate to and experience through the words and visuals. The show-and-tell nature of magazine advertising allows products to speak for themselves and demonstrate results. Although diverse in nature, many products appearing in magazines are exclusive or unique, and expensive to own. Other products are more mainstream, and their features may be indistinguishable from the features of their competitors' products.

Products boasting higher price tags are less likely to be purchased on impulse. Before buying, discerning consumers will research a product's benefits and features, identify where the product fits into their own lives, and determine which problems it can solve. When used in IMC, magazine advertising should make information readily available to assist the consumer in making an informed buying decision.

Very different from the discerning consumer is the trendy shopper who uses magazine advertising to look at all the competing products within a category. With little to differentiate one brand of sneakers from another, product features take a backseat to how consumers are affected by the advertised message, and consumers are convinced to purchase by how they will look, feel, or be perceived in the sneakers.

When image and product features are prominent, price plays a more subordinate role in the design; the focus is placed instead on the benefits of owning or using a product or service. Because of this, visuals tend to play a more dominant role, as does lengthy, fact-based copy. By creating a strong visual/verbal relationship, the advertised message can tap into a reader's rational or emotional tendencies by allowing him to see the product being worn or used; to learn what colors and sizes are available; and to review safety information and warranties.

MAGAZINE ADVERTISING'S ROLE IN IMC

Unlike publicity and newspaper ads, a magazine's message has a long life span. Because of the highly individualized content of magazines, consumers tend to hold onto them longer, often trading with other enthusiasts or friends. This gives advertising a second chance to make a first impression and reach out to a larger portion of the target audience.

A magazine's editorial content plays an important role in the advertising that appears between its covers. For example, advertising found in a home-decorating magazine will promote products such as barbecue grills, paint and wallpaper products, and furniture and carpeting, as well as patio and pool items.

THE VARIETY OF MAGAZINES

There are three basic categories of magazines: *consumer, business* or *trade*, and *farming*. Each of these three categories is broken down further into special interests, so that there are consumer magazines about fashion, sports, cars, and hobbies; and trade publications about advertising, marketing, public relations, and so forth.

Consumer Magazines

Consumer magazines make up an eclectic group of periodicals, comprised of articles and advertising either loosely targeted to a broad audience or specifically targeted based on special interests or hobbies. Let's take a closer look at each category by breaking them down further into two distinct types: *general-interest* publications, including local and regional editions, and *special-interest* publications.

General-Interest Magazines

General-interest magazines such as *People, Time*, and *TV Guide* enjoy national circulation and large, indistinct target audiences. This type of magazine supports advertising with a more generalized appeal, such as ads for cars, food and beverages, cold and flu medications, and so on—in other words, products that can be sold across geographic and demographic boundaries.

Metropolitan magazines are published for consumers in a particular city. Titles most often reference the city in which they are published, and editorial content reflects topics of local interest. This type of magazine allows local advertisers to reach those targeted consumers in their community only, eliminating advertising waste.

Geographical editions of national magazines are published for specific regions of the country or for individual states or cities. This allows clients to appear in a national magazine for a regional price, again narrowing the target and eliminating advertising waste.

Special-Interest Magazines

Special-interest magazines feature editorial material directed specifically to a targeted group having a specific interest in the magazine's featured topic. Because of this, advertising that appears in these publications generally matches the editorial content; here, it's guaranteed to reach those consumers most likely to use the product or service.

The more specialized the magazine, the more the advertising creative team knows about the consumer who will see their client's advertising. Dog lovers read dog magazines, car lovers read car magazines, and clothing lovers read fashion magazines. This kind of specialized readership challenges the creative team to create an environment that allows readers to participate in the advertising based on personal experience. And this specialized interest produces readers who are loyal, and who subscribe to the magazine or pick it up regularly at the newsstand.

The target's special interest in a magazine's editorial material allows for advertising with longer, more fact-based copy that can educate and encourage product trial. Full-color photographs and informative copy can be intimately tied to the self-image of the target audience, creating a perception of need and inducing loyalty.

Business, or Trade, Magazines

When selling products to *businesses*, the best way to reach this conscientious market, other than through expensive personal-selling tactics, is to advertise in business-specific, or trade, publications. Those in charge of purchasing actively seek out both the editorial content and advertising for the newest innovations in their specialization, making advertising in business publications advantageous. Business consumers not only need to buy but *want* to buy the newest products or business-related equipment that will increase both productivity and profits. The relatively small size of almost all business markets makes targeting easier than in consumer magazines.

In order to more precisely determine which business magazine(s) will reach the audience, business magazines can be broken down into two distinct types: *general business* and *specialized business*.

General Business Magazines

If advertising efforts are trying to reach upper-level managers or those in executive positions, business magazines such as *Forbes, Business Week,* and *Fortune* are some of the best bets. Editorial material and advertising content in these publications cover industry on a broad and generic scale.

Specialized Business Magazines

Just like special-interest consumer magazines, specialized business publications deal with various types of industries, such as industrial (including manufacturing and research and development), trade (including retail, wholesaling, and advertising), and professional (including medical, engineering, computers, etc.).

Farming Magazines

This very diverse and highly targeted type of magazine deals with both consumer and business issues. Most are technically based and deal with the newest innovations in farming. They are often published regionally because of the diverse planting, soil, and weather conditions across the country.

How Magazine Advertising Builds a Relationship between the Product and the Target Audience

Magazine advertising does a little better than newspaper at being consumer focused. Because of their highly targetable nature, it could be argued that magazines are both interactive and educational. Advertising efforts can talk directly to the target's special interests by tapping into the target's self-image. The ability of magazine advertising to build a relationship, and thus brand loyalty, is a result of the product image transferring to the target's self-image, creating a bond.

What magazine advertising cannot do is develop a dialogue with the consumer. The advertised message is a monologue directed at an often passive and distracted

CJ French

audience. In order to create a dialogue, advertising must be used to move the target to the next step: seeking out more information by using a toll-free number, or visiting a website to obtain additional information or place an order. A small degree of interactivity can be introduced through the use of coupons, samples, pop-ups, website addresses, or folds that can be opened and/or closed to find hidden information—any of which can involve the target in the reading or viewing of the ad. Magazines are a good choice if the goal is to inform with long copy or dazzle with color. They are also great at promoting trial by associating the product or service with an activity the target enjoys, and they're great for developing image or brand identity. Magazines bring elegance, prestige, and beauty to the product—and thus to the target's image.

Image-based products are often referred to as *high-involvement* products. The target's wallet and self-image are tied to the brand's identity. If magazine advertising is used for a new product launch, introducing any type of sales promotion at this early stage could affect a brand's perceived exclusivity in the mind of the target. However, sales promotion might be used to promote trial or to create initial interest, through contests or sweepstakes.

Direct marketing can utilize magazine advertising by offering a form within the ad, which the consumer can use to place an order or request additional information. Other direct-marketing devices used for ordering or making inquiries might include a bound-in postal reply card or a freestanding postal insert, also known as a *blow-in*.

By placing a Web address within the magazine copy, an advertiser can direct consumers to the Internet to acquire additional information, or for advanced purchase—which is another way of making the sale personal, interactive, and exclusive.

Magazines are a bad choice to use with any type of current publicity, unless planned or manufactured, because of the limited printing schedules and long lead times associated with publication. New, old, and reinvented products with messages based on image or innovation are ideal for magazine use. However, unlike a new or reinvented product, the image of a more mature product will not be affected by the sale mentality of pairing newspaper with magazine advertising in the promotional mix.

Design for magazine advertising will work with the same objectives as design for the other members of the promotional and media mix: strategy, key benefit, and visual/verbal message. It will speak with the same tone of voice, and use the same imagery, as other communication efforts used in the IMC campaign, for ease of recognition by the target. This applies to elements such as type, color, spokesperson, and layout style.

PROS AND CONS ASSOCIATED WITH MAGAZINE ADVERTISING

When deciding whether magazine advertising is right for an IMC campaign, it may be helpful to look at some of the pros and cons associated with it.

The more notable pros associated with magazine advertising include:

1. Its select target market. The highly targeted and specialized nature of magazines allows copy to talk directly to the person most likely to purchase the product or use the service.
2. Printing capabilities. Better paper, better print quality, better color, and detailed visuals allow targets to imagine themselves using the product. Printing capabilities allow both large and small photographs to hold detail.
3. Life span. Due to the highly individualized content of magazines, consumers tend to hold on to them longer, often trading with other enthusiasts or friends, extending the life of the advertising.
4. Image. Since magazines reflect readers' lifestyles and interests directly, visuals and concept directions that address lifestyle directly address image. Full-color visuals and detailed copy work in tandem to build or retain a product's image.
5. Its informative copy. Copy can be longer, since readers selectively spend more time reading a magazine.
6. Creative options. Creatively speaking, about the only restrictions in magazine design are the inability to dynamically demonstrate a product or service and budgetary restrictions.
7. Geographic selectivity. Local or regional advertising efforts can reach those most likely to use the product or service, without waste.

The more notable cons associated with magazine advertising include:

1. Early deadlines. Advanced deadlines require designers to work often months ahead of a publication date. These advanced deadlines need to be watched closely in order for magazine advertising to coincide with other IMC publication or print dates.
2. Cost. Magazine advertising is indeed more expensive to produce than most other forms of print advertising.
3. Clutter. Unlike in newspaper advertising, where the issue is clutter on the page, magazine advertising has to compete with the enormous clutter of ads that appear in any one magazine.
4. Sparse publication schedules. Magazines have fewer publication dates—ranging from weekly to quarterly—making the presentation of time-sensitive material more difficult.

DEVELOPING THE PROMOTIONAL MIX USING MAGAZINE ADVERTISING

Magazines are a time capsule, capturing lifestyle and values and immortalizing trends. Magazines can offer up the key benefit in brilliant color and, if necessary, with detailed copy points. The more that is known about the target's interests, lifestyles, and general demographics, the better. Strategy development designed to meet the special interests of the reader makes isolating a key benefit more individualistic and can accomplish the stated objectives more precisely.

Strategically, magazine advertising is not a good choice if the product or service is not image based or the budget is tight. The decision to use magazines as a part of the media mix will depend on the objectives. Magazines are best used for consumer-based strategies where brand image, lifestyle, or brand attitude can be specifically addressed through the visual/verbal message.

Before determining whether magazine advertising is right for an IMC campaign, here are some additional questions that need to be addressed: Is color needed? Is magazine advertising in the budget? Where is the relationship being developed? How will advertising in magazines help reach the target audience? Will magazines be used as a part of the campaign launch or as a support vehicle? What is the life-cycle stage of the product or service? Does dialogue need to be created, or does image just need to be reinforced? What will need to be done to create interactivity? Is it important to direct the target to customer service or a website? Do all IMC communication efforts work toward building both loyalty and equity?

Objectives that benefit from using magazine advertising might include generating interest in a new or reinvented product, or reinforcing the decision to purchase an expensive product or service by showing the benefits of ownership. Additional objectives might include creating awareness, positioning, or building or maintaining a brand attitude.

Carrying the strategy through each of the media or promotional mix options in an IMC campaign will require a strong sense of how the target thinks. Strategically, the objectives, key benefit, and visual/verbal message will dominate in each media vehicle. A strong tone of voice and equally strong visual imagery must resonate with the target's self-image.

WHAT TO AVOID AND WHAT TO INCLUDE IN MAGAZINE ADVERTISING

Since magazines sell an idea or an image of affluence, beauty, or even intellect, prices should not be prominent in magazine advertising. Often these ads have no price at all, and they generally include little copy; they let the image sell the product. Consumers should be able to experience the benefits associated with the product or service through the visual/verbal message and be encouraged to call, visit a website, or visit their nearest retailer for more information.

Depending on the product, this is also an opportunity to develop a storyline or plot that ties the benefits and image of the product or service to the target's needs and lifestyle. When creatively written, longer copy can sustain a reader's interest long enough to educate and inform. However, the printing surface of magazines is ideal for detailed photographs that show the product's benefits or attributes without the need for lengthy copy. A magazine ad can use a broad range of color; it can set a mood or recreate a time period; it can present a visual "discussion" through

**When the situation gets ugly,
call Maalox for the bubblies!!**

Fast acting for the most serious
indigestion.

Maalox Max.

Michele Lawson

photographs, illustrations, or graphics that show a product in use; and it can assist with image development, create a trend, or evoke an atmosphere of exclusivity or fun.

The highly targeted and well-informed nature of magazine readers allows copy to talk directly to the person most likely to purchase the product, the person who clearly understands its benefits. This is one of the few instances in which "been there, done that" is a positive concept, as consumers relate their experiences to those the product can solve.

Magazines should be avoided if high message frequency is required or if deadlines are an issue. Unlike the twenty-four-hour turnaround of most newspapers, magazine deadlines or submission dates range anywhere from a few weeks to a couple of months before the magazine appears on newsstands.

THE CREATIVE VOICE OF MAGAZINE ADVERTISING

Everything about designing for magazines is more creative and more exciting than designing for almost any other medium. Elite products allow the designer's fantasy world to come alive. The numerous products without independent identities present a design challenge. *Product individualism,* or what sets a client's product apart from the competition, is achieved through strategy development, layout, and/or type choices.

Magazines reflect personal image. Image portrayal means that it's the creative team's job to make targets see themselves driving this car or using this perfume, or to make them understand the envy friends will feel when they're seen in this piece of Tiffany jewelry. It is the goal of magazine advertising to assist consumers with their buying decisions by making them feel, see, taste, and imagine the product in their lives.

Advertising that appears in the pages of a magazine should provide a visually stimulating and informative experience for readers. Visual images should develop an identity and create a visual personality for the product or service. Copy should take the reader on a fact-finding adventure. Product image and user image should be woven throughout this personalized visual/verbal relationship.

Concepts that address lifestyle directly address image. Full-color visuals and dynamite copy work in tandem to create the appropriate consumer response.

Photographs bring the product or service alive with enhanced details, by offering an exclusive viewing opportunity. Textures are magnified, emotions are highlighted, and colors pop off the page. Storylines can be developed to promote uses; scientific studies can be cited; features can be demonstrated; purchase options can be enumerated; and trends can be created.

Graphic designs or colorful illustrations attract attention by showcasing interesting shapes and brilliant color variations. Design styles and color usage can recreate time periods and suggest liberal or conservative views. Bold, colorful graphics suggest youth and energy, while subdued colors reflect relaxation and stability.

VISUALLY AND VERBALLY INVOLVING THE TARGET

The varied concept approaches used in magazines must all prompt a purchase or promote additional research on the part of the consumer. Good interactive or educational devices might include encouraging test drives, employing some novel design option such as folds or pop-ups, or providing samples or order forms.

Testimonials also successfully create consumer involvement, by evoking curiosity. Informational ads are great educational vehicles, as are recipes that accompany food-product ads. Emotional appeals, how-to ads, and product demonstrations all work well in magazine advertising.

COOPERATIVE ADVERTISING AND MAGAZINES

As with newspaper and other members of the advertising media or promotional mix, it is not unusual for magazines to participate in co-op opportunities, to sell compatible products, or to support a special event.

The benefit co-op advertising brings to the target is the ability to combine two viable products into a package-savings deal. Product pairing, when done consistently, makes the target think in terms of "package" rather than separate products when considering repurchase.

LET'S FOLD SOMETHING

One great interactive device common to magazine advertising is a fold. The type of fold found in magazines is called a *gatefold*. A gatefold can be one or more folds that fold in toward the ad's center when the magazine is closed, and can fold out for viewing.

A gatefold can vary in size, but most often it is a nearly full-size third panel, 1/16 to 1/8 inch smaller than the page size; this allows the magazine to close without rumpling or folding the ad. Another common option is a partial page fold, which can vary in size but is usually around 2 1/2 to 3 inches wide and 8 1/2 inches deep.

Gatefolds are used to extend the ad, to add grandeur, and to invoke curiosity. Extending the photograph entices readers to open the panel, involving them in the ad and holding their interest a few minutes longer. Usually, small gatefolds overlay the bottom photograph (making it important that registration be exact during printing). Coupons, or contest or sweepstakes information, can often be found on or under these smaller folds.

BUYING MAGAZINE

The first choice media buyers need to make is whether advertising needs to be placed locally, regionally, or nationally. Second, the media buyer must consider the editorial content of magazines, differentiating among consumer, business, and agricultural publications.

Buyers can choose from a limited selection of specialized placement pages, such as the inside front or back cover, the center spread, or the back cover. If special placement is not required, the ad will be placed at the publication's discretion. The buyer can also buy space for a preprinted insert, consisting of one or more pages specially sized and designed to be bound into the magazine during printing.

The choice to use the visually stimulating pages of a magazine to bring prestige to a product and reflect the target's interests, self-image, and lifestyle is a business and design journey into the study of human nature. Magazine advertising can be fun, sexy, serious, colorful, imaginative, and visually/verbally informative. It is perfect for developing a new product's image, maintaining an established image, or rebuilding or repairing the image of a reinvented product.

CHAPTER ELEVEN

OUT-OF-HOME ADVERTISING

Ryan Vinett

I do not regard advertising as entertainment or an art form, but as a medium of information.

—David Ogilvy, *Ogilvy on Advertising*, 7.

WHAT IS OUT-OF-HOME ADVERTISING?

Any advertising you see outside your home, with few exceptions, is known as *out-of-home*. Considered a mass medium, it is one of the least expensive media vehicles and typically includes over thirty different types of outdoor and transit vehicles, shelters, stations, and terminals.

"Minimalism" is the best way to describe the look of out-of-home advertising. Although this medium is blessed with an unusual variety of shapes and sizes, copy is limited to five to seven words, and viewing time is often restricted to only a few minutes or even a few seconds. As a media and creative device used in IMC, out-of-home must present a visual/verbal relationship that relates to and supports any other pieces used in the campaign.

Although it seems to be everywhere, out-of-home advertising is not as dominant as it may seem, amounting to less than 1 percent of all advertising in the United States. But it is growing. Overall growth can be attributed to increased creative options, and to media vehicles that stand out and step up the viewing experience, in order to deliver what it takes to attract today's distracted, uninvolved audience. Out-of-home is one of the few media vehicles that do not need to compete for audience attention. In many cases, viewers are a captive audience for the duration of the traffic light or the trip to or from work. Because of this, consumers can't turn the ad off, throw it in the trash, change the channel, or hit the mute button.

Outdoor boards represent out-of-home's largest voice, and transit is its most mobile. Combined, their job is to reach consumers while they move about their day.

Carefully placed out-of-home advertising can be found in urban and suburban areas of large and midsize cities; in small towns; in or on public transportation; and along interstate highways nationwide. Personalized or generic messages can be developed for products sold locally, regionally, or nationally, but the majority of all out-of-home concentrates specifically on local businesses and products.

In an IMC campaign, out-of-home vehicles work as great support media, and are a great way to build or maintain awareness and reinforce other IMC media.

OUT-OF-HOME'S ROLE IN IMC

In keeping with its role as a supplemental or support medium for other, more traditional media, out-of-home works best when used for introducing new products, as reminder advertising, or to maintain a product's or service's brand image. The best way to do this is to show rather than tell. To do this effectively, advertising efforts must have three elements picked up from other vehicles in the IMC campaign: a bold visual, a short message, and a logo or package used as an identifier.

Out-of-home media vehicles do not have enough room or time to tell a product's or service's full story. Its main job is to remind the public about a product or service. Copy should be simple, so the message can be absorbed easily. Bright colors will attract attention, and bold visuals will help to remind consumers about a product's or a service's story. The best copy is a strong slogan or tagline, to tie out-of-home to other media vehicles used in the campaign. Sometimes it will take a combination of several elements to help with product recognition and/or a brand's image.

Let's look at two of the more popular out-of-home vehicles.

Outdoor Advertising Has Been Around a Long Time

Outdoor boards, one of the oldest forms of advertising, can be traced back to the Romans, who used wall signs to direct travelers to rooms for rent and local taverns. Their purpose has changed little over the centuries.

Outdoor boards, once known as *billboards*, are no longer used for roadway advertising alone. At one time they came under fire for marring the landscape. As a result, the Highway Beautification Act of 1965 was enacted to regulate outdoor placement on interstate highways. Regulation was a direct consequence of complaints by consumers that outdoor advertising was visually polluting the environment. It didn't help that alcohol and cigarette advertising and poor creative execution dominated the ads. The Institute of Outdoor Advertising works to continually push for improved designs and to ensure that signs are placed in locations that do not offend or impede the view.

Nationally, in the early 1990s, hundreds or even thousands of boards were removed, and Congress permanently banned the construction of any new boards on U.S. interstates. Regulation, and the granting of any necessary permits at the state level, is controlled by each state's department of transportation.

Since the 1990s, creative ingenuity, along with improved technology, has greatly improved the image of outdoor advertising. Modern consumers believe that outdoor boards offer helpful travel and business information, and they enjoy the creative options.

Today's big, bold, often technology-based "in your face" form of advertising is creative and attractively done, and it's placed into a diverse array of public places—such as office buildings, subways, buses, airport terminals, and shopping malls. It is becoming more attractive to marketers who feel the public isn't paying attention to more traditional advertising efforts. Because of the availability of diverse locations, this mass-media vehicle can often be highly targetable. Based on where the boards are placed, they can focus on specific neighborhoods or ethnic groups.

As a vehicle that must entertain and educate to capture attention, an outdoor board has only about six to eight seconds to deliver its intended message (when not located near an intersection where traffic lights help divert and hold the driver's attention). Because the message has to be brief in order to be read quickly, it must be memorable.

The fun of out-of-home advertising is its diversity of size, form, and location. Design options are limited only by budget and the creative team's imagination. Outdoor boards come in two different varieties: the more traditional painted bulletins and poster panels, and the newer and more creative electronic LED boards.

Working With the Painted Bulletin

Painted bulletins are hand-painted images, whereas *posters* are created using sheets of preprinted images that are glued directly to the board. Painted boards have evolved into vinyl-coated or single-fabric sheets that are stretched across the board. This new technique has greatly improved image quality, rivaling that found in magazines.

Bulletins are large boards. Their sheer size makes them great for placement on interstate highways or heavily traveled routes. It is not unusual for bulletins to have extensions or three-dimensional additions. Each of these options operates as part of the design, extending it beyond the edges of the board. Some boards use the existing landscape as a part of the design. Bic, for example, leaned a large three-dimensional razor against a board in an open field where a stripe the width of the razor had been mowed. Cingular cut a hole in the middle of one of their boards and dropped the piece onto the sidewalk below. The board asked the question, "HATE DROPPED [insert the hole here]?" The missing piece on the sidewalk held the word "CALLS."

This type of board is usually purchased for a longer period of time, often on a one- to three-year basis, making them more permanent and more expensive than posters.

Moving the Image onto Poster Panels

Posters are smaller in size than painted bulletins, and are created in sections or "sheets" rather than painted on site. These types of boards are usually rented by the month, and will most often be found in heavy-traffic areas and along highways. Overall cost is based on the amount of time the board will be used, the size, whether the design has bleed or is illuminated, and the location. Boards purchased for more than thirty days can be purchased at a discount.

Poster panels are preprinted in the shop on paper or vinyl sheets, then transferred to the board's location and mounted. The most common poster panels are *thirty-sheet posters*, measuring 10 feet 5 inches × 22 feet 8 inches. The name "thirty-sheet poster panels" is actually a relic: before printing techniques improved, it used to take thirty sheets of paper to create a board; today that number has been reduced to eight or ten sheets of paper, or one full sheet of vinyl.

Smaller, eight-sheet posters known as *location signage* are often used to mark the location of a business or promote a product near the point of purchase—increasing both reach and frequency, as well as building brand awareness and/or reminding consumers about a product or service. Visual/verbal messages include at least a logo, and perhaps a graphic or visual and a short message along with the logo.

Taking Outdoor to New Heights

Even outdoor boards can't escape the long arm of technology, with the introduction of *LED boards* to the landscape. These lighted and computer-controlled billboards host several different advertising messages that rotate every eight seconds, holding the commuter's attention. A single board can deliver several different messages for a single product or service, like a campaign, or it can advertise multiple products. Moveable outdoor boards are both attractive and entertaining; because of this, they have made outdoor advertising one of the fastest-growing media vehicles—second only to the Internet, according to the Outdoor Advertising Association of America.

A computer can quickly and easily change signs in minutes, compared to the forty-five minutes and the labor required to change traditional boards. On a smaller scale, taxicabs can be fitted with global positioning hardware, so that this same type of sign can change based on a cab's location within a city. This allows local advertisers to promote their messages close to their business locations.

Large and bright, these types of boards can often be seen from quite a distance on interstate highways. However, most boards are placed in low-speed, high-traffic locations that feature a four-way intersection, where drivers are stopped long enough to see a board's full rotation.

As an IMC device, marketers can use several boards that show the same or different messages in varied locations throughout a city, ensuring that vehicles along the route will see an integrated stream of messages.

LED boards are creative, attractive, and colorful; they don't fade or tear after prolonged exposure to the elements; and they are easy to change. The only downside is that several cities have banned the boards as too bright and as posing a driving hazard, because drivers lock onto the boards' continually moving messages.

Digital boards offer diverse creative opportunities and make the outdoors more

Start Your Vacation before the Airport.

1-800-BLUE-VAN

Let Us Drive You There!
Super Shuttle

Krissy Parson

targetable toward varied demographic groups than ever before. Many consumers favor these new LED boards, considering them to be attractive and entertaining, while others find them distracting and potentially dangerous.

Sizes

Outdoor boards come in the following sizes:

- 30-sheet posters (10 ft. 5 in. × 22 ft. 8 in.)
- 30-sheet *bleed* (i.e., color or visual goes to the edge of the board, leaving no white border) poster (9 ft. 7 in. × 21 ft. 7 in.)
- 8-sheet small (5 ft. 11 in. sheets)
- Painted bulletins or LED boards (three standard sizes: 14 ft. × 48 ft., 20 ft. × 50 ft., and 20 ft. × 60 ft.)

Whether one is using more traditional boards or technology-based boards, each design should sport a bold visual and be short, sweet, and to the point, using no more than five to seven words. Because of this, outdoor boards are often considered to have a limited creative palette. However, that is untrue: the medium's sheer size and flexibility, and its suitability to bold colors, add up to a broad range of creative options, which only expand further with the use of extensions or three-dimensional designs.

Say It While on the Move: Transit Advertising

Transit advertising, another form of out-of-home, targets the millions of urbanites who use public transportation or see public vehicles while they're on foot—or from their motor vehicles, bicycles, or office windows. The diversity of shapes, sizes, and canvases offers an abundance of creative opportunities and challenges. Public transit includes taxis, buses, trains, elevated trains, and subway and airport terminals. Canvases include buses (both interior and exterior, as well as entire bus wraps) and exterior taxi signs. Additional options include stations and platforms and bus shelters, benches, and three-dimensional kiosks. Basically, if there is a flat surface on any moving vehicle, or room where the vehicle arrives and departs, it's ripe for transit advertising. Transit, like outdoor, has limited advertising space and thus requires a short message—making it another great support vehicle. Since most public transportation is located in cities, advertising is targeted to middle- and working-class urban consumers. Let's take a closer look at some of these diverse vehicles.

Interior and Exterior Bus, Taxi, Train, and Subway Cards

These varied vehicles often offer space for a little more than a few words and perhaps a small visual. Often these cards are printed on both sides, so the message can be changed out from time to time. It can also be a great direct-response vehicle when offering tear-off pads of applications or order cards, known as *car-cards*. Passengers can use the car-cards at a later time to request more information, place an order, or apply a discount toward a purchase. Interior vehicle cards come in a number of different sizes and are placed in frames above the vehicle's windows.

Frequency is the reason to choose transit as a media option. Riders travel back and forth to work on a day-to-day basis. The fact that these consumers are "trapped" for a set period of time allows messages to be read repeatedly. Because space constraints keep advertising clutter to a minimum, memorability is increased.

Bus Side and Trunk panels

Sheer size makes bus advertising like a moving billboard, reaching people who are walking and in their cars. Design should be bold and entertaining to commuters.

Exterior bus displays come in three categories: king- and queen-size posters, and full bus wraps. The type of display chosen is based in part on a bus's route.

King-size posters display the advertised message on both the curb and street sides of the bus. Queen-size posters appear on the curb side only.

Full-size bus wraps are giant wraps that can creatively carry a storyline around the bus, making use of the front, the back, the side panels and the windows. Care has to be taken to ensure that riders' views out the windows are not blocked by the design. When you buy a wrap, you buy the entire bus, from front to back and side to side. Designs will almost always make use of the windows. Most wraps are airbrushed directly onto the bus's surface.

Bus Shelters and Benches

Transit shelters are the places where riders wait for the bus. They offer a very creative canvas, which can often be lit from behind by the sun. They attract both riders and those passing by on foot, in cars, on bicycles, or in public transportation vehicles.

Shelter ads are large (usually 4 ft. × 6 ft.), four-color panels. Like most out-of-home advertising, they use a visual, a logo, and perhaps a slogan to introduce the public to, or remind them about, a local product or service. Some shelters also have a bench that can also be used to support other, more traditional media vehicles.

Wall Murals

Wall murals are billboards that are painted on the sides of older buildings, usually located in urban areas. Wall murals offer a larger canvas and are more permanent than any other types of out-of-home media vehicles.

Taxi Advertising

Illuminated, two-sided *taxicab advertising* usually appears on the roof of a cab. Poster designs are also available for the doors and trunk.

Subway, Airline, and Train Terminal Posters

Terminal posters are large, usually local, ads located in bus, train, subway, or airline terminals. Many of these posters will be illuminated for greater impact. These posters often advertise local products that visitors can enjoy while visiting a city or that locals can find near the stop or station. Often the station posters can be coordinated to match smaller advertisements found inside the transportation vehicles. Glass floor displays are also common; these are known as *kiosks* and are used when showing the product will make a greater impact than a photograph would.

When ingenuity is added to traditional advertising techniques, it will always catch people's attention. For example, the San Francisco transit system (BART) showcased "mini movies" as a part of an advertising campaign in downtown tunnels. The "movie" used a flipbook technique that relies on a series of posters, strategically spaced, that are "activated" as the train passes by them, making the posters look like they are moving.

Moving Billboards

One of the newest forms of outdoor advertising appears on the backs and sides of semitrailer trucks. The trucks are hired to drive up and down the highway and streets during rush hour, when the audience is virtually a captive one.

How Out-of-Home Builds a Relationship between the Product and the Target Audience

Like all of the mass-media vehicles we've talked about, out-of-home is not consumer focused, but is a monologue that talks at the consumer. Because of this, it must be more creative, more targeted, and more flexible than two-way media vehicles.

As a support vehicle, out-of-home will not build a relationship or encourage brand loyalty; but it will keep the product or service front and center in the target's mind. The more creatively delivered the message the more favorable the image.

Seen every day as consumers travel, out-of-home is a friendly but persistent reminder that the product makes a great lunch or dinner choice, entertainment stop, investment, gift, or news-program choice.

Aside from promoting car purchases, it is not a canvas for image-based products. But it can entertain and stop attention. Outdoor works especially well for teaser advertising before a new product launch, and transit is ideal for long-term maintenance advertising. Transit in particular is great when tied to a direct-response campaign.

Since all products can be purchased locally, out-of-home can always direct the consumer to the next step in the buying process by including an address.

Pros and Cons Associated with Outdoor Advertising

When deciding whether out-of-home advertising is right for an IMC campaign, it may be helpful to look at some of the pros and cons specifically associated with outdoor and transit.

The more notable pros associated with outdoor advertising include:

- Availability. Out-of-home-advertised messages are there all day, every day.
- Reach. Depending on location, large numbers of people can be exposed to the message on a twenty-four-hour basis.
- Frequency. Since most consumers will see the board traveling to and from work, the message will be seen on a regular basis, increasing memorability.
- Demographic diversity. Since out-of-home is not as highly targeted as some other media vehicles, generic products can reach all age, sex, income, and education levels.
- Visual impact. Size and creative options can make outdoor advertising very attractive and visually stimulating.
- Creative potential. Creative options are boundless, limited only by the budget and the creative team's imagination.
- Location. Since most boards are placed in high-traffic areas, the message is sure to be seen.

The more notable cons associated with outdoor advertising include:

- The fleeting nature of its message. Outdoor boards have only six to eight seconds to get the message to a mobile and often distracted public.
- Visual and environmental contamination. Even the most creative boards are a blight to city streets and the landscape.
- The uncertainty of its impact. Although large numbers see the boards, it is difficult to determine how many read and remember the message.
- Maintenance. Media buyers cannot inspect each board for condition.
- Lead time. It can take anywhere from six to eight weeks for an outdoor board to go up.
- Location. Success is all about location, location, location. Unfortunately, good locations are limited in number.
- Lifespan. Most boards are purchased for thirty days, making the board's message and creative appeal critical in attracting attention.
- Brevity of the message. With only five to seven words, messages must not only get to the point—they must be simple. Outdoor boards can do little more than repeat a headline, slogan, and logo.

Josh Cantrell

PROS AND CONS ASSOCIATED WITH TRANSIT ADVERTISING

The more notable pros associated with transit advertising include:

- Exposure. Consumers riding public transportation spend an average of twenty-five minutes commuting back and forth to work, giving them time to read the message several times.
- Repetition. Consumers are exposed to the same message every day they go to work.
- Memorability. Since riders are exposed to only a few messages, and because they may have nothing else to do, messages are read, reread, lingered over, and remembered.
- Cost. Transit, like outdoor, is one of the least expensive media vehicles available to marketers.
- Creative options. Although more limited than outdoor, transit advertising is flexible, boasting numerous sizes and shapes, and color and printing options.
- Customizable messages. Messages can change with the time of day or location. The use of GPS systems in some larger cities allows messages to be quickly changed based on location.

The more notable cons associated with transit advertising include:

- Poor targetability. Transit is a mass medium that is constantly in motion, making it impossible to reach a highly selective audience.
- Potential negative impact on brand image. If the transit vehicle is dirty or in disrepair, it can reflect poorly on the brand.
- Clutter. Cities are full of advertising messages, both stationary and moving, which bombard the consumer. It is difficult for a single message to be noticed among the advertising noise.

- The limitations of location. Not everybody lives in the city or takes public transportation, and this limits exposure.
- Message limitation. All transit advertising has limited space, restricting how much can be said. This relegates transit advertising to a support role within the campaign.

DEVELOPING THE PROMOTIONAL MIX USING OUT-OF-HOME ADVERTISING

The choice to use out-of-home is based on the need to provide supplemental support for other major media vehicles such as broadcast or print. Strategically, out-of-home vehicles are great for new product launches or to maintain or reinforce existing advertising efforts for mature products or services.

All out-of-home is meant to build awareness and remind the public about a product or service; or persuade them to do something like come into a brick-and-mortar store or visit a website. Companies most often using out-of-home include local restaurants, media companies, retail stores, travel-related businesses, entertainment providers, and providers of package goods.

As a member of the media mix, out-of-home can do little more than creatively highlight the key benefit (which is covered in greater detail in other vehicles within the IMC campaign) with a bold visual and minimal copy. This medium can be highly targetable, because consumers employ repetitive travel patterns. Reach and frequency are maximized if the advertising is placed in diverse locations.

When working with supplemental vehicles, there are many questions that need to be addressed. For instance, will supplemental vehicles help to accomplish objectives? Does the target live in a major city or travel often? Does the target take public transportation or use other means of exposure, such as walking or riding a bike to and from work? What types of boards or transit signs do various city officials allow? Is the ad placed in a location the target is sure to see? Is some kind of interactive device required, such as car-cards or revolving outdoor boards? Where is dialogue talking place? Do advertising efforts need to support that or introduce something?

Possible out-of-home objectives might be to fortify a current campaign; to reacquaint the target with, or introduce her to, a brand or service; to give directions regarding how to get more information; or to reinforce an image.

THE CREATIVE VOICE OF OUT-OF-HOME

Even though out-of-home plays a supportive media role, it offers almost unlimited creative options due to its size and visual impact.

Most out-of-home is simply but boldly designed. It should be able to visually and verbally tie back to other media efforts used in the campaign. It should be brightly colored and creative, use bold visuals, and, if applicable, showcase a spokesperson or character representative, a headline, a package design, or a slogan.

Messages should get to the point in no more than five to seven words. Copy should be set in a typeface that is easy to read from distances of up to 500 feet. Spacing between letters should be slightly exaggerated, and "all caps" avoided, to increase readability and legibility.

If the design and statement are unique, it will stand out from the clutter of other out-of-home efforts in the area, as well as meeting with less specific resistance from opponents of outdoor advertising.

As in magazine and newspaper advertising, cooperative opportunities are available for local companies and national brands to team up and share the cost of advertising.

Buying Out-of-Home

Out-of-home advertising of all forms is usually purchased on a monthly basis, allowing for frequent changes or turnovers. Media buyers now have the option of buying larger blocks of time and more locations than ever before, and they will usually buy out-of-home options in a package, to maximize reach and exposure in any one market. The introduction of technology has increased costs; an LED board in particular is about three times the cost of a traditional poster or painted board.

It's important to understand that when buying out-of-home, a buyer doesn't just buy the board and location; he also buys maintenance, ensuring that the boards are not torn or full of graffiti and that they remain fully lit. Maintenance is part of the contract, because it would be impossible for the buyer to view every vehicle in every city across the country.

When buying transit advertising, a buyer can often make a deal with the individual transit unit, based on a percentage of the advertising revenues.

BROADCAST ADVERTISING: RADIO

Rachel Kennedy

Many a small thing has been made large by the right kind of advertising.

—Mark Twain, quoted in Edward F. Murphy, 15.

WHAT IS RADIO ADVERTISING?

Radio permeates our world. We are exposed to it everywhere: in the car, at work, while on hold on the phone, in the doctor's office, and while shopping. Because of this, radio has the distinction of being one of the few media vehicles that can be used to reach the targeted audience close to the time of purchase.

As a verbal medium, radio is often considered to be handicapped when compared to other media vehicles within the promotional mix. Limited by its sound-only format, radio is nonetheless burdened with delivering both the visual and verbal message. Looked at another way, radio can be considered the ultimate IMC strategic vehicle. Creative teams who try to make radio advertising conform to the same visual/verbal or show-and-tell standards as print and television inhibit targets from truly imagining "themselves" using the product or service, without the assistance of a predetermined visual stimulant. Radio is the ultimate strategic use of the target's imagination.

A radio ad should attack the listener's visual imagination with a verbal narration that outlines the features and benefits associated with the key benefit. To make listeners create a personalized picture, the verbal message must be colorful and informative, and it must be tied to their personal experiences, so that they will be enticed into placing the product in their visual perspective.

Great for building awareness, radio can be used as a primary advertising vehicle for local advertising, and as a support or secondary vehicle for regional and national advertisers. As a support vehicle, radio is a great way to prompt the target into action or reinforce other communication efforts within the promotional mix.

RADIO'S ROLE IN IMC

Radio advertising has changed very little over the years; about the only difference is that current messages are shorter than older storylines, and have a greater sense of urgency.

Today, delivering simple, low-cost messages to a small but specialized group of consumers is radio's specialty. Radio spots can be written, produced, and aired in as little as a few days. Changes or updates to existing spots are easy and relatively inexpensive to make, keeping material timely and making the medium adaptable to changing market conditions.

Radio's very personalized nature builds relationships with the target, especially if a popular radio personality reads the spot on the air, giving the product or service credibility, and effectively tying the product identity or image to that of the DJ.

One way to maximize brand awareness is to tie the product or service to an ongoing sponsorship—such as sponsoring the news or the weather. Sponsorships highlight the product's name and are guaranteed to run at the same time every day, adding extra emphasis to the product's name and image beyond the advertised message.

As one of the least inexpensive media vehicles available, radio allows for more advertising to reach the right target. Cost is determined by the length of the spot—fifteen, thirty, or sixty seconds—and the time of day the ad will air. The two most popular and expensive advertising slots, known as drive times, comprise weekday mornings from 6:00 to 10:00 and weekday afternoons from 3:00 to 7:00. Midday and evening hours are less expensive, as listenership drops off when listeners arrive at work in the morning and when they return home in the evening. Other costs associated with radio include production-related costs, such as the hiring of talent or the inclusion of sound effects (SFX) or music; and the frequency with which an ad airs.

Since people are often distracted by other things while listening to the radio, spots must be aired repeatedly in order to catch the listener's attention. It is also important to remember that the target audience will probably not listen to only one station; so multiple buys on multiple stations will be required to reach all the intended targets.

Airtime can be purchased on either AM or FM radio stations. Determining what stations will best reach the targeted audience depends on the station's programming format. The two most basic types of radio formatting are talk and music. A station's format defines the listening audience; because of this, radio advertising can talk directly to the target's special interests.

Because radio is sound only, it's important that what is said, read, or played in other media used in an IMC campaign be repeated on radio. This might include a jingle; sound effects; the distinctive voice of a spokesperson or character representative from television; or a slogan, tagline, or headline from print.

Radio is not considered interactive, nor is it a great image-building option. Although radio is a monologue, it need not be passive. Jingles are a great option, especially if they can be turned into participatory sing-alongs in the old-fashioned but well-loved "Hokey Pokey" style. *Remote broadcasts*, or broadcasts that take place from a location other than the radio station, are another way to get the target involved; they are the best way to use radio to encourage two-way communication between buyer and seller.

In radio, image is created verbally. But radio can be visually stimulating if an ad is written to support the target's perceived self-image. If the target can see herself using the product, her image will be much stronger than one manufactured by the creative team. This is especially true if the image was first introduced elsewhere in the promotional mix, and radio is being used as a support medium.

When radio is a part of the media mix, the advertiser will need to decide if the message will run nationally, with the same generic message in all markets, or locally, with the message adapted for each market. The generic form of radio advertising is known as *national network advertising*, while the more geographically tailored messages are known as *local* or *spot advertising*.

The national generic message is not used very often. It goes against everything that radio is: a highly targetable, highly specialized, and highly personable medium. Local radio is where most advertising is placed. This relatively inexpensive medium offers small, local business owners and national advertisers the same opportunity to tailor their messages demographically, based on a station's musical format (which is psychographically related to lifestyle), as well as geographically.

How Does Radio Build a Relationship between the Product and the Target Audience?

This very verbal medium must imprint the product's benefits on an inattentive mind. One of the best ways to do this is to make radio as interactive as possible. Radio ads should give the target an activity—for example, by letting him sing, hum, or clap along to a catchy jingle, the kind that intrudes upon an unconscious mind whether the ad is airing at the time or not. Radio also offers promotional opportunities through contests or sweepstakes such as trivia games, where a listener calls in with the answer in order to win a prize (such as a gift certificate or product sample). Remote broadcasts can encourage listeners to stop into a particular location and take a test drive, pick up a giveaway like a T-shirt or a CD, or meet a celebrity or local DJ. Another approach is to take a page out of an old radio script and create an ongoing, "visual," slice-of-life vignette. If you use intrigue, humor, or some other curiosity-building device to tell a compelling story, the target will tune in to get the next piece of the puzzle or learn how the next episode turns out.

Unlike in television, the majority of all radio advertising is local. Radio's highly targeted broadcast formats (rock, country, pop, talk, etc.) make reaching the intended audience relatively easy. Whether they are listening or paying attention is something else. Radio is a filler; it fills our lives with background noise while we are reading, driving, or working on a hobby. Because of this, messages need to be ear-catching; and they need to be simple, in order to be remembered. Radio advertising is fleeting: the target will not always have a pencil handy to write the information down, and there is no opportunity to reread important or difficult points. Radio is not the media vehicle to launch a new product. It is great for reminder and maintenance, or to announce where the product can be found, when, and for how much.

Radio programming is diverse, with stations offering all music, all talk, all news, or some type of combination. Each category of programming can be subdivided further into formats such as rock, country, pop, and so forth. Network and syndicated radio programming is sold to local stations throughout the United States. Commercial content is usually made up of a mix of national and local products.

Radio is often used in public relations, to promote events such as blood drives or collection drives, or even for new product launches.

Unlike in print, where it is easy to ignore advertising by turning the page, the radio audience is captive to the message unless they switch stations or turn the radio off. This is less likely when listeners are involved in other activities while listening.

Radio and newspaper advertising can be a powerful combination when adapting to changes in the marketplace, since messages can reach the public quickly and inexpensively. Radio, like newspaper, is not meant to educate, but rather to excite the target to action.

If price plays a major role in the communication efforts, radio advertising may be a poor choice, as its fleeting nature makes remembering price points difficult.

Like magazines, radio is able to deliver a specialized message to a small niche market. However, radio is not as useful as magazines for big-ticket merchandise or detailed copy.

Radio can also be used to reinforce and localize messages seen on television. The verbal message from television can be used on radio, keeping the cohesive IMC message going. Listeners who have been repeatedly exposed to the televised commercial will be familiar enough with the message that they will be able to replay the visual message, or *video*, from the television commercial in their minds.

PROS AND CONS ASSOCIATED WITH RADIO ADVERTISING

When deciding whether radio advertising is right for an IMC campaign, it may be helpful to look at some of the pros and cons associated with it.

The more notable pros associated with radio advertising include:

1. Cost. Radio is very inexpensive to use when compared to most other media vehicles in the promotional mix.
2. Targetability. The varied music formats of radio stations make targeting to a specific audience easier.
3. Portability. Radio can easily be taken anywhere by the target.
4. Turnaround time. Messages can be quickly developed and heard on the air within a matter of days, sometimes even within hours.
5. Interactivity. Listeners can become involved in the message by calling in to receive free samples or stopping by a remote broadcast location for free gifts.
6. Imaginative impact. Radio is an imaginative stimulus. It is a verbal message visualized in the mind of the consumer.
7. Local and national adaptability. Radio spots can be easily adapted for airing in any location.
8. Frequency. Radio's relatively low cost allows messages to be aired more often, to ensure that they reach the targeted audience.

The more notable cons associated with radio advertising include:

1. Its status as background noise. Radio gets little direct attention. Advertising must be clever, in order to catch and hold the attention of a target who is doing something else while listening.
2. Its dependence on sound only. Radio depends on the consumer's ability to

imagine the message. Messages must be written in a visually stimulating way, since the target can only hear the message.

3. The fleeting nature of the message. Lengthy, informational messages are impossible; the message is gone in fifteen, thirty or sixty seconds. Listeners cannot go back and review the message.

4. Fragmented audiences. In larger markets, radio ads need to be aired on multiple stations, since the target has many options with the same or similar formats from which to choose.

5. Clutter. Radio stations run a lot of ads between songs or talk programming. Radio is a cluttered medium, airing anywhere between fifteen and twenty minutes' worth of advertising in an hour.

6. Listener loss. Radio is being replaced by personal portable music devices such as iPods and MP3 players.

DEVELOPING THE PROMOTIONAL MIX USING RADIO

Nobody "listens" to the radio any more; it has been relegated to background noise that keeps us company while we work, drive, shop, or get our teeth cleaned. For radio advertising to work, it must do one of two things: have a catchy tune or jingle associated with the message—or just be downright intrusive.

Whether radio is strategically right for an IMC campaign will, of course, depend on the key benefit, the objectives, and the strategic approach used. Anything that can be told in story form will work on radio. It is an excellent media vehicle for bringing a character representative or spokesperson to life, and it gives immediacy to any message. Anything that has to be demonstrated, or be spelled out through lengthy copy in order to educate, will not work on the radio.

Effective communication objectives might include immediate sales, loyalty programs, increased store traffic, product or service inquiries, test drives, or development of brand awareness.

Strategically, radio is well suited to a product-based approach, since it is easy to tell a product's or service's story verbally. The type of strategy used to deliver the message can be either emotional (jewelry, perfume, sports cars) or rational (basic food and clothing) in nature, but the emotional appeal does offer more imagination-based options.

Radio is not a good choice if the strategy is based on a USP, since this often must be visualized to be understood, especially if it involves some kind of new technology, look, or use.

A good media mix might include a combination of out-of-home, radio and television, and magazine. Out-of-home can repeat radio's verbal slogan and the visual from television or magazines, tying all the pieces together.

THE SOUND OF RADIO DESIGN

Radio stations can air prerecorded spots or present material live through on-air personalities. Since DJs are as much a part of the listening pleasure as the music or talk format, the product gets an added boost of credibility when a DJ delivers the ad. On-air personalities are not provided a script from which to read, but a list of the product's features and benefits, which they present for the next thirty to sixty seconds in their own words.

Radio ads need not employ only spokespersons or on-air personalities to deliver the message; they can also use music and sound effects to activate a listener's imagination.

If it's true nobody's actively listening, then it's the creative team's job to find a way to get the listener "tuned in" to the message—and this must be done within the first three seconds. This can be done through the use of specialized voices (or voices that are unique to the ear), sound effects, or music.

There are a number of different execution techniques that can be used to deliver a radio message:

1. Music and jingles
2. Narrative drama
3. Straight announcement
4. Spokesperson or character delivery/single voice
5. Live donut
6. Dialogue
7. Multiple voices
8. Sound effects
9. Vignette
10. Interview

Music and Jingles

If the message can best be delivered attached to music, then use it. If the creative team wants to create ambience or evoke certain emotions, they might consider using music from popular culture or a "golden oldie." Music, especially an oldie, attracts attention by dredging up memories and feelings from the back of the consumer's mind. These imaginative musings will enhance and enrich the current message.

Jingles are intrusive. They creep up on our unsuspecting consciousness when we least expect it: in the shower, at a meeting, or at the movies. Jingles are interactive and memorable, and they're a great way to prolong the life of any message.

Narrative Drama

If there is a lengthy story to be told, then a narrative approach is the best way to go. *Narrative* dramas take a little slice out of life and deliver it to the listeners as dialogue between characters.

Straight Announcement

A *straight announcement* is just that—an announcement, most often delivered by an on-air personality.

Spokesperson or Character Delivery/Single Voice

If an IMC campaign has a *character representative* or *spokesperson*, he or she should speak on behalf of the product in the radio spot.

Live Donut

A *donut* uses a prerecorded opening and closing message. The center, or "donut hole," is filled in live by an on-air personality.

Dialogue

A *dialogue* between characters is a good way to structure discussion of the product and its uses, benefits, and features.

Multiple voices

In a *multivoice* approach, multiple characters carry the message, not by talking to each other, but by talking directly to the listener.

Sound Effects

If there is a repeatable sound, like the drum banging of the Energizer Bunny, it can be used to attract attention or bring a visual image to the verbal message.

Vignette

A *vignette* is a brief episode that forms part of an ongoing storyline. The various episodes are tied together by some repeated device such as music, a jingle, a slogan or tagline, or a spokesperson.

Interview

The *interview* approach is a good way to use testimonials.

DELIVERING THE MESSAGE

Radio, like television, is created in three different phases: preproduction, production, and postproduction. *Preproduction* includes writing copy; determining what music or sound effects, if any, will be used; and hiring a production company, the talent, and, if need be, jingle writers and musicians. *Production* includes the actual run-through and taping of the radio spot. *Postproduction* includes editing and the manufacture of copies to send to various local and/or national radio stations.

Music and sound effects can be included at the time of production or added during the editing phase. *Sound mixing* is the process of adding effects and music during editing. The final ad is placed on what is known as a master tape, and then reviewed by the creative team before being duplicated, or *dubbed*, and sent out to local and/or national radio stations.

THE SOUND WE HEAR AND ITS EFFECTS

Sound effects are the noises we hear in ads, such as doors slamming, dogs barking, or babies crying. They should be used to capture attention and move the copy forward. In other words, they are not used to create noise alone; they must have a point.

Sound effects should aid the listener's imagination by creating an image in his or her mind. Music can also be used as an attention-getter. It is important to note that although music is a sound, it can be used either to get attention or to create a mood or set a tone.

THE CREATIVE VOICE OF RADIO

Radio Scripts

The copy sheet used in radio advertising is known as a *script*. For the copywriter, a script is like an artist's canvas; descriptive words and visually constructed sentences are used like paint to create a picture in the mind of the consumer.

It is important in any script to make the copy flow in a conversational manner, and to give the person reading the script visual cues as to what is coming (such as music or sound effects).

The script can be prerecorded by talent hired by the agency or read live by an on-air personality. Radio spots can be of various lengths, but the most common are thirty- or sixty-second spots. The script must be able to be read in its entirety, without being rushed, in the time allotted. A thirty-second spot is approximately

60–70 words long, and a sixty-second spot is approximately 150–180 words in length. The number of words used will depend on who is reading the script, how fast he or she has to read, and whether the ad contains any complicated word combinations or technical jargon. Two speakers in conversation will take up more time. See table 12.1 for additional word counts.

Choosing Talent

The person chosen to speak the dialogue for an ad should represent the product's image and the target's demographics. If the product is a lawn mower, a young person speaking the copy could talk about how easy it makes his or her summer job. But if the message is relaxation time at the end of the day or price, an older speaker will be required. It is also important to be sure every word is clearly spoken, so the message can be understood. See table 12.2.

Ear-catching, informative messages keep listeners, especially those in their cars (i.e., close to the buttons), from changing channels during commercial breaks. Messages with a sense of urgency can hold attention.

BUYING RADIO ADVERTISING

Media buyers will buy radio time by market and format. Packages are often purchased to maximize both reach and frequency, as well as to lower overall costs.

Formats buyers can choose among include national versus local, as well as different commercial lengths (fifteen, thirty, or sixty seconds). They will also look at program formats—such as rock or country—that match the target audience, as well as considering the time of day, or *dayparts*, in which the ads will run (e.g., the popular morning or afternoon drive times).

One way media buyers will maximize their buys is to purchase a package rate, known as a *total audience plan*. This will guarantee that a select percentage of spots will air in a single market, or multiple markets, during drive times.

In the end, it is important when using radio that copy be both visually and verbally stimulating to the listener's imagination in order to incite action. The fact that it is low cost, portable, and highly targetable makes radio advertising an attrac-

Table 12.1. Word Counts

10 seconds	20–25 words
15 seconds	30–35 words
20 seconds	40–45 words
30 seconds	60–70 words
60 seconds	150–180 words

Table 12.2.   Sample Radio Script

Advertiser:	Target:
Run Date:	Strategy:
Length:	Key Consumer Benefit:

SFX: TERRIBLE COUGHING FIT.

ANNOUNCER: "Feeling a little under the weather, Mr. Billy Bob?"

(Straight dialogue should be typed in caps/lowercase and should include quotation marks. If you are not using a recurring character, label the speaker as ANNOUNCER or SPEAKER.)

BILLY BOB: "Ah (COUGH) ha."

(If you need a quick sound, place it within the dialogue. If you're introducing a recurring character, then give him or her a name.)

ANNOUNCER: "Then you need Cough Reliever. It will fix you right up and get you back in the swing of things."

BILLY BOB: "Cough Reliever?"

MUSIC: PITY MUSIC PLAYS IN THE BACKGROUND.

SFX: TERRIBLE COUGHING CONTINUES.

(Do not be afraid to intersperse the spot with ear-catching sound effects. It will help to hold the listener's attention.)

ANNOUNCER: "When you're this sick, be sure to pick up Cough Reliever. Available at your nearest Walgreens Drug or CVS."

(Be sure to close with the product name and, if applicable, the location where the product can be found, including landmarks, and/or a phone number or website address if it is easy to remember.)

tive media option. Although most often used as a support vehicle for other media in the IMC promotional mix (because it does not build image or promote a dialogue), radio is still a great choice when it is important to build or maintain brand awareness and localize the product's message.

CHAPTER THIRTEEN

BROADCAST ADVERTISING: TELEVISION

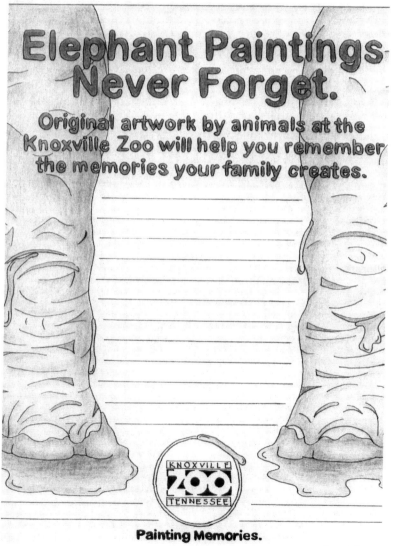

Elephant Paintings Never Forget.

Original artwork by animals at the Knoxville Zoo will help you remember the memories your family creates.

KNOXVILLE ZOO TENNESSEE

Painting Memories.

Amanda Sherrod

You have only 30 seconds. If you grab attention in the first frame with a visual surprise, you stand a better chance of holding the viewer. People screen out a lot of commercials because they open with something dull. . . . When you advertise fire-extinguishers, open with fire.

—David Ogilvy, *Ogilvy on Advertising*, 111.

WHAT IS TELEVISION ADVERTISING?

On average, an American will spend about one and one-half years watching television.

Advertising we see on television influences what we wear, drive, use domestically, and aspire to own. Its show-and-tell style can bring the product's or service's story to life, set a mood, demonstrate a use, create a memory, initiate a fad or trend, or define a style.

Despite its cluttered environment and overall expense, television is still one of the best mass-media vehicles available for reaching a target audience, building awareness, and maintaining or developing an image.

Through the use of sight, sound, and motion, television can attract and retain the target's attention, giving the ad the opportunity to entertain and inform. Its ability to reach the target through very specialized programming allows the product's story to be personalized to match the target's lifestyle, interests, and needs.

When used as a primary media outlet, television is ideally suited for use with new product launches, reminder advertising for mature products, or the repositioning of an old product in the mind of the consumer. However, it is too expensive to use if the product or service is not unique in any significant way or does not possess an inherent drama that only sight, sound, and motion can dramatize.

Television as a source of entertainment keeps television sets turned on and viewers tuned in. Millions of consumers watch television programming and are exposed to a lot of commercials; but that does not mean they watch the commercials. Today's television environment is cluttered with back-to-back commercials, further fractionalizing consumer interest. Getting the attention of any consumer who wields a remote control or owns a fast-forwarding VCR, DVD player, or DVR requires that advertising not only be entertaining but also useful.

DVRs are not hastening the death of television commercials as much as was originally feared. Predictions of the eventual demise of television advertising as we know it have not come true. Digital recording devices and remotes do allow the consumer to change channels or avoid advertisements altogether. However, consumers are not ignoring commercials in the numbers originally thought. A study by the Nielsen Company shows that when consumers do record programs, they still watch an average of two-thirds of the advertising shown.

Research done by the TiVo people did find, however, that when viewers do skip through commercials, they watch the last commercial in a break more often than the others, followed closely by the first spot aired. Unfortunately, buyers cannot buy a specific spot, like they can in newspapers and magazines.

Nielsen also found, not surprisingly, that younger viewers not only record more programs than older viewers but also skip more commercial messages.

To attract the attention of skippers, advertisers like Visa are using brighter colors to attract attention as the viewer speeds through the commercials; in other words, they make their ads stand out and create interest. But the more popular route is to develop ads that entertain rather than educate or inform, with advertisers relying on other members of the media mix to provide the details.

Avoiding commercials is a new American pastime that can take the form of *zipping, zapping,* or *grazing.* According to Dean M. Krugman, Leonard N. Reid, S. Watson Dunn, and Arnold M. Barban in their book *Advertising: Its Role in Modern Marketing,* zipping, zapping, and grazing constitute one of the most serious concerns advertisers have to contend with. The fact that television commercials are considered a nuisance is nothing new; however, it's only recently that viewers have gained the power to do something about them. Commercials considered uninteresting or irrelevant can be "zapped" with a channel change. Commercials recorded along with television programs can be "zipped over" with just a push of the fast-forward button. And today's channel surfers can lovingly caress their remotes while "grazing" through channels.

So what's an advertiser to do? First, get more creative, and target the audience with more accuracy than ever before. Second, consider weaving some form of interactive response into the commercial. Television advertising often asks the target to visit a showroom, go online or call for additional information, or make a purchase. Third, consider creating a contest or sweepstakes where the target can be the first to own the product or use the service; or use added-value incentives or free gifts as motivators to order now.

Another option is to creatively and uniquely present the product and hope that with a little bit of luck, the brand, concept, or slogan may evolve into a fad or trend. Fads come and go, leaving little lasting impression on society. A trend can evolve from media and advertising exposure, and can be influenced by movies, music, travel, politics, or other aspects of pop culture.

Traditional Advertising versus Interactive Advertising

Research for an IMC campaign identifies the target audience, the programs they are watching, and how they view family, fun, health, and leisure time. A creative team takes great pains to ensure that their message entertains and informs, in the hope of enticing the intended target to read, view, or listen to their message. This traditional interaction between buyer and seller is known as a *passive monologue.*

For television advertising to survive, it needs to take on technology and become more interactive and less passive. The next evolutionary step is known as *direct-response,* or *interactive, television.*

Direct response involves the target in the message process by asking her to call, visit a website, stop by for further information, or make a purchase. Interactive television allows the viewer to click on a link appearing on his TV screen, using a remote or a keyboard. If so inclined, the target can order immediately.

Interaction requires contact. Each commercial should display a toll-free number or website address where the target can find additional information, technical assistance, or help in placing an order. This interaction is active and takes place in the form of a dialogue. The target identifies the message, digests the information, and can then get a direct response from the advertised source with just the click of a mouse or push of a few buttons. Advertising clutter is reduced because the target chooses what he wants to see and when he wants to see it.

Traditional advertising delivers an uninvited message to a distracted target, and can take weeks or even months to build brand awareness and motivate the target to purchase. Direct-response advertising is immediate, allowing the consumer to buy while the commercial is still running. There is often a bonus offering if the consumer buys in the next few minutes or is one of the first 100 callers. Active involvement shortens the amount of time needed to build awareness, because consumers pursue additional information on their own time.

Most direct-response products, on the other hand, have little or no competition and thus make the decision to purchase generally easier and faster. Writing for direct response is simple: grab the listener's attention within the first three to five seconds; make the offer simple, especially with regard to ordering information; use experts, testimonials, or studies to validate the product; demonstrate how the product works or what it's like; make ordering easy; and repeat the most important information frequently.

Writing a direct-response ad may be simple, but to say it all takes a little longer than traditional advertising, requiring around 90–120 seconds. This extra time is needed to lay out the specific selling points and it allows the viewer to see the product in use. A direct-response commercial is basically a shorter version of the infomercial.

INFOMERCIALS AND THE USE OF DIRECT-RESPONSE TELEVISION

Most direct-response commercials will be found on cable stations, which are less expensive than the networks and have a more specialized programming format. The two most commonly seen forms of direct-response advertising are infomercials and home-shopping channels.

Infomercials are simply long commercials, usually about thirty to sixty minutes long. This extended commercial message allows time for a demonstration of how the product works; testimonials from satisfied customers; perhaps a professional endorsement or two by engineers, health professionals, or scientists; and, finally, the payment and ordering options. The basic premise of these long commercials is no different from that of their smaller, fifteen-to-thirty-second cousins: entertain and inform the viewer while making a sale. Infomercials are growing in popularity and effectiveness due to their use of toll-free numbers, the availability of credit cards, and ease of return.

Home-shopping channels allow consumers to purchase anything from jewelry to mattresses from the comfort of their own recliners, by dialing a toll-free number or logging in at a website. Special prices or payment options are prevalent, and returns are easy.

TELEVISION'S ROLE IN IMC

How Television Breaks Down

Television advertising can be categorized into five separate areas: *network, spot, cable, syndicated,* and *public.*

Network Television

Network television is home to the big four networks: ABC, CBS, FOX, and NBC. Each receives a sizable share of the available advertising revenue and viewing audience. There are also two Spanish-language networks, Telemundo and Univision.

Network programming is cluttered with advertising. For instance, the Academy Awards—an example of *special programming*, and one of the least cluttered programs—airs 11–12 minutes of commercials per hour, while the Super Bowl airs 13–14 minutes per hour. By comparison, weekly primetime network programming airs around 18 minutes of commercials per hour.

Because of this, look for future programs to take a step back in time to one or two products sponsoring programs as was done in the early days of television. Those products that have taken the plunge with this new/old idea have reported favorable results, with consumers remembering the advertised products better.

Despite clutter, televised events still offer advertisers great exposure. The biggest event of the year is the Super Bowl, followed by the Academy Awards and the Grammys.

Network affiliates are local television stations, located across the country, that are paid to air network programming at a predetermined time. When network programming is not filling the schedule, local stations will fill airtime with local broadcasts or nationally syndicated programs.

Spot Television

Spot television gives advertisers the opportunity to run their ads in individual markets rather than on a national basis. These commercials air between programs, while network advertising airs during programming. Most local advertising revenue is generated from spot ads.

Cable Television

Viewers can receive the big four networks and any additional local stations in their homes for free, but *cable television* is a subscription service. Because of this, cable

Student Name:_____

15 or 30 second spot (Circle One)

Name of Television Spot:_____

Grade:_____

Student Name or Group Name:_____ 15 or 30 second spot (Circle One)

Name of Television Spot:_____

Open: (Open on Tonka the elephant from right side with easel in front)
Camera: STILL
Music In: MUSIC IN (Musica) and UNDER
SFX: (Elephant Trumpet Blast)
Tonka: "So you came to the Knoxville Zoo with your family..."
CUT TO: (Beret on chair)

MCS:
Tonka: "... you see the exhibits. You laugh and learn..."
CUT TO: (Tonka's trunk picking up the paint brush)

MCS:
Tonka: "...about who we are and how we live and play, but you cannot take it home."
CUT TO: (Tonka behind the easel)

FS:
Tonka: "So I, Tonka, and my animal artist friends..."
WIPE: (FS of Tonka behind easel to MS of family in zoo shop looking at paintings)

MS:
Tonka: "...want to commemorate your family's zoo experience with a masterful original place of art."
CUT TO: (Behind family sitting and looking at purchased painting in house)

CS:
Camera: DOLLY FORWARD (to wall)
Camera: STILL
Tonka: "Take home the memories you make with the art we create."
CUT TO: SUPER (of the Knoxville Zoo logo on green background)

MCU:
VO: "Change one day's experience into a lifetime of memories. Animal art only from the Knoxville Zoo. Painting Memories."
SFX: SFX (Elephant Trumpet Blast)
Music Out: MUSIC (Musica) OUT

Amanda Sherrod

receives revenue from both subscriptions and advertising. Cable advertising is less expensive than nationally placed advertising, and the highly selective and special interest–oriented programming on many channels makes reaching a specific target audience easier. Unlike network programming, which offers a more generic schedule of shows, different cable channels offer very specialized lineups, including news, movies, documentaries, history, sports, and children's programming, with most channels running twenty-four hours a day, every day.

Broadcast Syndication

Programs that are in *syndication* are produced independently and then sold to individual local stations, with no consideration being given to any one network affiliation. Syndicated programs can also include reruns of older programs. Local stations are granted some of the commercial airtime, while the syndicate sells its portion to national advertisers.

Public Television

Public television is largely noncommercial. It is supported by individual viewers and, in part, by nonprofit organizations and state and local governments. Corporate sponsors often underwrite certain programs, but the use of traditional advertising methods on public television is rare. While sponsored announcements have in some cases evolved into shorter, less-aggressive versions of commercial advertisements, most sponsorships are understated and use only a logo, a tagline or slogan, and an address or phone number.

How Television Advertising Builds a Relationship between the Product and the Target Audience

Television involves the viewer through sight by introducing the product; with sound that sets the tone or mood; and through motion that allows the target to see the product in action. Used together, sight, sound, and motion place the product in the target's imagination and life. Television is a very expensive mass-media vehicle. It is important when using television to be sure the target is watching. The hit-and-miss mentality of years gone by has been replaced with a high degree of selective targeting. Cable allows advertisers to select specific channels and programming that can reach the intended target in the same way magazines and radio can.

Each of advertising's media vehicles, with the exception of newspaper and out-of-home, takes advantage of audience fragmentation and focuses on reaching the consumer through selective targeting—based on special interests that make it easy for advertising to build brand awareness or brand image. A corporation can use public relations to toot its own horn. Newspapers promote time-sensitive offers and low prices. Magazines offer tradition, status, prestige, and class. Radio offers events and introduces promotions. And out-of-home keeps the brand name in the public eye. Television can demonstrate the product in use.

Magazine, out-of-home, and television can be a powerful combination if the objective is building or projecting a product's image. Used together, these three vehicles can deliver unique, unusual, and creative solutions to an image-based strategy.

Magazines, cable television, and radio advertising are all great vehicles for selective and specific targeting. Reaching and affecting the target is made easier because special-interest magazines and programming allow advertising to talk directly to the target's self-interests.

When used as a support vehicle for television or other media within the promotional mix, radio allows listeners to take part in the message by imagining themselves using, wearing, or tasting the product; and purchase can take place quickly.

By including an interactive component, television can draw the target to a website or to customer service representatives. Information found there can be used to build a relationship between buyer and seller and contribute to building brand loyalty and equity. Television may be a monologue, but the information presented can encourage interaction through additional research or even trial.

PROS AND CONS ASSOCIATED WITH TELEVISION ADVERTISING

When deciding whether television advertising is right for an IMC campaign, it may be helpful to look at some of the pros and cons associated with it.

The more notable pros associated with television advertising include:

1. Impact. Television delivers sight, sound, and motion, allowing the target to view the product, see it in action or in the proper setting, and hear the message, all at the same time.
2. Selectivity. Between the networks and cable, television offers enough diverse programming to selectively choose the exact program the target will be watching, eliminating hit-and-miss placement and cutting down on advertising waste.
3. Audience size. As a mass-media vehicle, television reaches a lot of people. Although network television does not reach the numbers of viewers it did in the past, it is still one of the best ways to reach a target. Network television's national reach allows advertising to introduce, maintain, or reposition a brand's image.
4. Trends and fads. Television sets trends and influences the way we look and talk; we believe what we see on the screen. We are influenced by what we watch and adapt it to our vernacular or wardrobe. Programming and advertising often roll over into our personal and work environments, as we talk about what we saw on television the night before.

The more notable cons associated with television advertising include:

1. Cost. Television advertising is expensive. The length of the commercial, the program airing, and the time the commercial will run all determine cost. It is important to know where the target audience will be and what they will be watching when considering television as a viable media option.
2. Clutter. There are a lot of commercials running in any given time slot, some running back-to-back. In order to fight consumer apathy and remote-control rampages, an ad must stand out visually and verbally by specifically addressing the target audience and its needs.
3. The fleeting nature of the message. Television commercials are fleeting; the creative team has only fifteen or possibly thirty seconds to make a point to a group of people who need sandwiches or bathroom breaks. Concept development must repeat major points and use music to make the target stop, look, and listen. If someone missed the ad the first time around, then the music can announce a repeat performance.

DEVELOPING THE PROMOTIONAL MIX USING TELEVISION ADVERTISING

Writing for television is not an easy task. Copywriters must balance their words with the video portions of the commercial. They must also ensure that the proper information is included to strategically promote the key benefit and ultimately accomplish the stated objectives.

How does a copywriter tell a story in only fifteen to thirty seconds and still accomplish the objectives set up in the creative brief? What will make the key benefit stand out strategically? Consider some of the following:

1. Research should guide copy.
2. The key benefit needs to be relevant to the target.
3. Copy should talk to the target audience in words and about situations they can relate too.
4. Copy should open with the key benefit.
5. It is important that the commercial stay on strategy and on target, and reflect the same visual aspects and tone of voice as the other pieces in the IMC campaign.
6. The tone or execution technique chosen needs to complement and highlight the key benefit and accomplish the stated objectives.
7. If it can be shown on television better than it can be said, then it needs to be shown on television.
8. Copy needs to get to the point and hammer it home, frame after frame.
9. Audio and video must work together as a cohesive unit.
10. Copy must be written to the target. Each announcer or voice-over should

talk directly to the target, and on-screen talent should be shown dealing with situations the target can relate to.

11. The product's name and packaging should be mentioned and shown repeatedly, so the target will remember them.
12. The key benefit is the star of the commercial, and it should be clearly pointed out to the target.
13. The advertiser must involve the target in the commercial by showing how she will look in the product, or how it will keep her kids safe, or how it will make her clothes whiter; she should be informed about the benefits the product or service delivers. The target should be given an interactive activity, such as visiting a website or calling a toll-free number for more information.
14. The commercial must be the right length. The announcer or talent should be able to speak and move at a natural pace, without rushing. Any holes should be filled, when there is no action taking place.
15. The last frame in the storyboard must be either the logo or a final shot of the product with the logo showing. To assist with recall, especially for a new or reinvented product, it is preferable to show both logo and product.

The creative team must remember that the key benefit must be sold in every frame. It cannot be mentioned or shown just once. Television's short life span, fleeting messages, and inattentive audience require that the key benefit scream out for fifteen or thirty seconds.

Objectives best suited for television advertising include product demonstrations and concepts that entertain, excite, or have a social or personal impact.

Strategically, the creative team is armed with a toolbox of creative opportunities to show and tell, demonstrate, and activate the target's imagination.

THE SIGHT, SOUND, AND MOTION OF TELEVISION DESIGN

Television is more than just the random use of *sight*, *sound*, and *motion*. It is about determining the most appropriate setting for the product, the correct choice of talent to deliver the message, the right lighting to set the scene, and the appropriate props and music to set the mood or make a point. Finally, the pace or delivery of the message must be in keeping with the overall look and tone of the message. Television is the *coordination* of sight, sound, and motion.

THE INS AND OUTS OF A TELEVISION SHOOT

Designing, planning, and shooting a television commercial is a complicated and lengthy process. Very little is done on a whim or at the last minute. Most commercial shoots take anywhere from several days to several weeks to complete. Before any actual footage is shot, the creative team, along with the director, must walk through the shoot and go over any changes; hold auditions; look at possible locations; gather up the product, props, and costumes; and go over the various technical aspects of the shoot, such as lighting and sound, with the production crew.

Additional decisions, such as whether the television commercial should be produced on film, videotape, or digital media, are made at this point, as are decisions about media placement. Most decisions will be made during the preproduction, production, and postproduction phases.

Preproduction includes the development of the script and storyboard, budgeting, and the hiring of talent, a director, and a production crew. The production stage includes the actual shoot, and postproduction includes the editing process.

BIG, SMALL, AND ELABORATE PRODUCTIONS

How and where a commercial is shot depends on the product, the budget, and the strategy. Commercials can be done relatively inexpensively, when shot and produced locally. This type of shoot is relatively simple and contains few bells or whistles. The goal is to get the message out as quickly and effectively as possible.

Nationally produced commercials, on the other hand, use all the bells and whistles necessary to attract the targeted audience. These spots are usually produced, and often shot, in the major advertising markets and then delivered to the affiliates or cable television stations.

Many national spots are produced right in the studio, sometimes employing expensive computer graphics. Real or animated talent may be developed in order to attract attention or to create a specialized atmosphere or some type of special effect.

Another, and often equally expensive, option is to shoot away from a production studio, or *on location*. In this instance, a remote location is used for the background of the commercial. Locations may be exotic or mundane, and are determined by the commercial's overall strategy or concept. Being shot on location gives a dose of reality to the commercial, allowing consumers to see the product in the setting in which it might be used.

THE CREATIVE VOICE OF TELEVISION ADVERTISING

Scripts and Storyboards

Television commercials have two components: a verbal item known as a script, and a visual/verbal combination know as a storyboard.

Television Scripts

A *television script* is a very detailed document. Not only does it include what will be heard (such as dialogue, music, jingles, and sound effects), but it also details any special instructions to talent, camera, sound, and editing people, as well as any information concerning scene changes.

Storyboards

A television commercial begins as a *storyboard*. This storyboard consists of two parts: the visual aspects, or *scenes*, and the *script*, or what will be said and heard. Television scripts are much more detailed than radio scripts; because television requires a lot more people to produce a spot, the storyboard and accompanying script must talk not only to the client but also to talent, directors, camera operators, lighting and sound people, producers, editors, composers, food stylists, and computer animators.

Scenes

The visual aspects of a television commercial are known as *scenes*. Each scene is confined in a *frame* on the storyboard. Each individual scene depicts a major piece of action or location change. Any given scene may require additional shots from a variety of angles, but there is no need to show them all. A fifteen- to thirty-second spot usually consists of four to six frames; a longer, less common sixty-second spot will need six to eight frames.

Under each frame appears the accompanying dialogue, sound effects, and music—the *audio* portion of the commercial, or, in other words, the portion of the script that corresponds to that scene. This therefore amounts to an exact reproduction of the script and visual action combined. A storyboard is how the commercial will be presented to the client and any other major production players. The script alone will be used almost exclusively by the talent, although members of the production team may also consult it.

The storyboard lays out the action. It is impossible and unrealistic to show every scene; just the most important ones should be presented, or those that will move the commercial forward and that show concept direction.

The actual television shoot is exhausting and stressful; two or three seconds of actual footage can take several hours to shoot. It is important to have a detailed script to keep the enormous number of people it takes to shoot one thirty-second spot on the same page. Copies should be distributed to the talent, the director, the client, and the various members of the production staff. If everybody is on the same page when shooting begins, the commercial will be much more likely to stay on budget and shoot on schedule.

The cost of shooting and producing a television spot is huge. Television airtime needs to be bought, and this is a major chunk of the budget. The spot must be designed, the script written, and the talent and production crew hired. If plans include going on location or use of a celebrity, the cost skyrockets even higher. A detailed storyboard is imperative. It must be very tight and very detailed; the schedule and budget can be significantly affected if the storyboard is incomplete or requires changes of any kind once shooting begins. A good storyboard lets the entire production team know in advance where they need to be and what needs to be done.

Beyond dialogue, sound effects, and music, a storyboard will also specify where the camera should be placed and how closely it should zoom in on the action, as well as how the action will move between frames.

Table 13.1 shows a sample script.

THE LENGTH OF A COMMERCIAL MESSAGE

Length depends on budget, but the most common is thirty seconds. It is not uncommon for advertisers to purchase a thirty-second spot and then break the commercial time in half, producing two related commercials. This allows the advertised message to deliver two separate points in succession, building awareness one feature or benefit at a time. If the dual messages are mutually dependent, this technique is called *piggybacking*. If the budget allows, a sixty-second spot offers more time to drive the point home.

Table 13.1.   Sample Television Script

	FRAME 1
OPEN:	(Open onto a grocery store checkout line full of people).
MCS:	
CAMERA:	STILL.
SFX IN and UNDER:	SFX IN (a lot of people complaining and mumbling in background) UNDER.
WOMAN 1:	"Why don't they get some more help around here?
SFX OUT:	SFX (of people complaining and mumbling in background) OUT.
CUT TO:	(Another grocery store where another woman is checking out her own groceries.)
	FRAME 2
MFS:	
CAMERA:	PAN (grocery store, notice all the available check-out lanes) LEFT AND RIGHT.
CAMERA:	STILL.
WOMAN 1:	"Grocery shopping is always fast and easy."
MUSIC IN and UNDER:	MUSIC IN (It's a Hot Time in the Old Town Tonight) UNDER
ANN:	"At So So Bees, you will never have to stand in line. Open 24 hours, for your convenience. Located on 1234 Main next, to Taco Meat and Cheese."
SFX OUT:	SFX (It's a Hot Time in the Old Town Tonight) OUT
SUPER:	(Logo on parking lot, with grocery store in the background.)

WHO IS GOING TO TALK THE TALK AND REACT TO THE SOUNDS WE HEAR?

There are many sounds in a television commercial, whether spoken, created, or musically based. Let's take a short look at each one.

Talent

Talent refers to the individuals who will be seen on camera reading the copy or dialogue; it also includes any off-screen announcers who will be heard delivering the copy. It is important that the talent visually and/or verbally represent the product and target image.

Voice-Over

When an announcer is heard reading the dialogue but is not seen on camera, this is known as a *voice-over*. A voice-over can be used to deliver all the dialogue or just the closing. This is often a good place to consider using a recognizable celebrity voice. Using a celebrity in a television commercial is less expensive when the celebrity is only heard and not seen.

Announcer

An *announcer* is both seen and heard on camera, delivering the dialogue. This is a great way to associate, introduce, or use a character representative or spokesperson as the voice and face of the product.

Music

Music is used to set a mood. Imagine a movie without the sound track: we wouldn't know how to react or what to expect when the action finally took place. Music can be used to replace words, represent an emotion, or assist with placing the viewer in the proper emotional state. Volume can also be used to set a mood. Music should be used in the same way that talent and dialogue are used to tell the story.

Sound Effects

Sound effects replicate reality. We can relate to the headache of a slamming door, the tension associated with screaming babies, or the calming sound of the ocean. Sound effects should support the message, not get in the way of it.

COMMERCIALS CONSUMERS LOOK FORWARD TO

Commercials during the Super Bowl are as much a part of the experience as watching the game itself. It is one of the few times advertising is considered not an intrusion, but a part of the enjoyment that's anticipated.

The Super Bowl works for marketers because, first of all, it's one of the most watched TV events of the year; second, it's all about the next day's buzz, not only with respect to the game but also with regard to the commercials; and, finally, it is almost always watched live.

So why, you might wonder, doesn't every product want to advertise during the Super Bowl? First, its cost, at $2.6 million for nothing more than a thirty-second piece of air, is prohibitive to anyone but the biggest companies. Second, its only job is to remind and maintain image, rather than tell a product's detailed story. And third, certain food products, such as pizza, have no need to advertise, since they do more business on Super Bowl Sunday than on almost any other day of the year.

To keep viewer interest, the 2007 Super Bowl became the canvas for amateur-produced commercials for products like Doritos and the NFL, giving national television an interactive aspect that could be reviewed on various Internet sites. Promotion for the spots began months before the game, building interest through contests and ongoing publicity efforts.

Using contests to promote the project generates positive publicity, especially word of mouth, for the products involved for months before the big game, and it spotlights them during the game. This is a great way for consumers to get involved with a product or service.

According to an online *BusinessWeek* article from February 5, 2007, Super Bowl ads that have stood the text of time based on creativity and memorability are "Apple's 1984 ad, Coke's Mean Joe Green spot, and the Budweiser Clydesdales bowing their heads toward Ground Zero."

BUYING TELEVISION

Television is probably the hardest and most detailed of all media buys. A media buyer must work with both local and national media representatives in order to buy available commercial time. These representatives will let her know what is available, matching as closely as possible the product's or service's objectives, the target audience's viewing habits, and the overall costs.

Buyers must then decide which options are cost-effective and attempt to negotiate a deal. Most negotiations can be based on several approaches: (1) a *bulk buy*, or package rate; (2) *run-of-schedule*, in which the station is allowed to determine when the ads will run; (3) a *fixed buy*, the most expensive, because the spot is guaranteed; or (4) a *preemptive rate*, a less expensive option with greater risk, in which the advertiser understands that she may be replaced if another advertiser is willing to pay the standard fee.

Television has a great amount of influence on who we are, both as individuals and as consumers. We watch a lot of television, making it a great choice for an advertiser launching a new product; maintaining or reinventing an existing product; building or maintaining awareness; or developing both a product and a consumer image. Although expensive to use, television advertising can be highly targeted; and, with the right message, the use of sight, sound, and motion can attract and hold the target's attention long enough to make a message or image impact. If television is appropriate as a member of the media mix, it should entertain and, by asking the target to do something, be interactive.

CHAPTER FOURTEEN

DIRECT MARKETING

Join the Knoxville art circle that inspires.

The Knoxville Museum of Art offers membership on all levels.

For those who are serious, the Collector's Circle brings art to you.

knoxville **km@** museum of art

Visual Intoxication

Justin Cooter

That is the kind of ad I like. Facts, facts, facts.

—Samuel Goldwyn, U.S. film producer, quoted in Robert Andrews, 18.

WHAT IS DIRECT MARKETING?

Direct marketing is the first of the three promotional devices we will look at. You may be wondering what the difference is between advertising and promotion. *Advertising* is all about educating the consumer on a product's features and benefits to encourage purchase. *Promotion*, on the other hand, makes a proposition by offering package deals or some other incentive to induce immediate purchase.

The Direct Marketing Association (DMA) defines direct marketing as an "interactive system of marketing which uses one or more advertising media [to] effect a measurable response and/or transaction at any location."

When advertisers need to know exactly who the target audience is and want to talk to them one-on-one, direct marketing is a great alternative to traditional advertising vehicles.

Direct marketing is all about creating a dialogue between buyer and seller. Communication is coordinated and individualized through the use of multiple media vehicles and databases. The information collected in databases allows direct marketing to reach a target based on past buying history, demographics, psychographics, behavioristics, and geographics.

Knowledge about the consumer allows for the creation of a more personalized message, eliminating the more generic mass-media messages delivered through traditional advertising methods. This more intimate environment makes reaching, and talking to, the target in a language she can relate to, about a topic she is interested in, easier and more successful. The result is the development of a set of interpersonal relationships among the client or marketer, the product or service, and the target. These relationships constitute one of the foundations needed to build and maintain brand loyalty. The availability of toll-free numbers and access to the Internet carry these interpersonal relationships one step further by allowing the target to communicate directly with the advertiser.

Traditional advertising is where advertisers and their agencies have historically turned to build brand awareness, accomplish repositioning, and eventually build brand loyalty. Today, the cost of advertising—especially on television—and the fractionalization of media are changing the way consumers receive messages. Advertising simply doesn't reach the target as well as it used to. The interactive and more personalized nature of direct marketing makes it a better alternative for building a brand's image.

Direct marketing is everything traditional advertising efforts are not. As a mass-media vehicle, advertising delivers a message to thousands—often millions—of readers, listeners, or viewers, most of whom, in many cases, are not a part of the targeted audience. Direct marketing can personalize its message on an individual basis, addressing the target by name.

Traditional advertising requires more time to entice the target into action. Its impersonal format requires more frequent messages to reach, educate, and then remind consumers to purchase the next time they are at the grocery store or the mall. Direct marketing eliminates the middleman and makes purchase or additional inquires as easy as the click of a mouse or the push of a few buttons. To receive a quick response, direct marketing often employs the use of sales-promotion devices such as coupons, contests and sweepstakes, samples, giveaways, and rebates.

Because traditional advertising offers few interactive opportunities before purchase, the target remains anonymous, and it is difficult, if not impossible, to know where his exposure to the message took place. The highly targetable and interactive nature of direct marketing makes sales efforts easier to measure, especially if advertising materials include an identifying *marketing code*, often a combination of letters and/or numbers, that pinpoints the medium in which the order or inquiry originated. Most importantly, since direct marketing is sent to a specific person, it is easy to track who responded to the message and who did not. Ultimately, this information will be used to help determine whether the proper media mix was employed.

Because it is so individualized, reaching the target audience through direct marketing is much more expensive than advertising. As a mass medium, advertising is seen and/or heard by a large number of people who may or may not be interested in the product or service advertised. Direct marketing, on the other hand, targets one individual whom research has deemed most likely to buy the product or use the service advertised, increasing the overall interest and purchase rate.

Trust in direct marketing has grown steadily over the years, mainly because advertisers have delivered reliable products, included guarantees, and made purchase and returns easy. Additional elements promoted in direct marketing efforts might include some of the lowest prices anywhere, opportunities to be the first to own, exposure to limited-time offers, and additional incentives, such as free gifts or rebates just for buying in response to a televised or direct-mail message.

The goal of both advertising and promotion is to elicit a purchase. However, when direct marketing is a part of the IMC promotional mix, its role may not be to generate an immediate sale. Sometimes it is used just to generate interest or to encourage information gathering. Additional prepurchase research on the target's part may require an appointment with a salesperson, a trip to a retail location, or a test drive.

Before looking at the diverse list of media voices that direct marketing employs, it's important to look at why it can personalize a sales message, what makes it a relationship-building tool, and what makes it a successful alternative to mass-media advertising. The answers lie in direct marketing's use of database information.

A *database*, when internally created, begins life as a short list of names, addresses, and phone numbers. Database marketing as an IMC tool requires several years of data collection. Individual customer data is culled from previous interactions with a company, such as purchases or requests for more information. This data is used in customizing future communications and building customer loyalty. By developing their own databases, marketers can save money. More extensive lists can be purchased from external sources, based on the target's demographic or psychographic information.

Where do these names come from? Companies a target has done business with in the past may sell names, and additional names may be acquired from other outside sources such as telephone directories, the U.S. Census, warranty cards, credit card companies, and professional organizations.

Database information ultimately helps marketers develop messages that are tailor-made for the target audience based on their likes, needs, and lifestyles.

Privacy is an ongoing concern for consumers. Gathering and selling a consumer's private information without his knowledge or permission is becoming an unacceptable, and avoidable, way of doing business. Many corporations and services are refusing to sell their customer lists in order to protect their target's privacy.

DIRECT MARKETING'S ROLE IN IMC

Direct marketing uses a diverse array of contact vehicles, including mass media, the mail, the telephone, and personal contact. The most typical forms of direct marketing include:

1. Catalogs
2. Direct mail
3. Infomercials
4. E-mail
5. Direct response
6. Telemarketing
7. The Internet

Catalogs

Catalogs, whether they are solicited or not, are often opened, read, and lingered over. Like magazines, catalogs are often saved for later use or shared with friends or colleagues, which extends the catalog's life and reach. Ordering is made easy using toll-free numbers, the mail, or the Internet; and guarantees allow most, if not all, items to be returned for a full refund if the customer is not entirely satisfied.

Many of the larger catalog companies create what are known as specialty catalogs. These are smaller versions of a larger catalog, and the specialized content reflects those products the target is most likely to buy based on past purchase history.

Direct Mail

Direct-mail pieces are like bills: they find their way into consumers' mailboxes unsolicited and eventually into their hands unwanted. Direct mail isn't actually as hated as most people would think. Many consumers respond to the personalized messages because often such messages specifically address their diverse interests and lifestyles.

Direct mail, also known as *database marketing*, is a highly targetable, personal, and measurable form of direct response. The consumer can respond to an advertised message by sending in an order form or visiting a website to place an order, receive more information, or give feedback about the product or service. A toll-free number can also be used to speak directly to a customer service representative about colors or sizes, shipping, or guarantees or to place an order. A typical direct-mail kit can arrive in almost any shape or in any form; but basic pieces include an outside envelope, a personalized pitch letter, an informational brochure, and an order form and return envelope or business reply card for mail orders.

As an informational tool, direct mail can be used as an announcement device or a brand-building tactic. It can be used as an incentive to entice consumers into trying a new or existing product or service; to reward loyal, long-term users; or to persuade nonusers to switch.

As an involvement tool, a multipiece mailer requires the target's attention to sort through and read through the various pieces, play with the movable parts, or scratch off a game piece. The more time the consumer has to spend with the piece, the more memorable and involving it will be.

A good direct-mail response rate is around 2 percent of the total mailings. For direct mail to succeed, it is important that it be mailed to the right audience and present the right message. Too often, names are duplicated, wasting money and annoying targets. Another problem for direct mail is caused by postal rates. Economically, postal rate increases have a direct effect on both magazines and direct mail.

As a media option, direct mail is very diverse. It can be used as a sales or promotional device or as a primary or secondary media vehicle for almost any product or service. Currently, the heaviest users of direct mail are insurance companies, financial-service firms, and department stores.

Direct mail needs time to work. Marketers should not make the mistake of thinking their first mailing will be their only mailing. A few gentle nudges may be needed to get the target moving.

One lesser-known form of direct mail is the statement stuffer, also known as a *piggyback*, because it hitches a ride with a credit card bill, financial notice, or anything else a consumer might receive on a regular monthly basis.

Direct mail also includes magalogs and polypaks. A *magalog* deals with a single product; but instead of using a letter, brochure, or circular format, it features a layout more like a magazine and presents information in the form of articles. Purchase options and order forms are identical to those used in a direct-mail kit.

A *polypak* is a set of index cards, used to advertise a variety of products, that are bundled together and delivered through the mail. Often in color and double-sided, each card has about enough room for a picture and headline on one side and the order form on the other. These are often used to generate interest in a product, asking the consumer to call, mail in, or go online to receive additional information.

Infomercials

Infomercials are thirty- to sixty-minute-long television commercials that allow the consumer to order immediately from information provided on the television screen. Infomercials use the sight, sound, and motion of television to demonstrate a product, to educate, and to entice a consumer to buy. Infomercials take the time to create interest in a product through the use of testimonials from current users and/or endorsements from celebrity users or technical advisors. Consumers are offered purchasing options with varied guarantees or return policies. A successful infomercial should:

- Place facts into a storyline that speaks to the target's special interests.
- Break down potentially complicated information into easy, demonstrable steps.
- Use a celebrity or expert to talk about uses or key features and benefits.
- Summarize key features and benefits and then repeat them regularly throughout the program.
- Repeatedly tell the target what they need to do.

Ryan Vinett

- Make ordering easy by showing a toll-free number and credit cards accepted.
- Outline the guarantee or return policy.

E-mail

Direct-marketing messages delivered through *e-mail* are the newest version of direct mail. Personalized messages can be delivered to a target's e-mail address more quickly, more often, and for a lot less money than traditional direct mail. Now we see direct marketers hooking up with the Internet, using e-mail in lieu of or as a supplement to current direct-mail use.

Direct Response

Direct marketing often employs the use of mass-media vehicles such as newspapers, magazines, radio, and television, where the consumer can directly *respond* to the message via the telephone, the mail, or the Internet.

Newspapers

Newspapers bring news value to direct-response efforts and can be used to target specific geographic areas. Audience size suggests that products with a more generic appeal should be placed in newspapers. However, audiences can be targeted to some degree by placing the advertising in the appropriate special section. If a standard ad won't do, another option is the use of newspaper inserts, which are often full-color and can range from a one-page FSI with perforated coupons to a multipage booklet.

Magazines

Magazines, like radio and cable television, have very specialized formats for a very select target market. Magazine advertisers should use the opportunity to show the product in color and in a setting the target can relate to, reinforcing the product's or service's image.

Additional options include a multipage insert that is bound into the magazine, or a bound-in reply card appearing beside the ad, which can be torn out and used to order.

Television

Because *television* allows the consumer to see the product in use, it is the ideal medium for direct-marketing efforts. Direct marketing uses television to make a sale, create leads, or build awareness, and it works well as a support vehicle or companion piece for direct-response advertising appearing in other media.

Telemarketing

Companies that engage in *telemarketing* use the telephone as a media device and employ a salesperson to deliver the message personally to select members of the target audience. This is known as *outbound telemarketing*. Databases are used to identify and contact members of the target group who have a known interest in the product or service, or who are seen as potential buyers based on past purchase history. When a customer initiates contact with a company for any reason, usually through the use of a toll-free telephone number, this is known as *inbound telemarketing*.

The Internet

The *Internet* is an important player in direct marketing. Full of information, the Internet allows consumers to search out the answers to questions and compare products, in order to make an educated buying decision. A Web page can highlight sale products or suggest accompanying purchases without sales pressure, as well as make purchasing fast and hassle free.

Businesses that take advantage of the Internet for sales and ordering might also find it profitable to offer a catalog or create a direct-mail kit, initiating additional contact points and offering customers a choice of shopping venues.

As this list illustrates, direct marketing has grown beyond just direct mail. Some of the biggest changes, like the use of the Internet, text messaging, and infomercials, have come about because of product reliability and quality, the availability of credit cards and toll-free phone numbers, and guarantees and easy return policies that lower the risk of buying what can't be touched or smelled.

HOW DIRECT MARKETING BUILDS A RELATIONSHIP BETWEEN THE PRODUCT AND THE TARGET AUDIENCE

Direct marketing brings customer service and personalized messages to the IMC table. Nowadays, consumers will not always accept a generalized message as incentive to buy; sometimes they want informative, personalized service, and they often want their purchases to be adaptable to meet their needs. If they have problems or need help, they want to be able to talk to someone quickly and easily. Today, brand loyalty is built not only on the quality of the product but also on the quality of the interactivity.

The Internet allows today's savvy, educated consumers to shop from their homes, allowing them to instantly compare products. The need for additional information and research plays a particularly important role when larger, more expensive purchases are under consideration. Advertising that includes a website address or toll-free number encourages interaction and can be used as a great response device for prompting a consumer to request a catalog, brochure, or price list; a free consultation; a sales promotion package; coupons; or even a limited-time discount offer.

Consumers like direct marketing because it's convenient. Visiting retail outlets searching for the best product at the best price is a thing of the past. Direct marketing comes into the consumer's home announced. Consumers decide when to shop and what messages to seek out. They are not overly inundated with unwanted messages or rude or pushy sales clerks. Purchasing is fast and easy, requiring only a credit card and a few minutes of their time.

The Internet has made information seeking and comparison shopping easy for today's busy consumer, as previously discussed. There is little differentiation between brands in most product categories, so AEs and creative teams have to find ways to make their clients' products stand out from the competition. One way is the creative message. Strategies and promotional efforts must be unique and offer the target more than the competing brands by knowing what the target finds important, useful, and necessary. If the creative is very good, it can successfully grab and hold the target's attention and introduce him to a brand new product or service he didn't even know he needed. But the most lasting way to create product differentiation is through the development of a long-term relationship based on knowledgeable, courteous, and reliable customer service or technical assistance that is available twenty-four hours a day, seven days a week.

Once the options are known, the next step is to determine the message and the best media vehicle or combination of media vehicles needed to reach the target and accomplish the objectives.

Internal and external public-relations efforts are critical to the success of direct marketing. The dialogue initiated between the target and customer or technical-service representative must be easy, informative, and satisfying to the target. Customer service representatives need to be familiar with any current promotions, such as sales or coupons, to knowledgeably assist the consumer and support existing advertising efforts. Good public-relations techniques must be employed at all times when talking to consumers over the phone or responding to e-mail inquiries.

When print ads or out-of-home vehicles are used as a direct-marketing device, they can be simple and direct, and make the ordering process easy by attaching an order form or including a toll-free number or website address.

Newspapers are a great place to find coupons, for example in freestanding inserts or larger product or retail booklets. Newspapers are also a great vehicle for encouraging a visit or a trial or for last-minute event reminders.

Magazines are great for setting the product's image and use in the target's mind. Direct marketing can be used as a follow-up to encourage immediate purchase.

Out-of-home is a great reminder vehicle, promoting action-oriented ways to reach customer service representatives, visit a website, or make a note of an address where the product can be purchased.

Television is ideal as a direct-response vehicle because its ability to demonstrate allows the target to see the product in use, and often in the setting in which it will be used. Because of cost, direct-response television is usually found on cable. Its highly specialized programming is also better for reaching special-interest groups.

PROS AND CONS ASSOCIATED WITH DIRECT MARKETING

When deciding whether direct marketing is right for an IMC campaign, it may be helpful to look at some of the pros and cons associated with it.

The more notable pros associated with direct marketing include:

1. Personalization. Direct marketing can personalize communications, to speak to individual members of the target audience by name.
2. Measurability. By placing a marketing code on direct-marketing pieces, or color-coding order forms, the marketer can tell which vehicle the inquiry came from.
3. Database use. Databases provide target information. This information allows direct-marketing pieces to address specific individuals and their unique needs.
4. Customer response. Direct marketing builds relationships by offering two-way communication between the marketer and the target. It also allows the customer to give feedback that might influence any changes in the product or service.
5. Its attention-getting nature. Having the right database for targeting individuals is the first step toward ensuring that the target will open and read the direct-mail piece. Creating a piece that is both attractively designed and personally and correctly addressed generates interest and encourages investigation. Once opened, the piece must hold the target's interest through entertaining and informative copy. This might be the trickiest step of all, since a piece ending up in the trash unread closes the sale for good.

The more notable cons associated with direct marketing include:

1. Cost. One of the biggest advantages to direct marketing is also one of its biggest drawbacks. The personalization of each message makes direct marketing expensive, as compared to other forms of advertising. Additionally, if a company does not have its own database of names, it will have to purchase a list.
2. Annoyance clutter. If targets are not interested in the message, they can deal with direct-marketing messages in the same way they deal with other media: turn off the television, throw away junk mail, or screen telemarketers' calls.
3. Limited reach. The highly personalized nature of direct marketing limits the number of consumers that can be reached with any one message.
4. Time constraints. Depending on the numbers required and whether the piece is a traditional letter or a more involved mailer, direct marketing can take a great deal of production time. Add the time needed for basic folding, stapling, envelope stuffing, and third-class mail, and you have months invested into pre- and postproduction.

DEVELOPING THE PROMOTIONAL MIX USING DIRECT MARKETING

The job of advertising is to sell to a large audience. Although the known target is a part of this large audience, there is no way to ensure that the target will receive a mass message. As we now know, mass-message advertising is no longer the only way to differentiate a product or service from its competition. This is where IMC comes in. IMC understands that the efforts of the promotional mix (public relations, advertising, direct marketing, sales promotion, and the Internet), properly combined, will not only help to meet objectives but will also assist with positioning, creating brand awareness, and building brand image and brand loyalty more efficiently and effectively than any one medium ever could.

When deciding what media mix will best reach the target and accomplish the objectives, IMC considers two different techniques: advertising, which entices the target into a sale or gets the target thinking about purchase, and promotion, which solicits immediate purchase of a packaged offer. Together, advertising and promotion can be used as building blocks in an IMC campaign: one can inform while the other encourages purchase.

Effective communication objectives that lend themselves to direct marketing include generating sales, building consumer loyalty, enhancing a corporate or brand image, and encouraging an inquiry or product trial.

Like advertising, promotional efforts may target both a primary and secondary target audience. Determining the need for a secondary audience will depend on the target's overall knowledge of, or past history with, the product or service and whether it can, or would, be purchased by a family member, friend, or professional associate. Additional factors affecting both the promotional mix and the strategy include how far each audience is from trial, repeat purchase, and brand loyalty.

The decision to use an emotional or rational appeal depends upon the product and the consumer's knowledge about the product. The personal, interactive style of direct marketing walks a fine line between talking to the target like an old friend and getting too personal and inadvertently offending the target. It's important to remember that direct marketing is still a business relationship and that direct marketing should inform first and build a relationship second.

Finally, the ability to tie the key benefit to the target's lifestyle is crucial in direct marketing, because it helps personalize the message.

Using direct mail to launch an IMC campaign can be very effective. It makes a great teaser or announcement device. Teasing the target about a top-secret new product launch or grand opening can build curiosity. Direct marketing can also be used as a status device, for example by delivering invitations to grand openings or private sales.

Once a campaign is launched and interest begins to build, direct marketing is a great support to other media efforts, and can make buying the product from home—avoiding traffic, parking hassles, long lines, and moody salespeople—easy. Detailed information can be supplied through copy and/or demonstrations, allowing any di-

Ryan Vinett

rect-marketing vehicle to close the sale quickly and conveniently from the target's home or office.

THE CREATIVE VOICE OF DIRECT MARKETING

Direct marketing is so diverse creatively that it is impossible to address all the creative options available to the creative team effectively here. Instead, let's take a quick look at one of the best known, and often most creative, promotional devices available in direct response: direct-mail kits.

Direct mail consists of any advertising material sent by mail to a targeted consumer to solicit a sale or further inquiry. The personality that is direct mail reflects a variety of faces, shapes, and sizes. It is not unusual for simple direct-mail kits to employ a mixture of letter formats, informally handwritten notes, postcards, scratch-off cards, die-cuts (i.e., pieces with shapes or holes cut out of them), pocketed folders, brochures, price lists, CDs, calendars, key chains, and/or menus.

More creative direct-mail pieces may incorporate three-dimensional designs that use pop-ups or pop-outs, or designs that employ moving parts or sound. Such pieces are often spectacular. But not all mailings are as imaginative or expensive as that: most are functional, with a strictly business appearance.

Almost 50 percent of all direct mail, known better by the derogatory name of "junk mail," is never opened. Why? Because it does not create interest or curiosity. It's considered junk for two reasons: it comes unwanted into the target's home, and the overall design is junk. There is nothing that can be done to change the former, but the later can be changed—and that's the one that will get the piece opened.

A direct-mail kit is a design whole. One piece should not stand out alone; all pieces in the kit must work together in creating one visual/verbal message. The kit should reflect the key benefit and strategy as defined in the creative brief, and use the same tone of voice, and reflect the same overall appearance, as the other pieces in the IMC campaign of which it is a part. A direct-mail kit will most often include multiple pieces that must be tied together by headline or type style, color, layout, or the use of a spokesperson or animated character. An overview of concept and creative devices will help the designer decide how to tie the kit to the rest of the campaign.

In the end, direct mail gets a bad name because it's usually poorly thought out and often even more poorly designed. When pieces are inconsistent and offers are buried in the copy, the target will not act on the promotion. The envelope should be used to stop attention but also should say something relative to the target. Each kit should highlight one key benefit that is pushed throughout the copy. The kit should back up claims with testimonials, and it should also include a guarantee. Additionally, every kit should have a letter or short note from the president or CEO of the company, covering the company's history, quality, and commitment to customer service, as well as providing a quick and easy way to order. Color, promotional devices and visual images should further the message, not get in the way by giving the piece a junky or circus feel.

As a member of the promotional mix, direct marketing talks directly to the target and initiates a dialogue—an IMC must. Messages are personalized and address the target's known interests based on past purchasing behavior. Most forms of direct marketing are less intrusive than any of the other media we have looked at so far, allowing the target to decide what message to respond to, when to respond to it, and where to make further inquiries or purchase decisions. If the goal is to introduce a new or reinvented product; remind, or encourage retrial; or update the consumer on product changes or additions, direct marketing will reach the target in a shorter amount of time, and more effectively, than traditional advertising efforts.

CHAPTER FIFTEEN

SALES PROMOTION

At least she won't hide from her Kool-Aid.

Everything's better with Kool-Aid.

Racheal Bell

The advertising man is a liaison between the products of business and the mind of the nation. He must know both before he can serve either.

—Glenn Frank, quoted in John P. Bradley, Leo F. Daniels, and Thomas C. Jones, 13.

WHAT IS SALES PROMOTION?

Sales promotion is fun: it gives the consumer a gift or incentive to elicit an inquiry or encourage purchase. Sales promotions are intended to quickly increase sales or interest through discount pricing or other motivational devices available for a limited time. By comparison, advertising takes longer to make a sale and has little personal or immediate effect on an individual consumer.

Sales promotion differs from advertising in its approach. Advertising influences attitudes and tells the consumer why she should buy, answering the question, "What's in it for me?" Sales promotion gives the target an incentive to react quickly to the advertised message.

Incentives can take many different forms. Some of the most commonly used include coupons, premiums, sampling, contests and sweepstakes, in-store displays, rebates, and discounts. The choice of sales promotion vehicle should reinforce the advertised message, reflecting the strategy and both the target's and product's image.

When advertising and sales promotion are coordinated together in an IMC campaign, it's known as **integrated brand promotion** (IBP). IBP takes place when the brand's image (advertising) is integrated into the promotion (sales promotion). To do this effectively, the brand-building message of advertising has to coordinate with sales promotion's incentive to buy. In other words, they must work with each other rather than against each other. For example, coupons arriving in the mail or appearing in a newspaper, in combination with an advertised image of elegance and sophistication, adds up to a mixed message. Instead, advertising efforts might direct the target to a website or toll-free number for more information or to set up an appointment. And if the message is young and upbeat, promotional items might be distributed at concerts or in the mall.

The most distinctive characteristic about sales promotion is its intent. While public relations, advertising, and direct marketing bring a product and message to the target, sales promotion sidesteps the message and brings the target to the product, making it a great interactive device.

The basic premise behind sales promotion is to give the target something for purchasing or for remaining a brand-loyal customer. The job of sales promotion is to attract first-time buyers, stimulate impulse buys, and entice users of a competitor's product to switch brands. It's also a great tool for raising brand awareness through "try me" promotions, effectively increasing product demand for a limited time. This is important to IMC efforts because initiating trial is the first step on the long road to obtaining brand loyalty.

The use of sales promotion has steadily increased over the last several years, due to the overwhelming number of often-indistinguishable products available to consumers in any one category. By spotlighting one product, sales promotion can help consumers with a purchase decision by offering an incentive to try the product or use the service.

SALES PROMOTION'S ROLE IN IMC

The success of all communication efforts rises and falls with the economy. Sales promotion can be used as an incentive to buy when a poor economy causes consumers to purchase conservatively. However, side effects are numerous. For example, it's easy for marketers and their products to get caught in a vicious cycle of promotion, where they find it hard to get even loyal users to buy when there is no current promotion—customers are simply waiting for the next one.

Other side effects include the devaluation of the brand in the mind of the consumer, the overall expense, and an end-of-promotion drop in sales. Excessive or unnecessary use of sales promotions can lead to the erosion of brand loyalty, brand image, and eventually brand equity.

When deciding whether or not sales promotions should play a part in the IMC strategy, it's important to determine whether inducing an immediate sale is a prerequisite to accomplishing the objectives. Can awareness or loyalty be built using a form of bribery? In the end, that's what sales promotion is, and if it is overused it can tarnish the brand's image.

Although sales promotion can do a lot of things, it cannot, all by itself, build brand loyalty, cover for a poorly promoted or poorly made product, or save the life of an aging brand. These objectives will require the additional and combined efforts of other media in the promotional mix to promote, to educate, or to reinvent a product's or service's image.

There are a lot of options available when deciding on a promotional device. Some are creative, some are functional—but all are consumer motivated. Sales promotions can be broken down into two basic types: in-store and out-of-store promotions. A distinct few fall into both categories. Let's look some of the most popular.

In-store promotions include:

1. Coupons
2. Bonus packs
3. Price-off offers
4. Specialty packaging
5. Sampling
6. Point-of-purchase advertising

Out-of-store promotions include:

1. Refunds and rebates
2. Continuity programs

3. Product placement
4. Trial offers
5. Special events
6. Product warranties or guarantees

In-store or out-of-store promotions might include:

1. Contests and sweepstakes
2. Premiums
3. Giveaways

In-Store Promotions

In-store promotions are a marketer's last shot at influencing the target prior to purchase. The sales promotion devices employed are most often determined by price and purchase location.

Coupons

Coupons come with many different offers, such as cents-off discounts and two-for-one opportunities (also known as *buy-one-get-one-free* offers). Other coupons, often for higher priced items, might offer a percentage off. Whatever the offer, coupons initiate action and account for almost 70 percent of all consumer sales promotions.

Coupons can be found just about anywhere; but one of the most common places is within the Sunday newspaper, where FSIs are found. These perforated, usually four-color, 8 1/2 × 11 pages offer numerous coupons for one brand of product. Coupons can also be found within newspaper and magazine ads; in the mail, as a part of a direct-mail kit or polypak; and as bounce-back coupons on the outside of a product or placed inside packaging. The majority of coupons can be used immediately and are known as *instant-redemption coupons*. Others, like those used in an FSI, might be valid over several days or weeks, to encourage return visits.

Coupons can also be found on the Internet, where distribution is tracked and usually limited on a per-person basis; so it is unlikely the target will print coupons directly off a website. Instead, coupons are usually sent to the target by e-mail or traditional mail. A request for coupons directly from the consumer, either by toll-free number or through a website, creates an interaction between buyer and seller. The more time a consumer spends actively thinking about the product or service, the more likely the product is to move from her short-term memory to her long-term memory, assisting with recall when shopping.

Technology at the checkout counter has also jumped into the coupon game. One of the most commonly seen coupon systems is Catalina Marketing's checkout coupon. This form of coupon is distributed with grocery receipts. Which coupons are distributed is determined based on current purchases; they are not for the same brand, but are for other products in the same brand category. These checkout coupons cannot be used immediately, but may be used on the consumer's next visit—delaying purchase. If the consumer remembers to bring the coupons on his next shopping visit, this is a good way to encourage trial.

Crossruffing is another coupon opportunity. Here, two mutually compatible products team up to share one promotion. For example, a coupon for Pillsbury cookie dough might be placed on a package of Nestlé chocolate chips.

The better the offer, the more likely it will be redeemed. Consumers are also influenced by the origin of the coupon. On the negative side, in-store coupons require time-consuming decisions and extend the shopping experience. Other offers, such as bounce-backs or checkout coupons, cannot be used until a future visit. Polypak coupons are the least attractive, because of the time required to sort through the stack of cards. On the positive side, coupons that arrive via e-mail or land on the target's front doorstep in the Sunday paper are successful because they can be looked at and organized at the target's leisure. Coupons that arrive at the point of purchase with the target are more likely to be redeemed.

Coupons never go out of fashion; they just hit their stride. Most sales or promotions occur before and during a product's peak season. It is not unusual to see a summer promotion for barbecue grills or a winter promotion for hats, coats, and gloves. This might seem a little strange, because the products would most likely sell even without additional incentives. But remember, the whole point is to get people moving *now* in order to increase short-term sales within a specific time frame, rather than waiting for them to get around to a last-minute purchase. Believe it or not, most coupons are never redeemed, and many that are redeemed cause another problem: *misredemption*. This is when a coupon is accepted for the wrong product or used after the expiration date. Additionally, coupons do not always attract or reach new users, and are often redeemed by consumers who are already loyal to the brand.

Bonus Packs

Bonus packs are very popular. These give the consumer more of a product for the price of the original size, or include a related, bonus product in a "try me" size.

Price-Off Offers

Price-off offer is a fancy term for a sale. Unlike coupons, price-off deals often appear on the packaging or are announced by shelf signage. A sale can be anything from a cents-off offer to several dollars or even several hundred dollars off, depending on the product.

Specialty Packaging

Used to raise awareness and to attract attention, *specialty packaging* is often used when a product has been reinvented or repackaged. These offers are most common during holidays or in conjunction with a promotional event—such as the premiere of a movie that's expected to be popular with the target audience; a celebrity endorsement; or a sponsored event.

Sampling

Sampling is just what the name implies: the product is available for consumers to try at the point of purchase. If the goal is to entice consumers to try the product, it needs to be put in the target's hands, particularly if it is new or repositioned. Let them feel the quality, the weight, or the texture. Better yet, if it smells good, let the consumer have a taste at no charge.

Samples can also be distributed through the mail as a part of direct-mail kits, bound up in the Sunday newspaper, distributed at events, or even sent in response to consumer requests.

Point-of-Purchase

Point-of-purchase (POP) advertising is all the advertising you see while shopping, such as store posters, signage inside and outside the store, promotional kiosks that prominently display products either in the aisle or on the endcaps, and shopping cart signs. Shelf dispensers are a popular way to distribute POP coupons that can be immediately redeemed. POP makes the product stand out at the point of purchase, reinforces a brand's image, builds equity, and creates interactive opportunities between the product and the target.

Out-of-Store Promotions

Out-of-store promotions can be used to reward consumers for their loyalty, for purchase, or to draw attention to a brand or service.

Refunds and Rebates

Both refunds and rebates give cash back to the consumer. In the case of a *refund* it's possible for the entire purchase price to be refunded, with or without the original sales receipt.

The amount of return on a rebate can vary. *Rebates* often require the target to fill out a lengthy form and return the original sales receipt and the UPC code or model number found in or on the packaging. The target's willingness to give detailed personal and purchasing information in return for some kind of incentive is another great database-building tool.

Continuity Programs

One lesser-known type of sales promotion is the *continuity program*. Every time consumers use the program and/or make a purchase, they earn points toward some kind of reward or free gift, usually associated with the program's sponsor. Most

Amanda Sherrod

often used by restaurants and airlines, this is a great way to encourage repeat purchase and build brand loyalty.

Product Placement

When a name-brand product is clearly recognizable in a movie or television show, it is known as *product placement* or *brand placement*. The goal is to tie the product to a character image or plot in some favorable way.

Trial Offers

Trial offers, most often used for expensive items such as beds, larger lawn and garden tools, and exercise equipment, allow consumers to try products in their homes on a trial basis for a specified period of time, often thirty to ninety days, before buying.

Special Events

When a product or service attaches its name to an event, it is called *special events promotion*. As an event sponsor, a product or service keeps its name in the public eye, through public relations, sampling opportunities, logo identifiers such as cups and T-shirts, and positive word of mouth—all of which work to build or maintain both brand image and brand equity.

Sponsoring events allows the product to get close to the consumer, as well as allowing marketers to get product feedback from the target, creating an interactive dialogue rather than a traditional advertising monologue. Sponsors whose products are a good fit with the event and its target audience will experience a high degree of product awareness and recall.

Product Warranties or Guarantees

One of the best ways to generate trust or goodwill in a product or service is to offer a product *warranty* or guarantee. Consumers expect a 100 percent product warranty when shopping over the phone or the Internet. A warranty guarantees that if the consumer is not 100 percent satisfied, the purchase price will be refunded in its entirety.

A 100 percent product *guarantee* assures consumers that they will not find the product at a lower price anywhere. If they should find a lower price, the marketer will honor the lower price, refunding the difference. Many companies require some kind of proof, such as an ad or circular with the price clearly stated, while others simply take the consumer's word for it.

In-Store or Out-of-Store Promotions

Some promotions can be used whether the target visits a store location or purchases from a website or over the phone.

Contests and Sweepstakes

Contests and sweepstakes are among the few types of promotions that do not necessarily require a purchase in order to participate.

Consumers love the interactive participation of games of chance and competitions. The choice of whether to use a contest or a sweepstakes depends on the type of promotion and the desired outcome. *Contests* are games of skill that require participants to meet a certain set of standards in order to win. A *sweepstakes*, on the other hand, is based entirely on chance. Contests and sweepstakes are another great way to build up a database list; information from entry forms can be stored and used for future promotions.

Premiums

Premiums are wearable or usable gifts that are often given away at out-of-store sponsored events or through personal selling. In addition, they are often attached to in-store products. Usually emblazoned with a company or product logo and/or tag-line or slogan, these items include T-shirts, pens, calendars, coffee cups, and base-ball caps—basically, anything that can display a logo. When marketers decide to employ premiums, or *specialty items*, it is important for them to know that the quality of the item reflects well on the quality of the product or service; as a result, marketers are using more expensive gifts, ranging from three to five dollars in cost, as opposed to smaller, bulk items costing only pennies apiece.

Not all premiums are free; sometimes a few proof-of-purchase seals and/or a little cash to cover shipping are required.

Giveaways

A *giveaway* can take place in or out of the store. Although similar to sampling, giveaways rarely give the actual product or service away. Instead, a giveaway is often something that complements the product or service. For example, a DVD player might be promoted with an offer of free DVDs with purchase.

Studies show that the majority of retail purchases are unplanned. POP displays, samples, or trial offers can affect unplanned purchase decisions. Recognizing a logo, color scheme, slogan, or package design helps the consumer tie the display back to traditional advertising seen elsewhere.

How Sales Promotion Builds a Relationship between the Product and the Target Audience

Sales promotion brings customer contact to an IMC campaign. It can be used to reinforce an existing campaign message, stimulate trial or repeat purchase, or launch a new product.

A promotion is an interactive direct-response vehicle that often initiates a one-on-one dialogue with the consumer. Products can often be tested on site, creating immediate feedback between buyer and seller. Most sales promotions are personal.

Because sales promotion, like direct marketing, is so consumer focused, it is more expensive to use than either public relations or mass-media advertising approaches. Cost is dependent upon the size and length of the promotion and the number of prizes or premiums needed. Sales promotion runs the risk of generating big losses if participation is low.

Every buyer likes a bargain, but not all consumers will respond to a bargain. Consumers who are loyal to a product will not be tempted by sales or giveaways, while others live only for the next promotion, with brand playing little or no role in their purchase decisions. In between these two extremes lie the *switchers*, those who may be successfully tempted into switching from a preferred brand to a new brand. This is the group most influenced by sales promotion efforts.

Sales promotions are most often used in an IMC campaign to round out and reinforce the other advertising efforts that make up the promotional mix. The type of promotion used should be chosen based on the product and where it is in its life cycle. New product launches often use coupons, sampling, bonus packs, or contests and sweepstakes to encourage trial purchase. A product in its maintenance stage relies on advertising and requires little promotional assistance. The use of sales promotion is a great way to reawaken interest in a mature brand, and might be used to remind the consumer of its value, by means of crossruffing coupons, in- or on-pack offers, or flashy POP displays.

Enticing consumers to take advantage of offers is not always that successful, so sales promotions cannot be relied upon as the sole way to generate interest and increase traffic or short-term sales.

PROS AND CONS ASSOCIATED WITH SALES PROMOTION

When deciding whether sales promotion is right for an IMC campaign, it may be helpful to look at some of the pros and cons associated with it.

The more notable pros associated with sales promotion include:

1. Time limits. Sales promotions increase a company's cash flow on a short-term basis, since consumers are more likely to buy when they are offered an incentive, ensuring an influx of cash for a set period of time.
2. Trackability. Once a coupon is redeemed or a contest winner is found, results are easily tracked. The volume of sales made during the promotion, which determines success, is also measurable.
3. Product visibility. A good promotion can excite the consumer and get him to try the product. When a product is supported by a promotion, it can increase awareness by making the product temporarily stand out from a competing brand's, initiating trial or purchase. Promotions have been directly responsible for convincing consumers loyal to a competing brand to switch brands based on an initial trial.

The more notable cons associated with sales promotion include:

1. Negative sales effect. Once a promotion has ended, sales will often drop, as consumers move on to another product promotion. This is an unfortunate

side effect of using sales promotion. In order to quickly increase sales again, another promotion will be needed.

2. Damaged brand image. Overuse of promotions can damage a product's image in the mind of the consumer by cheapening its appeal. This directly feeds into the need to build and maintain brand loyalty. A product's image is the voice of advertising efforts. Excessive promotions can quickly erode the message, destroying consumer confidence in the brand.

3. Equity depletion. Excessive use of sales promotions can negatively affect the way the target views the product's image or worth, effectively depleting a brand's equity over time.

4. Cost. Sales promotion is expensive. A relatively small number of consumers will be reached, compared to other approaches, and inventory to cover prizes or premiums can be high in cost when compared to the actual number of sales.

DEVELOPING THE PROMOTIONAL MIX USING SALES PROMOTION

When should sales promotion be used? It works great as a secondary medium for public relations, advertising, and direct marketing to induce trial during small or inexpensive product launches. It is a useful tool for any product where a particular feature can be proved at the point of purchase—such as taste or softness. Products in highly competitive categories, where there is little or no product differentiation, can benefit from the use of coupons, bonus packs, price-off offers, or sampling opportunities.

So how does sales promotion fit into the promotional mix? A campaign advertising a mature product that is being repositioned might lead off with public relations, using the media to announce a new face on an old friend. Advertising will then begin building awareness and introduce the new image. A coupon could be placed in almost any print medium, but would most likely be found in newspapers, magazines, or direct-mail kits.

Direct marketing might use sales promotion in a direct-mail kit by directing the public to a store location, a website, or a toll-free number to receive a free sample or participate in a trial offer. Incentives such as samples, coupons, POP displays, or trial offers can be used to build brand awareness for a new product or reintroduce the target to a reinvented product.

Key benefits have nothing to say in sales promotion—but they have everything to show. The message, along with strategy, overall objectives, and target audience, should be the creative team's guide as to what the image of the promotion has to do with the image of the product and that of the target. Sales promotion efforts should be avoided for products with a strong brand image, with the possible exception of event sponsorships or continuity programs.

Effective sales promotion objectives might include encouraging trial or product switching by nonusers, supporting a new product launch, offsetting competitor promotions, gaining a larger market share, or increasing short-term profits.

The type of strategy chosen will depend on the desired outcome. If the focus is on the consumer, promotional efforts might reward purchase or loyalty. If the focus is on the product, trial might be the ultimate goal. Depending on the product's life-cycle stage, a good alternative emotional appeal is the reminder. If it's important to make a quick sale and increase profits for a limited time, then sales promotion is strategically a good choice.

THE CREATIVE VOICE OF SALES PROMOTION

Sales promotion must be an extension of the advertising message. The closer the visual/verbal relationship, the easier it is to excite consumer interest.

It is important to remember that in IMC there are no single messages with multiple images; only one message, with one image, will define a product's or service's brand image across all media vehicles within the promotional mix. So it is important to carry the visual/verbal message created elsewhere in the promotional mix through all sales promotion efforts. This is often easier said than done, because of the eclectic shapes, textures, and sizes of promotional materials.

Depending on the amount of available surface space, promotional devices such as special packaging; premiums; contest and sweepstakes announcements and/or game boards; POP displays; coupons and freestanding inserts; and special-event materials should take their cue from print or direct-marketing materials. Creative teams should consider adapting unique headline styles, color combinations, and typefaces or type styles; spokespersons or character representatives; logos; and slogans or taglines for use in sales promotion pieces. POP advertising that reflects the overall visual/verbal appearance of the other IMC components can assist with product recognition should the target forget the product name while shopping.

The job of this very consumer-focused approach is to get the product into the target's hands and push for an initial inquiry, a request for follow-up information, or a purchase. Sales promotion is a great way to introduce a new product or create excitement around it or to reintroduce an old product.

If the goal is to entice the target through trial or gifts and games, then sales promotion is the best outlet.

Sales promotion techniques may not seem to have the impact of traditional, Internet, or even direct-response advertising; but the majority of sales promotion techniques represent a marketer's last chance, either before or immediately after purchase, to educate consumers, interact with them, and remind them about a product or service.

CHAPTER SIXTEEN

THE INTERNET

On a binge. On a diet.

No Guilt. No Lie.
The only thing you should feel guilty about is how good it tastes.

_____
_____
_____
_____
_____
_____

Russell Stover.
Eat what you should. Get the taste that you want. www.russellstover.com

Leah Loudon

For marketers . . . the mass media are no longer the sole choice. Traditional media retains an important advantage: the "rub-off" credibility that accrues from being part of a broadcast or publication invited into the home. But for many marketers, media advertising is a shotgun. The new technologies provide rifles, which can target prime prospects.

—Stanley E. Cohen, 18.

WHAT IS INTERNET MARKETING?

The *Internet* has changed the way corporations conduct business and connect with customers. Through the Internet, advertising that once spoke to the targeted buyer can now actively interact with that buyer. Consumers can ask questions, get help or technical assistance, and make a purchase without ever leaving their homes or offices. The Internet allows consumers to decide when, where, and for how long they will view a message. The ease with which information can be gathered makes comparison shopping easier, faster, and more convenient; so when consumers elect to buy, they are much better educated on product use, quality, prices, guarantees, and return policies than ever before.

The Internet is the place to be for advertisers, with two out of every three Americans spending time surfing the Web. It is important that when consumers initiate contact, they encounter courteous and knowledgeable customer service or technical representatives who can answer questions quickly and professionally. Often, this is the only thing that separates one product in a category from another. The quality of this interaction is often transferred to the brand or service.

The Internet is the fastest-growing media vehicle, growing almost 14 percent in the second half of 2006, as compared to the first three months. According to a recent Harris Poll, 77 percent of adults within the United States use the Internet at home, school, and work, as compared to only 3 percent in 1995.

The Internet is the medium most consumers turn to for initial or additional information. The majority of Internet users are technology savvy, educated, upscale individuals within the highly influential 18-to-30-year-old target. This is the word-of-mouth group that creates buzz, participates in chat rooms and blogs, and watches webisodes.

Because of this intense interest, the role of the Internet is still evolving. Its growth as an advertising or direct-selling tool will ultimately depend on how and why consumers use the Internet. Its use as a primary vehicle requires the target to initiate contact based on a personal need that begins with a search for information. In its current role as a secondary or support media source, the target is directed to a website based on exposure in a traditional advertising or promotional media vehicle.

Used together, traditional advertising and Internet marketing, also called **cyber-marketing**, are effective at building brand awareness, initiating interactive opportunities, and educating consumers about a product or service. As an educational and informational tool, the Internet is a great place to direct the target for information on current promotions, news articles, testimonials, tests or medical results, and advice or tips from relevant experts. Many websites also sponsor chat rooms and message boards where consumers can talk to, and exchange information with, other product users.

Why Do Marketers Need a Web Presence?

All companies big and small must have a presence on the Web to compete in today's technology-based business world. A decade and a half ago, the Internet was not considered a viable media vehicle. Its commercial value was not recognized until the late 1990s. At that time, marketers jumped on board the World Wide Web with little knowledge of how it worked or how consumers would use it. As a result, the initial efforts of many advertisers failed in 2000–2001.

Today, marketers better understand how to use interactive technology in an IMC campaign. Additionally, the growth of broadband, the introduction of advanced creative execution techniques such as streaming audio and video, and better research capabilities have helped advertisers understand and be able to measure potential use and current and future audience use, making advertising efforts more accountable.

Advertising has advanced from an informational device to one that must interact with and entertain consumers, in order not only to make an impression over competing products, but also to hold the attention of consumers with short attention spans and little tolerance for misinformation. The more inventive the entertainment value, the more memorable the experience and interaction with the product or service will be. Creating "buzz" or word-of-mouth advertising between consumers carries more sales value than any advertised message alone ever will.

Advertising has become a global sales tool, in part because of the rise of the Internet. The ease of reaching international consumers makes international sales a viable option even for the smallest company. Economically, the Internet offers smaller companies the opportunity to compete with larger ones, not only in product development, but also in terms of customer service and delivery. Globally, the Internet has exploded because shipping is faster, personal incomes are on the rise worldwide, and falling trade barriers make it easier for global consumers to purchase and surf internationally.

Businesses who choose to employ the Internet in their media mix will find that:

* It's where the target is.
* It is a great vehicle for delivering personalized advertising messages.
* It offers customer or technological service on demand.
* It allows them to provide in-depth product or service information.
* It enables quick, easy, no-hassle sales.

Internet Marketing's Role in IMC

The Internet offers 24/7 access, personalization, creative opportunities, and additional links to similar or cooperative sites for more information. It builds relationships, and it's a great way to build databased information on customers, a critical component of a successful IMC campaign.

The Internet is interactive, requiring the consumer to participate in the message by scrolling or clicking to retrieve information. This participation should take little thought, and, like any of the other media discussed, it should lead the consumer on an informative but structured journey. Interactive advertising vehicles can be as uncomplicated as a banner ad or as multifaceted as an entire website.

"Brick-and-mortar" retail stores may offer e-commerce sites for convenience or to promote sales. This consolidation is known as multichanneling. *Multichanneling* focuses on creating dialogue and building relationships between buyer and seller by providing multiple channels of communication to encourage consumer interaction and feedback. For example, a diverse media mix might include other interactive vehicles such as mobile marketing, CD-ROMs, catalogs and magazines, and interactive television, as well as more traditional vehicles like radio, out-of-home, or newspaper. The successful integration of interactive and traditional media is important to an effective IMC approach.

Traditional advertising, as we know it in print, does exist on the Internet in the form of pop-ups and banners; and some Internet service providers do sell message space at the bottom of each viewable screen. This type of message is more reminder than hard sell, and can be targeted to match the demographic of the viewer based on previous visits to the site.

Search engine sites like Yahoo! and Google can track what users read and purchase when on the Internet. Being able to follow a computer user around the Internet allows marketers to customize their advertising efforts to fit that user's particular interests. This type of information gathering is known as *behavioral targeting*.

Behavioral targeting will often replace the use of demographic information since knowing what a person is interested in or already buying is much more valuable than knowing age, sex, or income level. Agency senior vice president of Starcom IP Jeff Marshall, in a *New York Times* online article dated August 15, 2006, reports that "search behavior is the closest thing we have to a window onto people's intent. When people are gathering information to make a choice, that means they are often going to spend money."

In the same article, Les Kruger, senior marketing manager at Cingular, adds, "you are no longer targeting people you think will be interested in your product. We know based on your behavior that you are in the market, and we can target you as you bounce around the Internet."

Cookies are used by most marketing systems not only to track returning visitors to a site but also to personalize both messages and products for individual consumers. Cookies tell marketers whether a user is a first-time visitor to their site or a returning visitor.

Advertising on the Internet is less expensive than traditional advertising methods, is easier to revise, is much more targetable, and is less intrusive to consumers, since they choose when and where, and for how long, they will visit a site.

Internet use is on the rise, and advertisers are still learning the most effective way to deliver an advertised message to consumers. Making advertising interactive or participatory, rather than just visually and verbally interesting, is a new challenge. To creative teams, "interactive" means creating an attention-getting activity that can also inform. To marketers, it is a means of creating an informational vehicle for two-way communication with the target audience.

Internet advertising and promotional efforts, at their simplest, can take many diverse forms, such as banners and pop-ups, search ads, personalized e-mail or text messages, or opportunities to enter a contest or sweepstakes or pick up a coupon or two. More sophisticated options might include streaming audio and video, social networking sites, and interactive television.

Banner Ads

With a click of the mouse, a banner can transport a viewer to a sponsored Web page. *Banner ads* are mass-media Internet vehicles, usually found at the top of Web pages. In its simplest form, a banner is nothing more than a brightly colored rectangular bar featuring a logo and a small amount of type. Vertical banners known as *sky-scrapers* are another option, although they are not used as often. More complex banners such as interstitials, animated banners, and DHTML floating ads, to name just a few varieties, can use moving or blinking images to attract attention. It is important designers not get so caught up in what can be done with new technology that they ignore basic design principles. It is not a big leap from animated to tacky and annoying; care should be taken when deciding how the consumer should think about the client's product the first time she sees the banner.

Like traditional advertising methods, these often unpopular, intrusive, and un-wanted ads are paid for by the advertiser and placed strategically throughout the Internet, usually on very active or highly visited sites. These interactive advertising messages have little type; they briefly present the key benefit and/or a slogan or tagline with an accompanying logo.

When used as a more selective targeting vehicle, banners can be placed on sites that focus on a specific market. For example, a site on dental health might have a banner for a tooth whitening system. This option allows for less waste and creates more interest.

Rich Media

A form of advanced technology, *rich media* allows websites to use streaming audio and video and specialized effects. The use of rich media is a direct result of more consumers having access to higher bandwidth, allowing information to be trans-ferred to them faster.

Rich-media banners and badges allow advertisers the flexibility to present a lot of information in a limited space. More interesting, and thus engaging, than static banners, rich-media banners allow designers to use drop-down boxes, sound, anima-tion, and games. There are basically three types of rich-media banners and badges available to designers: HTML, plug-in, and Javascript. Available technology (i.e., whether the user has narrowband, better known as *dial-up*, or the faster broadband option) plays a role in the success and use of each one.

Using HTML banners and badges is probably the safest route, since they use existing browser technology, which makes them viewable within any browser.

Plug-in banners and badges require users to have Flash and/or Shockwave. Sites that use advertising featuring plug-ins need to also provide a link for viewers, so that those who need it can download the required software.

Banners and badges utilizing advanced functions such as Enliven or BlueStreak require users to have Javascript. Since most browsers have Javascript (though the user must make sure it is turned on), there is no need to download any additional plug-ins.

Interstitials

The ads seen in the main browser between two pages of a website are known as *interstitials*. These ads appear when a viewer clicks on a link. Instead of going to the linked page, he "stops" on an advertising page first. Once there, the viewer can stay, taking advantage of additional links that will take him to the advertiser's Web page; or he can wait approximately five to ten seconds to automatically be taken to the page originally requested. These types of ads have a very high click-through rate and are great for reinforcing brand image.

Advanced Banner Ads

Unlike traditional static banners, *animated banners* consist of moving images that follow a sequence, helping attract attention to the banner. Software used to create animated banners includes Flash, Director, Blender, Squeak, and nonlinear editing tools such as Premier, FinalCut, and After Effects, among others.

DHTML floating ads are another type of rich-media advertisement. Floating ads appear unsolicited on top of a loading Web page and offer designers a great deal of creative flexibility. Floating ads are viewable for only about five to thirty seconds, and may or may not feature a close button. These ads can jet across the page in an ongoing loop, and can be preset to land on a banner or badge, or to disappear off the page after a set period of time. Advertisers can also take advantage of the visitor's cursor. To do this, an image actually attaches itself to the user's cursor, creating an advertising image that follows the viewer as she moves about the page. Since this viewing option cannot be clicked on, it is most often used to attract attention to an ad or link appearing somewhere else on the page. Another option is to incorporate scrolling ads into the site. This type of ad is placed along the edge of the site and continually scrolls in time with viewer use.

Floating ads have about the same click-through rates as pop-up ads; however, since these ads offer movement and sound, they hold the viewer's attention longer, making them more memorable. The majority of floating ads include tracking capabilities that are able to keep track of the number of times the ad is clicked on, as well as how many times the viewer repetitively watches the ad.

Not all visitors to a site will be able to use all the technological bells and whistles. Rich-media sites may need to offer additional software, like Flash or Quicktime, in order to view video options. A visitor may also lack the high-speed connection necessary to view video options, so it is important that designers make sure all information can be accessed in multiple ways.

Pop-Up Ads

Pop-up ads are separate windows that "pop-up" on top of a Web page. Much like banner ads, these mass-media ads link the viewer to another site. Pop-up ads were originally conceived as a vehicle to drive consumers to the desired Web site; instead, consumers consider them an annoyance, making them even more unpopular than banner ads. Consumers are taking advantage of pop-up blockers offered by their service providers to keep pop-up windows from opening.

For now, banners and pop-up ads make up the largest part of the limited palette from which Internet advertisers can choose to deliver their message. Advertisers and marketers alike are asking, "What is the look of Internet advertising? Is it more like print or broadcast?" Banners and pop-up ads currently have more print characteristics than broadcast—and all the annoyances of both. Marketers are constantly working to come up with new and less intrusive ways to catch the target's attention and direct it to their websites. The Internet's visual/verbal growing pains might call to mind the nature of television ads in their infancy: long and boring, they sounded more like radio ads than the creative, informative productions we see today.

Search-Engine Advertising

Paid search ads are the newest form of Internet advertising and quickly replacing the annoying, uncreative banner or pop-up ads. How do paid search ads work? Consumers who use search engines will have advertising pop up next to their search engine results. Cost to marketers is based on the number of times the ad is clicked on. This type of pricing is known as *pay per click*. Results that pop up from a key word search have a hierarchy based on a fee (or bid) paid by the marketer. Every time a viewer clicks on a marketer's website, the marketer pays a fee. Marketers are making sure that words tied to search ads are also tied to slogans or jingles seen in current print or broadcast advertising, in order to tie Internet searches to current campaigns.

The biggest advertisers pay top dollar to have top-of-page listings. These top spots are also based on key word searches, and are sold to the highest bidder.

Search-engine marketing is directly related to advertising and should be considered a vital part of the cost of operating a website. Worth the cost, paid search-engine placement guarantees that the product gains both exposure and frequency.

E-mail Marketing

E-mail marketing is another way to reach the target electronically. E-mail makes printed copies and lengthy printing delays things of the past, and it is an inexpensive and dependable means of reaching the target. As an effective customer-service device, e-mail can be used to thank customers by name for their purchases and reinforce ways to contact the marketer with questions or comments. E-mail can also be used to verify the receipt of an order, alleviating concerns that it might somehow have been lost in cyberspace. It is also an excellent way to send a follow-up customer-comment sheet, allowing buyers to comment on service, product quality, and so forth.

Like other forms of Internet advertising, e-mail marketing gets mixed reactions. When consumers elect to receive e-mail messages, it's known as *permission*, or *opt-in marketing*. Elective e-mails might come from local retailers announcing sales, or from airlines or hotel chains advertising discounted fares or room rates. E-mail messages sent without permission are known as **spam**.

Opt-in e-mail gives information on upcoming events and sales that are of interest to previous viewers. The idea is to whet the target's appetite enough to make him come back and, hopefully, make a purchase. To keep viewers interested in the messages so that they're willing to keep opening and interacting with them, opt-in e-mails have to be more than just copy. The more fun an opt-in is, the better the chance for viral sharing of the e-mail with friends and family.

Another, more popular, e-mail option is **rich mail**. Rich mail is an e-mail ad that can include graphics and audio and video. When the receiver opens the e-mail, it automatically links her to an HTML page. Rich mail, since it is usually opt-in, has a good click-through rate. The downside is that the opt-in participant, in order to experience all the audio and video options, must have broadband.

For marketers, opt-in advertising cuts costs associated with more traditional direct-mail advertising and allows a hands-on, personalized interaction with the consumer.

For every e-mail consumers opt-in to receive, they get even more they don't want. **Phishing**, like spam, is an unwanted Internet road bump. A phishing e-mail arrives in your inbox as a legitimate-looking message. The problem is, it's not legit, and its main goal is to trick the receiver into giving up personal information, such as a credit-card number, for a bogus product or service. And if that's not enough, there is also spyware, along with a plethora of computer viruses just waiting for the unsuspecting consumer to click once too often.

CD-ROMs

CD-ROMs are not widely used by advertisers. A CD-ROM holds a lot of information in a small space, reducing shipping, updating, and printing costs. For complex messages, a CD-ROM is an interactive sales device that can tell the story of the product or service in words and pictures, simplifying the message.

When creative teams elect to use a CD-ROM, it is important for them to make sure an interesting visual/verbal story is told. It is not uncommon for a CD-ROM to be a text-only version of a company's website; but if the client is going to spend the money, the message should be as unique as possible. It should be visual, have some noise, and be interactive, to hold the viewer's attention.

Remember, traditional advertising is passive; interactivity brings consumers to the message and entertains them while involving them in an informational yet advertising-focused process. Any material placed on the CD-ROM should be easy to access and print. It is less expensive to distribute CD-ROMs at trade shows, through the mail, or as promotional devices than it is to print and distribute brochures or direct-mail kits.

Digital Coupons

One of the ways to reach consumers on the Internet is through the use of digital coupons. *Digital coupons* are another way to offer incentives online. Coupons may be used online, or in a brick-and-mortar location, for advertised promotions or specially marked merchandise. Digital, like traditional, coupons are used to promote an immediate sale.

Streaming Audio and Video

Streaming audio and video comprise the Internet version of radio and television advertising. A static image or link can be clicked on and played back, which creates a great opportunity to use demonstration or testimonial techniques or to give the spokesperson or animated character a role in the website. It takes a fast Internet connection to run streaming video and audio combinations; and because of technology limitations and variables, it is most commonly used, not as a straight advertising tool, but as an interactive supplement.

Webisodes

A *webisode* is one of a series of streams that use audio and video to tell a short story. They are often used to promote products or services, introduce music, or publicize news events.

A good example of a webisode was created by Dove. Titled "Dove's Calming Night," it was used to highlight and expand on points made both in print and on TV. Very interactive, this storytelling approach entertained and engaged the viewer and offered a direct-response component in that browsers could order samples online.

Weblogs

Weblogs, or blogs, allow consumers to discuss a product, service, or company. Discussions are uncensored and can deliver both positive and negative information, as well as involving crusades for change in product performance or company policies. Additional options include chat rooms and message boards, which allow users with similar interests to interact and share information. Many companies sponsor chat rooms or blogs dedicated to users of their products.

Wireless Communication

It won't be long before regular text messaging will be commonly used by marketers to deliver advertising via the target's cellular phone. How will it work? Targeted consumers will receive a text message and a link; if they are interested in the product, they can use the link to connect to the online sponsor. This type of contact is known as *wireless communication* or *mobile marketing*.

Mobile phones have evolved from just a social connection to a media device. Users can phone, text, browse the Internet, play music, watch streaming video, create personal organizers, e-mail, take pictures, record video, play games, enter contests, change ringtones, and listen to the radio, all by means of a device held in the palm of the hand. Potential customers can be targeted based on phone number, time of day, and location.

Mobile advertising is evolving because mobile carriers who are members of the Mobile Marketing Association—like Verizon, Sprint Nextel, T-Mobile USA, and others—have all agreed to release information about their customers to advertisers.

Mobile carriers know enough about their customers to make mobile advertising a very juicy morsel to marketers. They know the basic demographics, psychographics, and geographics of their customers, such as age and sex; what types of phone service they have; who they call; what games and music they play on their phones; as well as where they live and where they are when viewing any advertising sent.

The opportunities associated with cell-phone advertising are so talked about by marketers that the mobile phone is now referred to as the *third screen*, behind the television and the computer. Why? Because consumers are inseparable from their phones, and the demographic most desired by marketers consists of college students and affluent business travelers. These are the groups who most actively rely on their cell phones for entertainment and news. This is also the group most likely to have the newest generation of cell phones that can access the Internet, run audio and video, play music, take pictures, and send and receive more detailed text messages. The downside is that marketers don't pay for this potential advertising canvas—consumers do—and this limits how they will use and accept advertised messages. Since privacy is just as big an issue for mobile advertising as it is for the Internet, carriers are offering consumers incentives and allowing them to decide how they will opt in. For example, a consumer can elect to receive certain types of advertising at certain times of the day. Advertising for the sake of advertising will never work on a medium fully funded by the consumer; for mobile advertising to be successful, it must have a message that is creative, interactive, useful, and relevant. And although it will cost marketers more to advertise on mobile phones than on the Internet, the upside is that there will be fewer ads appearing on cell phone screens, increasing memorability.

In the future, it is possible that mobile marketing will advance *m-commerce* opportunities by providing consumers the opportunity to purchase products online by taking a picture of them. Carriers will continue to offer mobile search engines that will allow consumers to find the nearest locations selling the advertised product, and that will assist them in fulfilling personal needs such as finding a place to eat.

Additional interactive options include the use of banners that can be clicked on in the same way as Internet banners. By combining mobile advertising and tradi-

Justin Cooter

tional vehicles, advertisers can encourage phone users to input text codes (a functionality made possible through *short message service* technology) to answer trivia questions, download rings or screens, enter contests, or vote on specific topics. However marketers get involved, you can rest assured it will be as creatively delivered as possible.

More adventuresome advertisers are developing actual commercials known as **mobisodes** (mobile episodes) that will use the customer's cell phone to run audio/video messages. The first companies to explore and have some success with mobisode techniques are Toyota and Burger King.

Although the idea of cell phone advertising is acceptable to only a small number of consumers, it is a great way to establish a relationship with the target by creating personalized ads that lead to a one-on-one dialogue between buyer and seller.

As with any popular communication device, marketers and advertising agencies will find a way to use it to talk back to the consumer. Right now the best way to consistently deliver a message is through text messaging.

To date, there are no specific regulations aimed at mobile marketers. That makes it easier for unethical marketers to promote and send unacceptable content, such as ads for sexually explicit material sent to underage users.

Social Networking

The Internet is no longer just one surfer individually looking for information; it has become a place to be entertained and to network socially, with sites like MySpace and YouTube.

Social sites are a pop culture phenomenon that affects viewers both socially and culturally. These popular networking sites offer participants the opportunity to post personal profiles, including photographs; participate in blogs and chat rooms; post messages on bulletin boards; and listen to music or view videos.

Consumers' love of anything technical is boosting revenues on these social sites. Advertisers, ever behind the eight ball when it comes to new technology trends, are rushing to keep up. The newest advertising trend involves using amateur-directed videos, as well as more traditional Web-based video advertising, on sites such as YouTube.

Interactive Television

Interactive television, as previously discussed, is a mixture of television and the Internet. A television advertisement that features a link allows consumers to directly respond to the commercial message viewed on their TV screens by using their remote controls or keyboards to click through. Satellite television has offered interactive technology for years, allowing viewers to order movies through their remotes. The technology required to make television viable as a two-way media device is currently available but has yet to catch on.

DESTINATION OR INFORMATIONAL WEBSITES

The job of a website is to give company background and/or product details. There are two basic types of content sites: destination websites and informational websites.

A *destination website* is the place for a surfer to be. This type of site actively engages viewers through some form of entertaining activity, with the goal of building brand awareness and encouraging return visits. The ever-changing destination website can intrigue, entertain, and interact with visitors as a means of introducing a product or service. This type of approach works great for products that are generally purchased more spontaneously and products that are not technical in nature and need little explanation as to use.

A return visit requires initial interest, but the site must change constantly so that every visit is unique. Easy methods for keeping a website fresh include using promotional options such as contests and sweepstakes; sponsoring chat rooms where consumers can share unique uses for a product; or simply featuring news and/or weather updates or stock quotes. The key is to find a way to make visitors bookmark the site.

In order to keep visitors on their site, marketers must engage the browser or surfer. The more *engagement* a site delivers, the more exposure advertising on the site will obtain. Sites with high engagement can charge higher ad rates.

Since most surfers are on the go from site to site, they like sites that load quickly and that can be viewed as simply as possible. A simple visual/verbal format will be read more often than a time-intensive multimedia message. Streaming video and audio are great if consumers want to take the time to watch or listen; but even in this new medium, simple and traditional approaches work best.

Creating involvement on a site creates word-of-mouth discussion, such as the one developed by the milk industry. They decided to create the first "branded emoticon," to tie their traditional milk-mustache advertising to mobile, e-mail, and Internet copy's style. The "branded emoticon" adds a curly bracket to the standard smiley: :{)

The goal was to get young consumers to use the emoticon when discussing the campaign—first online, and then through other technological devices—thus attaching the new Internet image to traditional efforts.

An *informational website*'s primary job is to educate rather than entertain. This type of site showcases products or services, offers advice or promotional devices, and provides customer service or technical support. A typical page features descriptive copy with an accompanying visual. Although informational sites are not flashy, interactive opportunities exist through promotional efforts such as free gifts, additional information requests, contests, and "click and print" coupon offers.

HOW INTERNET MARKETING BUILDS A RELATIONSHIP BETWEEN THE PRODUCT AND THE TARGET AUDIENCE

This alternative electronic medium, called *Internet marketing*, or *e-commerce*, is voluntarily used by consumers to gather information, find entertainment, and make the occasional purchase. But most importantly, it creates interaction between the buyer and seller.

The Internet is as consumer focused as marketing gets without resorting to personal selling. Electronic media have brought the company to the consumer and made the consumer an active participant in marketing decisions. Marketers have moved a step beyond one-way communication (the message), to two-way communication (target response). This give-and-take creates a relationship between company and target (awareness), and target and brand (loyalty).

This type of advertising allows marketers to avoid mass-market selling techniques and focus more on niche marketing, where advertising efforts focus on a small group of brand-loyal customers.

The Internet is the only vehicle in the promotional mix that is not readily available at the same technological level to all consumers. The costly nature of technology, the subscription basis of Internet access, and the variety of connection options limit the Internet's universality. Before a consumer can go online and interact with a company, product, or service, he must first purchase access from a service provider, such as NetZero, EarthLink, or PeoplePC, to name just a few. The average Internet user is generally more educated than the average consumer, with search sites based on interests, and is attracted to gadgets and any form of new technology.

What are online shoppers looking for? Research shows cars, airline tickets, investments, and household items as the most researched products. The most important concerns of Internet shoppers are price and online-shopping security considerations. Other things desired by online shoppers are discounts; free shipping; sites that are easy to navigate, with prominently displayed prices; and customer comments.

Because Internet users are actively engaged in seeking information, consumer attitude is positive. Buyers choose to look at, or look for, messages; since the messages are not thrust upon them, Internet consumers are less apathetic. If, when visiting a website, a consumer's attention is drawn elsewhere, she can choose a convenient time to return to the site and finish gathering information or complete an order. The Internet offers a no-muss, no-fuss, shopping experience.

Internet users can also decide what they want to look at and how long they want to look at it. A poorly designed site that is confusing or difficult to navigate or read can be removed from the screen with the click of a button.

If a client's website has interactive capabilities, as it should, it must ask the consumer to do something: call, write, or e-mail for more information or a free sample. And when possible, the site should offer coupons to encourage trial or repeat purchase. Most importantly, the consumer should be encouraged to make a purchase or ask for assistance from a customer service representative or technical advisor. Interactive dialogue is the goal of Internet marketing.

CUSTOMER SERVICE IS AN INTERACTIVE MUST

For an IMC program that is trying to develop or maintain loyalty, customer service is critical. Customer service begins when the website launches; continues with informative messages and visuals, feedback, and ordering, and moves on to delivery, follow-up e-mails, and periodical reminder notes. Customer service and brand-building messages are the Internet's keys to success.

It is important to give the consumer a way to make contact. Once a consumer clicks on a customer service button, he needs to get a response. Knowledge is power; let the consumer know how long it will take to get a response. Whether a reply is almost instantaneous or takes twenty-four hours, let the consumer know. This helps to create an environment built on trust and reliability, rather than negativity and distrust.

There are two types of customer service: active interaction and passive interaction. *Active interaction* is live, via instant messaging, the telephone, or online chat rooms or message boards. Traditional e-mail works great for follow-up or reminder notices, order confirmations, and thank-you initiatives.

Immediate e-mail responses keep an impatient consumer happy. Consumers want their questions answered now, so it is important to incorporate contact e-mail links that will immediately connect them with customer service or technical representatives.

Toll-free telephone numbers make contact easy and familiar. Specific questions can be asked and answered with little or no effort. Many consumers are still concerned about making financial transactions on the Internet, so it is important to offer phone, fax, or mail order as options when encouraging purchase.

Passive interaction, on the other hand, involves a delayed response to questions from customer service representatives—such as receipt of a sample in the mail or a follow-up or confirmation e-mail response.

Consumers can then search for more information, ask for technical or customer service support, and even purchase. This familiarity builds brand loyalty. An unsatisfactory visit can turn a consumer off and prompt her to search elsewhere on the Web for the quality or assistance she is looking for.

With all the Internet's positive capabilities, it has a lot of problems that consumers need to be concerned about. In 2003, the FTC found that one in twenty-five adults were victims of identity theft. Fraud is also a concern. It 2004, the FTC reported that more than half of all fraud claims reported were Internet related.

PROS AND CONS ASSOCIATED WITH INTERNET MARKETING

When deciding whether Internet marketing is right for an IMC campaign, it may be helpful to look at some of the pros and cons associated with it.

The more notable pros associated with Internet advertising include:

1. Individualized messaging. Individuals or specific target segments can be easily reached through e-mail or through niche sites devoted to specific interests.
2. Databases. Individuals can be reached through existing databases or those

built based on inquiry or purchase history. This allows existing customers to receive personalized messages containing customized text and images.

3. Cost. Relatively inexpensive to use, the Internet costs about the same as advertising in print. Although it is expensive to initially create a basic website, its overall appearance will change little over time, saving money as compared to other media. Changes or updates are much easier and less expensive than reprinting individual pieces or whole campaigns.

4. Flexibility. Online messages offer convenient accessibility twenty-four hours a day.

5. Interactivity. Internet marketing allows for direct communication between the buyer and seller.

6. Simplicity of integration. The website address can easily be promoted in other IMC advertising efforts.

7. Its engaging nature. The consumer looks more favorably at the Internet as a communications tool, because he chooses when to be exposed to its message.

The more notable cons associated with Internet advertising include:

1. Clutter. There is a lot of information on the Internet so finding a way to make a site stand out is important. Traditional advertising methods are still useful in attracting readers or viewers, so the website address should appear on all advertising materials. The site itself should also be well organized and easy to navigate.

2. Niche segmentation. The Internet is still used mostly for information gathering and the sending and receiving of e-mail, and it is not available at the same technological level to everyone. Research has shown that most mass-advertising efforts on the Internet, including banners and pop-up ads, are considered an annoyance and are routinely ignored; this makes attracting new audience members more difficult.

3. Reach. The very nature of personalized, databased advertising means the message will be received by a small audience. Users tend to be relatively affluent and tend to browse or shop based on specific interests, leaving many sites unseen.

4. Privacy issues. The use of database information in other forms of advertising is also an issue with Internet marketing. The Internet has yet to fully address safety and privacy issues during purchase.

5. Difficulty of measuring. It is difficult to determine exactly how many consumers within the targeted audience actually visit a site. Neither click-through rates nor length-of-visit stats are a reliable measurement tool, as they cannot distinguish between those who end up on a site accidentally or leave their computer for a significant length of time, and those who specifically choose to browse the site.

6. Unbalanced technology. It is important to understand the customer's techni-

cal limitations and capabilities. User-friendly sites should be viewable by even those consumers with slow computers or dial-up Internet connections.

DEVELOPING THE PROMOTIONAL MIX USING INTERNET MARKETING

Internet marketing is an extension of traditional advertising tactics. Websites can be used to help personalize messages and build and maintain both brand loyalty and brand awareness, as well as increase equity and deliver an informational message. It is not a good choice for building brand image or for reinventing or launching a product. At its core, a website is no different from a brochure or direct-mail kit; what makes the Internet unique is that it allows the seller to interact with the customer, creating valuable dialogue through feedback. The website represents the product through overall appearance, ease of use, and customer service options, replacing retail outlets and salespeople.

Other media used as a part of the IMC campaign should feature the website address to encourage visitation and build interest. A company, product, or service cannot survive on Internet marketing alone. It is still necessary to use traditional media vehicles to get the word out about the site.

Internet marketing efforts should reflect other advertising efforts, both visually and verbally. It is important to know how the Internet fits into the promotional mix. Will it play a supporting role as an informational tool? Or will it be the primary location for picking up a coupon before buying or the only location to place an order?

Promotion is a big part of Internet-based advertising. Consumers must be able to order samples, download coupons, and enter contests or sweepstakes on the website.

In public relations, the Internet can be a very effective communications tool. Timely information can be delivered to all levels of the target audience and stakeholders, to announce job openings, provide information about sponsored events, or even link to other relevant sites.

Internet marketing combines elements and advantages of newspapers, magazines, television, catalogs, sales promotion, and direct mail, making it among the most versatile of all media vehicles. The Internet can use the strengths of each of these media vehicles to engage the viewer and successfully deliver the key benefit: print presents a visually and/or verbally dominant element; broadcast entertains; catalogs prominently highlight product features; sales promotion entices with a gift; and direct mail and out-of-home are eye-catching, attracting and holding the reader's or viewer's attention. Internet marketing uses all of these attributes to make information gathering easy and informative, visually/verbally stimulating, and entertaining to keep a viewer from leaving the site and going elsewhere.

Effective communication objectives include developing two-way communication, making sales, encouraging inquiry, developing information, and building loyal customers through interactive activities.

Not counting anything.

Counting everything.

No Guilt. No Lie.

The only thing you should feel guilty about is how good it tastes.

Russell Stover.

Eat what you should. Get the taste that you want.
www.russellstover.com

Leah Loudon

The strategic approach can be either product or consumer based. Consumer-based approaches work well because the Internet can be used as a relationship builder. Product-oriented approaches should tie the product's or service's features and benefits back to the consumer's self-image, lifestyle, and/or attitude.

Good websites are current and ever-changing, and they reflect the idea that news is old at the end of every day. Websites need to maintain initial interest, build excitement, create need, and encourage action.

THE CREATIVE VOICE OF INTERNET MARKETING

After advertising, a website is often the consumer's first concentrated impression of a brand or corporation. The consumer's initial website visit is like stepping into a brick-and-mortar store for the first time: the consumer will take notice of the furnishings, how the floor plan is laid out, and how products are displayed. A messy or haphazard appearance is a turnoff and reflects low budget and quality; a lot of white space and a clean atmosphere give the illusion of quality and exclusivity. As has been previously discussed, advertising in any medium is all about presentation and how the visual/verbal message is delivered.

From a design standpoint, the Internet is part print, part television. At its simplest, it is pure text with visual accents; at its most complex, it is sight, sound, and motion. However, the Internet is neither print nor television, so it has its own set of rules that must be followed to effectively accomplish the objectives and strategically highlight the key benefit. Keep it simple, keep it clean, make it interactive, and think of the page layout as print and the delivery of information as television.

Designers should not get caught up in what can be done electronically; instead, they should focus on what should be done to inform consumers. They are visiting a website, first and foremost, for information; only after the site has kept them from clicking away to yet another site will they plan on making an inquiry or purchase.

The Internet connects the target, the product, and the seller through information and dialogue. It is the only member of the promotional mix that the target actually seeks out for information on a product or service. It is important that this contact, whether initial or ongoing, be a positive one and that it be considered meaningful and productive by the target. This type of one-on-one contact with customer service representatives or techs is great for building loyalty beyond knowledge of the product.

When developing a website designers should:

- Keep the site free of clutter.
- Use increased leading to increase readability and legibility.
- Be sure to show the product in use.
- Tie copy to visuals, and use visuals to explain copy.
- Be sure to show both the product and the packaging.
- Use the logo on every page.
- Keep the site updated.
- Be sure the site matches the visual/verbal look of other media used in the campaign.
- Use color to project an updated look and match other pieces within the IMC campaign.

Websites have several jobs to do. They must showcase merchandise; offer informative copy; highlight visuals (especially those that show the product in use); prominently display prices; offer an easy way to contact customer service representatives or make a purchase; and offer a section covering frequently asked questions, as well as a section covering public-relations events and a company's public-service involvement.

If there is no need for a brick-and-mortar store, and if the site's major function is to make a sale, then it must clearly show the product, its uses, and it price. It must also make ordering easy, providing customers a choice of online order form, phone number, fax number, or mailing address.

Websites should be ever-changing, much like retail stores, which change out displays to encourage consumers to return. Changes usually include the home page. The site should be easy to read and easy to navigate. It should be easy to get help and easy to make a purchase.

As knowledge of what the Internet can and cannot do—and how the consumer will interact with and react to Internet advertising—continues to develop, creatives will be better able to define what good advertising on the Internet will look and sound like and how information should be displayed.

CHAPTER SEVENTEEN

ALTERNATIVE MEDIA

GUERRILLA AND VIRAL MARKETING

Daniel Sanders

Advertising is on its deathbed and it will not survive long, having contracted a fatal case of new technology.

—Roland T. Rust and Richard W. Oliver, 76.

WHAT IS ALTERNATIVE MEDIA?

Alternative media, also known as *new media*, is defined as those media used in advertising that do not fit in the standard or traditional media categories of broadcast, print, or out-of-home.

The definitive label for these new media is under debate. By definition, "new" is an apropos descriptor, because these vehicles are newer than traditional media vehicles. However, *alternative* is the more accepted term, since some vehicles falling into this category, such as the Internet, have been around for more than twenty years. At one time, alternative-media vehicles could be identified based on the fact that they were influenced by current technology. However, this no longer sets them apart. Traditional vehicles such as television and radio have been transformed by technology (e.g., with interactive television and satellite radio), making them an alternative choice when determining the promotional mix.

Alternative-media vehicles reach target audience members where they are, whether they elect to receive the messages or not; so making use of technology, and creative and informative ingenuity, will make these unsolicited messages more interesting to consumers as they go about their day. The majority depend on some kind of interactive device, while others employ the "WOW" factor (as in, "WOW, did you see that!") to make their messages memorable. Alternative media has been dubbed the "creative economy" by marketers, because it seeks to build excitement and create attention in very creative ways.

While consumers have greedily embraced this new visual/verbal voice of advertising, those in the industry have been less than enthusiastic about its use. In its infancy, alternative media was considered little more than an experiment by most marketers, often employed halfheartedly when budgets allowed. Today, it is becoming more mainstream, as marketers search for more consumer-focused, creative, and memorable ways to attract consumer attention. Some examples of alternative-media vehicles are:

- Satellite radio advertising
- Blogging
- Instant messaging
- Podcast advertising
- Online advertising
- E-mail marketing
- Mobile marketing
- Viral marketing
- Viral videos
- Advertising on social-networking sites

- Games
- Supermarket video displays

Although alternative-media vehicles often include out-of-home, Internet, e-mail, mobile, and social-marketing techniques (as discussed in previous chapters), many of these vehicles continue to use traditional sales methods. Vehicles discussed in this chapter create attention in ways consumers do not expect, and they not only hold their attention but also create viral opportunities.

Like traditional media before them, alternative-media vehicles have carved out a place in our fast-paced, instant-messaging lives; they have become a social, political, and economical force within our culture, helping us communicate and trade locally, nationally, and internationally. Each media vehicle offers marketers, creative teams, and consumers variety, convenience, flexibility, and personalization.

In 2006, alternative-media vehicles drove advertising's growth, outpacing traditionally used media vehicles by almost 30 percent. Overall growth can be attributed to marketers seeking vehicles that show a greater ROI and allow for fewer avoidance opportunities.

ALTERNATIVE MEDIA'S ROLE IN IMC

For decades, marketers have relied on traditional advertising vehicles to build brand awareness, reinforce an existing brand image, or launch a new product. In an IMC campaign whose objective is to reach today's media-blitzed, factionalized target audience, traditional methods may not accomplish these goals as well as alternative media or be as consumer focused.

Although most often used as a supplemental or support vehicle, use as a primary vehicle makes sense if the target is especially hard to reach through traditional means. In this case, taking the message directly to the target is a great alternative. For example, if urban youths make up the target audience, and the goal is to get them to try a new brand of sneakers, a promotional van, complete with an activity center, could take the shoes directly to the target consumers and allow them to try the sneakers on and to wear them while working out and perhaps playing some basketball. The goal is to encourage feedback and create interest by letting those who are most likely to purchase the product touch, see, and use it, letting word of mouth do the rest.

Let's take a look at three different types of alternative media vehicles: product placement, guerrilla marketing, and viral marketing.

Product Placement

Placing a product in a movie or in a television program is a common practice. *Product placement* puts a product in a scene, where the camera lingers on it longer than necessary, or incorporates the product into dialogue. The goal is to deliver a less-intrusive message to a captive audience and tie the product to a character's image.

The most famous product placement to date was the use of Reese's Pieces in the movie *E.T.* The use of the candy in the movie was not a paid endorsement by parent company Hershey's; however, they did agree to promote the movie in their advertising. Sales soared well over 50 percent, solidly placing product placement on the advertising map. Successful paid endorsements have included Exxon in *Days of Thunder* and Pampers in *Three Men and a Baby.*

Product placement does not work in all movies or television programming, or even in all video games. A product must fit the environment in which it is placed. Futuristic games and movies, for example, are often inappropriate for most products, unless the products are actually written into the games or movies.

Advertising plays a major role in entertainment. It is with us when we relax in front of the television, and it accompanies us to the movies—and back home again, with our movie rentals.

At the movies, the minute you enter the theater lobby there is advertising in lobby kiosks. There is advertising on popcorn tubs and drink cups. More controversial is the advertising appearing once you've taken your seat. Premovie commercials are often so annoying to consumers that they boo them. As a direct result, Disney has banned premovie advertising in all its theaters.

But it doesn't stop when you leave the theater. Should you decide to stop by the video store to rent a movie, advertising is just as big a part of the viewing experience.

With television, viewers can walk away; they can zip, zap, or graze; or they can record programs in order to skip traditional advertised messages. Placing products in the programming is less obvious, but it is less likely to be intentionally skipped or ignored.

Guerrilla Marketing

Guerrilla marketing can be defined as the use of nontraditional promotional methods to attract attention, increase memorability, and make sales. The more unique the technique or unusual the locale or surface, the better. Its rise in popularity can be directly attributed to media-blitzed consumers ignoring most traditional advertising messages; however, when the message springs up in places and in ways that consumers least expect, the message breaks through the advertising clutter and engages that same inattentive mind. Its unconditional approach develops, introduces, and delivers pop culture directly to the target, and extends message life through word of mouth.

The use of guerrilla marketing techniques was originally envisioned as a low-cost way for small businesses to attract consumer attention in creative and unique ways. Increasingly, however, Fortune 500 companies are investing big bucks to create extravaganzas, rather than just small but innovative marketing/promotional events. Let's take a look at a few examples. OfficeMax, the office supply company, launched a guerrilla campaign in Chicago to introduce its new multicolored rubber-band-ball logo. Using GPS and a mobile projection system, OfficeMax projected its bouncing-ball logo off the sidewalks and buildings in downtown Chicago. The projection system was inside a vehicle that traveled up and down Michigan Avenue, and the ball's bounce and location were determined by the speed with which the vehicle was traveling. Not only did this guerrilla tactic help promote a new logo design, it was also in keeping with OfficeMax's new positioning as a company that represented "fun, passion and innovation."

In order to attract the attention of young urban consumers and promote its 2007 Altima sedan's push-button ignition system, Nissan North America initiated a guerrilla campaign that randomly placed over 20,000 key rings in various public places in major metropolitan cities. The idea was to get those who found the key rings to visit two separate websites, one that educated viewers on the ignition system, and one that gave them directions regarding how to enter a sweepstakes.

Another successful guerrilla campaign was launched by Microsoft, when they attached software to thousands of little parachutes that they then dropped on the city of Willow Springs, Illinois. Before dropping the small software paratroopers, Microsoft was careful to clear the plan with local police and city officials. This is an important step, since guerrilla tactics can often be costly and initiate negative press if care is not taken to follow city, state, and/or federal laws.

Guerrilla marketing tactics are so new that marketers don't always get it right. For example, a recent "Got Milk" campaign in San Francisco went sour when residents complained that ads placed at bus stops smelled like chocolate chip cookies.

It is important to remember that guerrilla-marketing techniques are meant to titillate, not terrorize. When guerrilla-marketing techniques are not well planned, they can get a corporation or brand into some pretty big trouble, as Turner Broadcasting (TBS) found out when it implemented the campaign for its movie *Aqua Teen Hunger Force*.

When small, battery-operated projection boxes were placed throughout the city of Boston without permission from city or state officials, they got more attention than TBS had bargained for. The devices were thought to be bombs, and large sections of the city were shut down to accommodate local bomb squads after someone spotted several of the 12-×-14-inch boxes in prominent locations across the city. After much ado, the boxes were determined to be nothing more than harmless light boards that projected characters from *Aqua Teen Hunger Force*, a TBS cartoon aimed at 18-to-24-year-olds. The guerrilla campaign was part of a promotional campaign to promote the cartoon's movie premiere. State and local officials were enraged, once it was realized that the boxes were part of a marketing campaign.

TBS could have avoided this misunderstanding with the city, had officials been notified of the campaign before the boxes were placed on city property.

Irate officials demanded that Turner pay the expenses the city had incurred in defusing the situation. TBS responded by using the local media to apologize to the people of Boston for any inconvenience they may have suffered in an effort to regain the respect of local residents. In the ad, Phil Kent, chairman and chief executive officer of TBS, said, "We never intended this outcome and certainly did not set out

Exotic stripes of the world in your home.

These life size stuffed animals bring your house into the wild.

F·A·O·SCHWARZ

Jessica Kelly

to perpetrate a hoax. What we did is inadvertently cause a great American city to deal with the unintended impact of this marketing campaign."

Although a public debacle for Turner, the stunt brought a great deal of publicity to the film. Nothing like this had occurred on such a scale since the 1938 "War of the Worlds" broadcast led radio listeners to believe that aliens had landed on earth.

The guerrilla campaign was designed to attract younger consumers and was meant to create a buzz among this jaded target. Generating word of mouth is known as **viral marketing**; like a virus, it is intended to "infect" (i.e., be talked about or shared with) others.

If marketers had warned officials in advance of placing the boxes throughout the city, Turner could have avoided this scandal all together.

As the disaster in Boston shows, guerrilla campaigns need more than just creative development. In many instances, marketers need to check with local police and city officials before launching the guerrilla aspect of a campaign. This is something that Chase Bank New York also did not do. Their guerrilla campaign seemed a simple and safe enough one: project the bank's logo onto city sidewalks. Unfortunately, the city of New York considered this a form of graffiti and declared that the images defaced city property, which resulted in the campaign being pulled.

Beyond the extravaganza are other interactive forms of guerrilla marketing, including stealth marketing, street marketing, and video projection, to name just a few.

Stealth, buzz, or *ambush marketing* uses people or devices to approach, jump out at, or interact with consumers in order to capture attention. Some approaches are so low key that consumers do not know they have been exposed to a promotion, which calls into question the ethics of some of these techniques.

Street marketing interacts with consumers as well, using high-traffic areas like malls, parks, clubs, or beaches to distribute samples or marketing materials. This type of guerrilla marketing is more blatant, bringing current advertising from the pages and screens of traditional media vehicles directly to the consumer and turning former viewers, readers, and listeners into participants who interact with the brand—often creating a great opportunity for additional word of mouth between consumers.

Video projection mimics both outdoor and television by projecting an image or a thirty-second commercial on the side of a building. The projection of logos, character representatives, spokespersons, slogans, or full commercials is a great reminder technique. This form of guerrilla marketing is used most often in large cities that boast a bustling nightlife and heavy foot traffic. Street teams and/or product samples usually accompany these video or static images.

These are just a few of the possible interactive guerrilla techniques available to marketers. Additional options might include word-of-mouth, blogs, letter-writing campaigns, direct-mail kits, lectures and seminars, and promotional brochures distributed in highly trafficked areas. The list is endless, limited only by the creative team's imagination (and sometimes by budget). The very uniqueness of these techniques, along with their interactive qualities, means that marketers have an opportunity not only to get in the faces of consumers, but also to get into their long-term memories, increasing the reach of the advertising as consumers repeatedly share their experiences with others.

Other guerrilla vehicles are just as diverse as the interactive campaign stunts. Simpler and less expensive to execute, they are no less creative in their visual/verbal delivery. In assessing all the bare, flat surfaces available to marketers, the key attributes that need to be considered include:

- Exposure
- Reach
- Creative flexibility
- Size, in conjunction with placement
- Coverage

The following is a short list of possible alternative media surfaces:

- Video games (product placement)
- Movies and television programs (product placement)
- DVDs (ads on boxes and/or attached to the viewed content)
- Sporting events
- Airplane banners
- Trade shows (displays)
- Bathroom stalls and urinal walls
- Sidewalks
- Parking meters
- Public phones
- ATMs
- Gas pumps
- Construction barriers
- Manhole covers

No matter the size, cost, or location, all forms of alternative media are important to marketers because they reach that critical, often hard-to-reach 18-to-39-year-old target group. Marketers who are currently using any form of alternative media recognize the need to incorporate some kind of viral aspect into their campaigns.

Viral Marketing

Interactive Internet technology has reintroduced a marketer's dream: consumer-originated advertising, known as *viral marketing, word-of-mouth*, or *consumer-generated marketing*. The more creative, informative, and interactive the message, the more likely the consumer is to share information with friends, colleagues, and family. The term *viral* refers to what happens when a consumer receives a message he likes and sends the "virus" (i.e., the message) to others—"infecting" them via positive word of mouth, one of the more powerful and trusted forms of advertising.

Consumer-generated marketing is an old/new media device that may be able to control the advertised message better than any other vehicle, by openly analyzing and discussing its content with current or potential users. Viral marketing efforts require that marketers stand behind claims that have been made; otherwise they expose themselves to dissatisfied consumers.

It is important that marketers do more than just monitor these active conversations. They must join in the conversation and address consumer input, good or bad. Employees who monitor blogging sites should have the power to quickly act upon concerns raised in the discussions.

Why encourage viral discussions? Because a 2004 study by Intelliseek found that consumers trust messages delivered by other consumers, whether through conversations with friends or family or via blogs, over the advertised word of corporate giants. This was not a surprise to businesses like Avon and Tupperware, who have been using consumer recommendations as their sales force for decades.

Although advertising on social websites or advertising messages in general may not sell the consumer on a product or service, it may encourage her to search for more information. Because of this, a marketer needs to invest in a well-designed website and develop a strong search-engine presence.

Geico capitalized on their product's popularity and positive word of mouth when they launched an interactive video featuring one of their caveman characters. The video opened with a greeting from our caveman. Casually dressed in a robe, he invites the viewer to read a magazine while he heads off to shower. While he's gone, visitors can snoop around and interact with items in his home—for example, by reading what's on his computer screen, turning pages in books and magazines, and rearranging the word-jumble magnets on his refrigerator. Like all good hosts, he will occasionally pop back in and check on his guests.

The Flash site never officially mentions Geico by name, although the company name does appear briefly, scribbled in a book on the caveman's shelf. The site's purpose is not to sell, but to keep the storyline alive between commercials and allow consumers to continue to build a relationship with the character(s) and, by extension, with Geico.

A viral site like the one developed for Geico keeps consumers aware of the brand by keeping them aware of what their favorite characters in the ads are up to.

Campaigns that create slogans that become a part of the public lexicon, or characters or events that intrigue and/or entertain and thus hold the public's interest, represent the best ways of creating buzz and the best uses of viral marketing techniques.

Referral, or Viral Messaging

We have all been victims of the popular *viral e-mail*. These are the e-mails that are sent to us by friends, colleagues, or family members because they are interesting or entertaining.

Viral messages offer links that will take the viewer to the advertiser's website. Research shows that over 80 percent of consumers who receive a viral e-mail pass it along, making it an excellent vehicle for building brand awareness.

Since it is difficult to measure the ROI of a viral, or *referral* campaign, the importance of this technique in an IMC campaign has yet to be determined.

Despite that, a viral effort can help sustain a campaign's message if it's creatively presented and tied to other media efforts in the campaign.

In order not to be considered spam, viral messaging must be creative, entertaining, educational, and interactive. Viral e-mail ends up in a consumer's in-box because the consumer has "opted-in" to receive it, or because he is receptive to viral deliveries by friends and family.

Josh Cantrell

HOW ALTERNATIVE MEDIA BUILDS A RELATIONSHIP BETWEEN THE PRODUCT AND THE TARGET AUDIENCE

The days of stationary and captive target audiences are fast becoming a thing of the past. Today's consumer is a moving target, flitting from one medium to the next. This constant and diverse interaction is known as *media multitasking*. So reaching this audience with the right message through the right vehicle requires a great deal of research, a lot of repetition, some pizzazz, and a little bit of luck.

First and foremost, the media chosen for a campaign should advance the brand. Second, when using multiple media channels, whether old (i.e., traditional or brand-centric) or new (i.e., consumer-centric), the campaign must deliver an engaging visual/verbal message throughout. If unique enough, it should create chatter among the target audience members, as they infect each other with information about the product or service.

As interactive and consumer focused as they are, alternative-media vehicles have yet to affect ROI in any significant way, making them a small part of most advertising budgets. The very fact that consumers flock to new technology and elect to use it makes it a great way for marketers to interact with them. More research will be needed before it becomes a marketer's first or only choice of advertising venue.

Replacing the static, uninvolved corporate messages of old, alternative vehicles bring not only creative diversity to an IMC campaign, but also interaction, by encouraging conversation between the buyer and seller as well as dialogue between consumers—making it an extremely consumer-focused member of the media mix. Dialogue, when positive, can be a very powerful and brand-building investment.

When used as an advertising tool, alternative vehicles offer marketers more than just an opportunity to talk to their target. Interaction with, and solicitation of feedback from, consumers makes them feel a part of the brand's success, making this dialogue a great way to build a loyal customer base as well as to build, further develop, or maintain brand image and brand equity.

PROS AND CONS ASSOCIATED WITH ALTERNATIVE MEDIA

When deciding whether the use of alternative media is right for an IMC campaign, it may be helpful to look at some of the pros and cons associated with it.

The more notable pros associated with alternative media include:

- Exposure. Many alternative media vehicles reach the target where they least expect it, while other vehicles deliver messages that the target has opted in to receiving.
- Creativity. Because it has such a diverse palette, the visual/verbal message can reach and often interact with a tuned-in audience.
- Its ability to create interest. The "WOW" factor keeps consumers talking to one another about the message or the experience. The interaction or dialogue taking place in chat rooms, on blogs, or via e-mail keeps the message alive. It also keeps corporations honest, and keeps them in the habit of listening to their targets.
- High targetability. Events can be created to reach a specific target, or the target can opt in to receiving the message.
- Its highly interactive nature. The target, in order to participate, needs only to log on or click a few buttons before receiving and reacting to a message.
- Cost. Most alternative media require little more than permission and a detailed database of target e-mail addresses.
- Lack of clutter. Because consumers elect to receive most messages, the environment is still relatively uncluttered as compared to other more traditional media.

The more notable cons associated with the use of alternative media include:

- Its intrusiveness. Since target audience members are often exposed to products, messages, or product representatives as they go about their day, or while relaxing as they watch movies or TV programs, many devices can be annoying or invasive.
- Ethical concerns. Many techniques are so subtle that consumers do not realize they are being exposed to advertisements or promotions, leaving some to question the ethics of advertisers who use certain forms of alternative media.
- Its limited effectiveness. It is only effective if the target opts in or chooses to participate in blogs or viral sharing.
- Cost. Guerrilla campaigns specifically can be very expensive and difficult to pull off as compared to other more traditional media.
- Life span. Buzz lasts only as long as consumers are talking about the product.

DEVELOPING THE PROMOTIONAL MIX USING ALTERNATIVE MEDIA

If the product or service needs to attract attention in order to stand out from competitors, the use of alternative-media vehicles will create memorable and creative visual/verbal messages, which will spread beyond the initial audience through the use of such vehicles as viral e-mailing and plain old word of mouth.

As a member of the promotional mix, alternative media can highlight the key benefit; remind; launch; reinforce existing advertising efforts; deliver a thirty-second commercial in unusual places; or create interest through grand promotional events.

Whether, and at what levels, new media should be used in an IMC campaign requires a detailed look at the brand, its strategy, the target, and overall communication needs.

Whether used as a primary or secondary vehicle, alternative media is a great way to keep the key consumer benefit and product name in the public eye.

Many alternative media vehicles are successful at encouraging impulse purchases, reinforcing brand image, improving brand awareness, and encouraging a brand connection at the point of purchase.

Alternative media can reach any target, anywhere, at any time; but its primary target is usually the hard to reach 18-to-39-year-old target group.

Objectives that require generating interest or announcing a change, or that involve demonstrating a product or discussing how it works, will perform well if showcased through alternative-media vehicles.

Strategically, because of its primary role as a support vehicle, it is great for building brand image or for reinventing the image of an older, established brand. If the product or service is on a maintenance schedule, reaching brand-loyal consumers with e-mail, product placement, or guerrilla marketing techniques will keep awareness high and deliver a way to distribute some kind of incentive or get product feedback.

It is perfect when used in conjunction with public relations to create buzz. Because of the sophistication of most alternative-media vehicles, it is best when used with other image-based vehicles such as TV, magazines, or public relations.

As a supplemental device, traditional vehicles such as newspapers can employ alternative options by updating their Internet presence and adding an interactive element to traditional advertising. A great example of this was employed by *Metro New York*, a free consumer tabloid. Their strategy was to offer advertisers the chance to buy scented newspaper ads. Although this was not a new concept—it harkened back to scratch-and-sniff ads used in magazine and direct response—these types of unusual and inventive efforts will certainly regenerate interest in newspaper readership, as well as being a new and interactive marketing tactic when incorporated into newspaper advertising.

The problems faced by traditional media vehicles, such as consumer fractionalization, avoidance, accountability (i.e., the number of readers or viewers), and the use of the Internet, are the very things that are facilitating the overall acceptance and use of alternative media vehicles by marketers.

Problems with New Media

Consumers are way ahead of marketers when it comes to adopting new media. Marketers who do not keep up with emerging technology will lose equity, as consumers tune in to listen to or watch messages that appear on the technology they use.

To keep up, marketers are jumping into new media almost blindly. As we have seen, research ultimately determines what decisions will be made in determining creative direction and the overall media mix. At this time, however, there is very little research available to help marketers decide what new steps should be taken—and when, where, and how they should be taken.

The newest media options available to agencies and marketing include social Internet sites like YouTube and MySpace; blogs; e-mail and mobile marketing; event sponsorship; product placement; and, to a lesser degree, gaming.

These sites and/or options offer the marketer an excellent opportunity to build her product's or service's image throughout a storyline, where the product is integral to the plot.

The Creative Voice of Alternative Media

Like the creative revolution developed in the 1960s by the likes of Bernbach, Ogilvy, and others, a new creative revolution lies in the unlimited array of creative possibilities associated with the use of alternative media. Here the advertiser can combine stimulating visuals or events with tantalizing copy that both entertains and educates, while still strategically meeting the advertising objectives.

Since alternative media has no standard form or format, it is impossible to determine or describe its creative voice; each use is unique, and depends entirely upon the target and on the overall concept and strategy. What is consistent is that outcome, no matter the budget or vehicle, must be memorable and repetitive, matching the visual/verbal personality of other members of the media mix. Since no current pattern exists to define its diversity, let's take a look at a few of the diverse surfaces and creative solutions currently being developed and employed by creative teams.

One of the newest alternative media surfaces has emerged in the field of air travel. Advertisers have struck a deal with the Transportation Safety Administration (TSA) to sell ads inside the plastic bins in which passengers put their belongings before passing through the X-ray screening at airport terminal entrances. Stipulations require advertisers to share revenues with participating airports and provide the TSA with the trays, plastic carts, and tables used at the checkpoints.

Although limited by time and attention span, these 12 x 17 inch reminder ads have enough space to accommodate both a visual and a logo and/or slogan.

Potential advertisers might include cell phone companies; the makers of luxury items, such as jewelry; and computer manufacturers.

Other alternative-media success stories include the collaboration between the Glad Products company, the nonprofit group Keep America Beautiful, and the New York City sanitation department. Ads for Glad trash bags were placed on the sides of New York sanitation trucks, in order to raise awareness for Keep America Beautiful and Glad's own Glad to Help foundation. To raise awareness, Glad also bought ads in the *New York Times* and the *New York Post*. The promotion was such a success that it raised the brand's market share and thus brand equity.

Just when you thought old could never be made new again, take a look at product placement's emerging interpretations. Advertisers are remaking and recasting unnamed products placed in old movies with new, name-brand products. AMC has cut a deal with pharmaceutical giant Johnson & Johnson to expose viewers to pop-up advertising that matches products used in movies. Here's how it works: Originally, when a character experienced a cold or allergy symptom, he or she took an unnamed pain medication. Today, AMC viewers will see an additional piece of action, an ad for a known Johnson & Johnson product that will pop up on their television screens at the same time the character is using the unnamed product.

If the consumer can't see the product, why not use sound to tell him about it when he least expects it? One brand-new alternative-media technique that is seeing widespread use is *audio spotlighting*, an audio technique that projects sound in a narrow beam, so that only the person passing by can hear the message—avoiding the need for loudspeaker announcements. Traditional speakers send sound out in all directions, whereas the audio-spotlight speaker focuses on one spot, making it an intimate message, specifically aimed at the person standing directly in front of it or underneath it. Quick, focused messages can be quietly used for a variety of purposes, in a variety of locations—such as grocery stores, museums, bookstores, and even car dealerships. Here's how it works: A grocery-store shopper passes a trigger attached to a certain product. Once activated, it delivers a quick and highly targeted message that only this consumer can hear.

Court TV used this new sound technology in the mystery aisle of several New York City bookstores to promote a new murder-mystery show. When activated, a whispering, disembodied voice asked, "Hey you, can you hear me? Do you ever think of murder?" Imagine the consumer's surprise as she looks around for the spooky, intrusive speaker, only to find out she activated the discussion just by walking through the mystery section. Although not yet widely used in this country, this technique is growing in popularity as marketers continue to test consumer reaction.

Glossary

advertising: A paid form of nonpersonal, mass-media communication in which the sponsor of the message is clearly identified. Advertising uses persuasion to sell, inform, educate, remind, and/or entertain the target about a product or service.

alternative media: Media used in advertising that do not fit in the standard or traditional media categories of broadcast, print, or out-of-home.

animated banner: A banner ad consisting of moving images that follow a sequence, helping attract attention to the banner.

announcer: An individual who is both seen and heard on camera, delivering the dialogue.

assorted media mix: The use of more than one medium in a campaign.

banner ad: A mass-media Internet vehicle, usually found at the top of a Web page.

behavioristic profile: A profile that breaks down the target audience by looking at how a person buys.

big idea: A creative solution that sets a product/service off from the competition, while at the same time solving a client's advertising problem.

bleed: A phenomenon associated with a photograph, illustration, background color, or graphic element that extends beyond the trim size or the size of the ad on one or more sides, leaving no complete outer edge of white space.

blog: As an advertising vehicle, a blog is a Web page that can be used by the public to post comments, concerns, or questions about a product or service.

body copy: The descriptive copy that works to make a sale or create an image. Body copy focuses on copy features such as color, price, and size, and/or features a visual/verbal message.

brand advertising: Advertising that promotes a brand's specific features.

broadband: Web access that is fast, allowing users access to streaming audio and video and video games.

business-to-business advertising: Advertising that focuses on wholesalers or distributors.

camera-ready art: Art is camera ready when all its pieces—headline, copy, visuals, and logo—are assembled on a computer screen in preparation for printing.

clip art: Publicly available line-art drawings that can be used without specific permission.

CMYK: The dots that make up a full-color photograph are composed of concentrated percentages of cyan (C), magenta (M), yellow (Y), and black (K). Combinations of these four colors create all colors found in a color photograph.

cognitive dissonance: The guilt or anxiety associated with decisions concerning extravagant or excessive purchases.

communication objectives: A set of goals that the client needs communication efforts to achieve. Communication objectives should describe what the target should think, feel, and do after exposure to the message.

concentrated media mix: A mix that places all advertising efforts into one medium.

consumer advertising: Advertising directed at the public.

continuity: The length of time a campaign will run, or be seen by the target.

cooperative advertising: A combined effort by two individual but compatible clients who pair up to share the cost of advertising and to encourage consumers to use their products or services together.

creative brief: Also known as a *copy platform*; a document developed from the marketing plan and creative strategy that defines the big idea or unique selling proposition. The creative brief also looks at the individual features and benefits of the product or service, outlines tactics, and redefines the target audience.

creative concept: An idea that imaginatively solves the client's advertising problem.

creative strategy: The part of the marketing process that outlines the creative approach needed to accomplish marketing goals.

creative team: A team is made up of at least a copywriter and an art director, who are responsible for developing the creative idea for the IMC program.

cropping: The removal of any unnecessary part(s) of a photograph, allowing the designer to dispense with information that is not necessary to the design.

cybermarketing: Marketing that uses the Internet as a sales device.

database: A collection of individual customer data that are developed from previous interaction with a company, such as a purchase or a request for more information. Databases help marketers personalize the communication message.

demographics: A science that defines the target market in terms of age, income, sex, marital and professional status, education and number of children, and other relevant factors.

detail copy: Small copy that features addresses, phone numbers, store hours, website addresses, credit card information, e-mail addresses, store hours, parking information, and other relevant information.

direct mail: Also known as junk mail; a direct-marketing tool that includes an outside envelope, a personalized pitch letter, an informational brochure, an order form, and a return envelope for mail orders.

direct marketing: A marketing strategy that uses databases and multiple media to talk to members of the target market individually.

duotone: An additional color added to a black-and-white photograph, adding depth and creating a faux full-color feel.

e-mail marketing: The use of e-mail to communicate directly with the target.

engagement: The amount of interest consumers have in an ad and their receptiveness to the message.

flighting: A scheduling approach that alternates between a heavy period of advertising and no advertising.

focus group: A representative sample of the target, usually ten to twelve people, that gathers together to use or try a product in a controlled environment.

font: A typeface's catalog of upper- and lowercase letters, numbers, and punctuation.

formal survey: A survey that relies on closed-ended questions, where participants choose from a predetermined set of responses such as "strongly agree," "agree," "disagree," and "strongly disagree."

four-color process photograph: A photograph or illustration that uses the four-color (CMYK) dot pattern.

freestanding insert (FSI): Also known as *supplemental advertising*; a full-color ad that is inserted into the newspaper, usually featuring coupons and/or announcing a special sale or promotion.

frequency: The number of times an individual is exposed to a message.

generic advertising: Advertising that promotes like products and uses.

geographic profile: A profile that breaks down the target audience by looking at where a person lives.

gross impressions: The number of possible exposures available from a specific medium.

gross rating points: A way to measure the amount of total exposure to a message that a household receives, without duplication.

guerrilla marketing: The use of nontraditional promotional methods to attract attention, increase memorability, and make sales.

gutter: A white space created by the inner margins of two facing pages of a magazine or book. Some of this area is used in the binding.

halftone: A black-and-white photograph that has been converted to a dot pattern.

headline: The largest copy in an ad. Its focus is on highlighting the ad's USP or big idea.

impression: An individual's exposure to a single ad on a single occasion.

infomercial: A thirty-to-sixty-minute television commercial that allows the target to order immediately based on information provided on the television screen.

informal survey: A survey that relies on open-ended questions, allowing participants to give their opinions.

integrated brand promotion (IBP): An IMC campaign that uses advertising and sales promotion in a coordinated effort.

integrated marketing communication (IMC): Also known as *relationship marketing*; a marketing method that uses databases to interactively engage a specific individual with a specific message through specific media outlets. The goal of IMC is to build a long-term relationship between buyer and seller by involving the targeted member in an interactive exchange of information.

Internet marketing: Use of the Internet as an interactive medium to allow the target to come to the product or service. Consumers can place orders or talk to customer-service or technical representatives from the comfort of their own homes.

interstitial: An ad seen in the main browser between two pages of a website.

kerning: The removal or addition of space between letterforms on the computer.

key benefit: The one element, or product feature/benefit, that will be stressed in all IMC efforts.

leading: A specific numerical value for the amount of white space that appears between lines of text.

legibility: The ease with which an ad can be easily understood when viewed quickly.

letter spacing: The amount of white space between letters.

line art: Black-and-white art that consists of a line drawing with no tonal qualities.

line spacing: The amount of white space between lines of text.

lobbyist: A person hired by a corporation to influence the legislative process.

logo: The symbol of a company or a product.

marketer: Also known as the *client*; the person or company who hires an advertising agency to promote products or services to the public.

marketing mix: Also known as the "Four P's"; a brand's marketing plan of action, including product, price, promotion, and distribution (or place). Each of the Four P's plays a vital role in message development.

marketing plan: A client's business plan. The marketing plan outlines the company's strengths and weaknesses, as well as the opportunities and threats affecting the product or service. It determines marketing objectives, profiles the marketing strategy, and looks at budget issues and evaluation tactics.

marketing public relations (MPR): The selling of a corporate or brand image to a specifically defined target audience.

media buyer: The person who buys media and negotiates the terms.

media kit: A direct-marketing media option that can include a news release, a fact sheet, a backgrounder, and a head shot. These kits are prepared for members of the press.

media mix: The media mix breaks the promotional mix down to specific media vehicles such as newspaper, magazine, direct mail, and so on.

media plan: A document used by both buyers and planners that serves as the road map for determining the best use of media, time, and space.

media planner: A person responsible for conducting research, developing the media plan, and determining the media mix.

message weight: The number of vehicles that will be used within a media schedule.

mixed media approach: An approach in which products are placed in multiple media vehicles.

mobile marketing: Advertising that arrives via the consumer's cell phone.

mobisode: An audio/video commercial message that runs on the consumer's cell phone.

narrowband: Web access that is obtained through a conventional telephone line and is very slow.

news release: A document that contains the latest news and information about the product or service in the form of a finished news article.

niche marketing: Advertising efforts that concentrate specifically on winning the attention of a small group of (usually affluent) consumers loyal to one specific product.

opt in: To elect to receive e-mails from a retailer.

out-of-home: Advertising seen outside the home, specifically transit advertising and outdoor boards.

outside influencers: Individuals or groups of individuals who are trusted by the primary target audience and who can influence their purchasing decisions.

overline subhead: An subhead that appears above the headline as a teaser or attention-getter.

Pantone Matching System (PMS): A series of colored chips that have each been assigned a number and which are separated based on whether they are coated (C) or uncoated (U) colors.

permission: See **opt in**.

phishing: E-mails that look legitimate but are not. They are meant to trick the receiver into giving up personal information or money.

pixels: A series of small colored or gray-tinted squares that create a photo's image and color variations on a computer screen.

planned contact: Reaching the target through advertising or promotion.

pop-up ad: A mass-media Internet ad that pops up over a website and contains a link directing the target to another site.

positioning: How a product or service is viewed by the target, as compared with the competition's product or service.

primary data: Data that are gathered by means of original research, for example through surveys, interviews, focus groups, observations, or experiments.

printing plate: A thin, flexible, metal sheet used in printing, which has the ad's image etched into its surface.

promotional mix: Any combination of public relations, advertising, direct marketing, sales promotion, alternative-media marketing, and/or Internet marketing.

psychographic profile: A profile that breaks the target audience down by looking at a person's lifestyle.

public relations: A mostly nonpaid form of communication that builds relationships with both internal and external audiences through communication efforts that reinforce, defend, or rebuild a corporate or product image.

pulsing: A form of media buy that alternates a regular amount of advertising with heavier seasonal use.

qualitative data: Data collected by means of open-ended questions that can be distributed through interviews, convenience polling, and focus groups.

quantitative data: Information represented by statistics, numbers, or comparative scales.

reach: The number of times different consumers are exposed, at least once, to a media schedule within a specified amount of time.

readability: The ease with which an ad can be read at a glance.

registration marks: Marks that are used to align layers while printing.

relationship marketing: See **integrated marketing communication**.

repositioning: A strategy to change the way a product is positioned in the mind of the target.

resolution: The size of the pixel needed to reproduce an image on the computer screen.

return on investment (ROI): The profit realized after advertising and other costs have been deducted.

rich media: A form of advanced technology that allows websites to use streaming video and audio.

roughs: Also known as *layouts*; full-size representations of the final design, with all elements in place and tightly rendered in black and white or color. Conceptual devices such as headlines, subheads, and visuals are readable and viewable.

sales promotion: A marketing strategy that gives the consumer a gift or incentive to entice an inquiry or to encourage purchase.

sans serif: A typeface that has no *feet*, or appendages.

scenes: The visual aspects of a television commercial.

scheduling: Determining the insertion dates, commercial lengths, and promotional activities for a product or service.

script: The copy sheet used in radio and television that indicates sound, camera instructions, and any spoken parts.

secondary audiences: See **outside influencers**.

secondary data: Data that has already been collected and is available from external sources such as the public library, the Internet, trade associations, and the U.S. Census.

serif: A typeface that features *feet*, or delicate appendages that protrude from the edges.

slogan: A statement that represents the company's philosophy or a product's or service's image, and is usually placed above or below the logo.

sound effects (SFX): The noises we hear in radio and television ads, such as doors slamming, dogs barking, and babies crying.

spam: E-mails sent by retailers without permission.

sponsored educational messages (SEMs): Corporately sponsored materials (such as multimedia kits, videos, or software) that are supplied to schools for free, or for a small fee.

spot color: The use of a spot of color to highlight a detail in a black-and-white photograph.

stock art: Existing photographs that can be purchased and used in an ad.

storyboard: An illustration of the visual portion of the commercial and the timing sequence between what is heard and what is seen, one frame at a time.

super comprehensives: Also known as *super comps*; representations of an ad created from the final roughs. Super comprehensives are generated on the computer and include all headlines, subheads, visuals, and a logo—and, for the first time, completed body copy in place—simulating exactly how the design will look and read.

talent: The individuals who will be seen on television or heard on radio, reading the copy or dialogue.

target audience: Also known as *target market*; the group of people research has determined is most likely to buy the product or use the service. A target audience can be broken down based on demographics, psychographics, geographics, and behavioristics.

thumbnails: Small, proportionate drawings that are used to get concept ideas down on paper.

trapping: A phenomenon that occurs when two different colors touch each other in a design. The darkest color will slightly overlap the lighter color to keep any white space from appearing between colors when printing.

trim size: The full size of the magazine page, including margins. *Trim* is also used when referring to the full size of an ad. *Trim marks* indicate where the ad or magazine will be trimmed during production.

type style: The form of a typeface used, such as boldface, italic, or roman.

type weight: The thickness or thinness of the typeface's body.

typeface: The name given to a specific design of type.

underline subhead: A subhead that appears below the headline and explains in more detail what the headline is saying, elaborates on the statement or comment made, or answers the question posed.

unique selling proposition (USP): A consumer benefit that is unique to a client's product or service (or a commonplace feature that is promoted as unique).

unplanned contact: An unplanned message that could be transmitted by word of mouth via conversations with friends in chat rooms, via viral e-mail sharing, or via blogs.

value-added program: A diverse media package sold by one media outlet to a buyer who wants to save money.

viral marketing: The use of interactive and/or entertaining advertising, often delivered via e-mail or on a website, to inform and "infect" the receiver with enough interest about a product or service to visit the marketer's website.

visual: A basic design element that can take the form of a photograph, an illustration, line art, or graphic design.

voice-over: Dialogue read by an announcer who is not seen on camera.

webisode: One of a series of videos, appearing on a Web page, that tell a story.

Weblog: See **blog**.

word spacing: The amount of white space between words.

Bibliography

Altstie, Tom, and Jean Grow. *Advertising Strategy: Creative Tactics from the Outside/In*. Thousand Oaks, CA.: Sage, 2006.

Andrews, Robert. *The Columbia Dictionary of Quotations*. New York: Columbia University Press, 1993.

Arens, William C. *Contemporary Advertising*. 9th ed. New York: McGraw-Hill Irwin, 2004.

Arens, William C., and David H. Schaefer. *Essentials of Contemporary Advertising*. New York: McGraw-Hill Irwin, 2006.

Azzaro, Marian. *Strategic Media Decisions*. Chicago: Copy Workshop, 2004.

Belch, George E., and Michael. A. Belch. *Advertising and Promotion: An Integrated Marketing Communication Perspective*. 6th ed. New York: McGraw-Hill Irwin, 2004.

Berger, John. *Ways of Seeing*. London: British Broadcasting Corporation and Penguin Books, 1980.

Betancourt, Hal. *The Advertising Answer Book A Guide for Business and Professional People*. New York: Prentice Hall, 1982.

Blakeman, Robyn. *The Bare Bones of Advertising Print Design*. Boulder, CO: Rowman & Littlefield, 2004.

Blakeman, Robyn. *Integrated Marketing Communication: Creative Strategy, from Idea to Implementation*. Boulder, CO: Rowman & Littlefield, 2007.

Bovée, Courtland L., John V. Thill, George P. Dovel, and Marian Burk Wood. *Advertising Excellence*. New York: McGraw-Hill, 1995.

Bradley, John P., Leo F. Daniels, and Thomas C. Jones. *The International Dictionary of Thoughts*. Chicago: J. G. Ferguson, 1969.

Burnet, Leo. *100 Leo's*. Chicago: Leo Burnet Company, 1991.

Burnett, John, and Sandra Moriarty. *Introduction to Marketing Communications*. Upper Saddle River, NJ: Prentice Hall, 1998.

Clow, Kenneth A., and Donald Baack. *Integrated Advertising, Promotion & Marketing Communications*. Upper Saddle River, NJ: Prentice Hall, 2002.

Cohen, Stanley E. "The Dangers of Today's Media Revolution." *Advertising Age*. September 30 1991.

Conover, Theodore E. *Graphic Communications Today*. 3rd ed. St. Paul, MN: West, 1995.

Duncan, Tom. *IMC: Using Advertising and Promotion to Build Brands*. New York: McGraw-Hill, 2002.

Hester, Edward L. *Successful Marketing Research*. New York: Wiley, 1996.

Krugman, Dean M., Leonard N. Reid, S. Watson Dunn, and Arnold M. Barban. *Advertising: Its Role in Modern Marketing*. Fort Worth, TX: Dryden Press, 1994.

Li, Hairong. *Advertising Media: Planning and Strategy*, 2007, www.admedia.org (accessed June 28, 2007).

McDonald, William J. *Direct Marketing: An Integrated Approach*. New York: McGraw-Hill, 1998.

Mencken, H. L. *A New Dictionary of Quotations*. New York: Knopf, 1964.

Moscardelli, Deborah M. *Advertising on the Internet.* Upper Saddle River, NJ: Prentice Hall, 1999.

Murphy, Edward F. *The Crown Treasury of Relevant Quotations.* New York: Crown, 1978.

Ogilvy, David. *Confessions of an Advertising Man.* New York: Ballantine Books, 1978.

Ogilvy, David. *Ogilvy on Advertising.* New York: Vintage Books, 1985.

O'Guinn, Thomas C., Chris T. Allen, and Richard J. Semenik. *Advertising.* Cincinnati, OH: South-Western College, 1998.

O'Guinn, Thomas C., Chris T. Allen, and Richard J. Semenik. *Advertising and Integrated Brand Promotion.* 3rd ed. Mason, OH: Thomson South-Western, 2003.

O'Toole, John. *The Trouble With Advertising.* New York: Chelsea House, 1981.

Pate, Russ. *Adman: Morris Hite's Methods for Winning the Ad Game.* Dallas: E-Heart Press, 1988.

Percy, Larry. *Strategies for Implementing Integrated Marketing Communication.* Chicago: NTC Business Books, 1997.

Rossiter, John R., and Larry Percy. *Advertising Communications and Promotions Management.* 2nd ed. New York: McGraw-Hill, 1997.

Rothenberg, Randall. *Where the Suckers Moon: An Advertising Story.* New York: Alfred A. Knopf, 1994.

Russell, Thomas J., and W. Ronald Lane. *Kleppner's Advertising Procedure.* 15th ed. Upper Saddle River, NJ: Prentice Hall, 2002.

Rust, Roland T., and Richard W. Oliver. "The Death of Advertising." *Journal of Advertising* 23, no. 4 (1994): 71–77.

Sheehan, Kim. *Controversies in Contemporary Advertising.* Thousand Oaks, CA: Sage, 2004.

Shimp, Terence A. *Advertising Promotion: Supplemental Aspects of Integrated Marketing Communications.* 5th ed. Orlando, FL: Dryden Press, 2000.

Sirgy, Joseph M. *Integrated Marketing Communication: A Systems Approach.* Upper Saddle River, NJ: Prentice Hall, 1998.

Surmanek, Jim. *Media Planning: A Practical Guide.* 3rd ed. Chicago: NTC Business Books, 1996.

Throckmorton, Joan. *Winning Direct Response Advertising.* 2nd ed. Lincolnwood, IL: NTC Business Books, 1997.

Vanden Bergh, Bruce, and Helen Katz. *Advertising Principles.* Lincolnwood, IL: NTC Contemporary Publishing, 1999.

Wagner, Elaine, and Amy Desiderio. *From File to Finish: A Prepress Guide for Art Directors and Graphic Designers.* Chicago: Copy Workshop, 2007.

Wells, William, John Burnett, and Sandra Moriarty. *Advertising Principles and Practice.* 6th ed. Upper Saddle River, NJ: Prentice Hall, 2003.

INDEX

Account executive, 38, 113, 146
Account planner, 38
Advertiser. *See* Marketer
Alternative media, 11, 92, 276
Anthropological research, 46
Art director, 39, 113, 117, 146
Assorted media mix, 14

Behavioristic profiles, 48, 49, 230, 258
Better Business Bureau, 29
Big idea, 84, 85
Bleed, 141, 146
Brainstorming, 113, 125
Brand, 12, 62, 64, 73
Brand advertising, 73
Brand attitude, 184
Brand awareness, 62, 64, 83, 93, 98, 126, 157,162,
   173, 192, 199, 202, 210, 214, 219, 228, 239,
   244, 250, 253, 256, 267, 271, 283, 286
Brand equity, 12, 43, 63, 66, 67, 83, 94, 121, 131,
   149, 155, 157, 158, 160, 162, 220, 245, 248,
   250, 271, 285, 287, 288
Brand identity, 64, 69,
Brand image, 12, 62, 64, 69, 72, 93, 106, 114, 131,
   149, 157, 158, 173, 184, 190, 196,219, 220,
   228, 230, 239, 244, 245, 248, 250, 260, 285,
   287
Brand image advertising, 83
Brand loyalty, 11, 12, 43, 60,62, 66–68, 83, 93,
   94, 155, 157, 160, 162, 173, 220, 230, 236, 239,
   244, 245, 249, 268,269, 271
Brand management, 159
Brand strategies, 79
Branding, 62, 69
Broad mix, 100
Business-to-Business advertising, 41

Cable television, 217
Character representative, 72, 121, 122
Classified advertising, 169
Client. *See* Marketer
CMYK, 142
Co-op advertising, 105, 175, 186, 200
Cognitive dissonance, 59
Cohort analysis, 48
Combination sales promotions, 250, 251
Communication objectives, 11, 14, 16, 76, 77, 79,
   80–82, 86, 112, 115, 117, 131, 160–62, 164,
   173, 176, 182, 184, 199, 220–22, 237, 239, 245,
   253, 271, 273, 286, 288
Competitive strategies, 78
Concentrated media mix, 14, 100
Consumer advertising, 41, 47, 272
Consumer behavior, 58
Consumer-Focused advertising, 171, 181, 196,
   254, 268, 276, 277, 285
Consumer generated marketing, 282
Continuous scheduling, 102
Copywriter, 39, 113, 117, 126
Coupons, 170–72, 246, 268
Cradle-to-grave brand loyal consumer, 31, 34
Creative boutiques, 40
Creative brief, 81, 112, 116, 126, 162, 221, 241
Creative concept, 116, 117
Creative director, 38
Creative strategy statement, 80
Cybermarketing, 256

Databased marketing, 10, 159, 230, 231, 233, 236,
   238, 285
Deceptive advertising, 28
Demographic profiles, 48, 49, 204, 230, 231, 264
Detail copy, 130, 175
Digital prepress, 134, 144
Digital proofs, 148
Direct-to-Consumer advertising, 24
Direct mail, 233, 236, 240
Direct-mail kit, 233, 236, 240, 241, 246, 248, 253
Direct marketing, 15, 182, 230, 251, 253, 254
Direct response, 15, 41, 93, 99, 106, 194, 196,
   215, 216, 233, 235, 237, 240, 251, 254, 263,
   287
Display advertising, 169

E-commerce. *See* Internet marketing
E-mailadvertising, 235, 237
E-mail marketing, 262
Emotional appeals, 58, 87, 99, 178, 186, 239, 254
Engagement, 72, 267
Evaluation, 79
Experiential marketing, 72
External audience, 154, 158, 237

Fact sheets, 165
Fad, 67, 215, 220
Federal communications commission, 29, 33

Federal trade commission, 28, 29, 33, 269
File transfer protocol, 139
Focus group, 47
Food and Drug Administration, 24
Freelance advertising, 42
Freelancer, 40
Freestanding insert, 170, 235, 237, 246
Frequency, 7, 96, 97, 192, 195, 197, 199, 205, 210

General interest publications, 179, 180
Generic advertising, 73
Geographic profiles, 48, 49, 204, 230, 264
Graphic design, 120, 186
Guerrilla marketing, 11, 15, 41, 278

High involvement, 101
Horizontal cooperatives, 176

Idea generation. See Brainstorming
Illustration, 120, 186
Image advertising, 27
Implementation strategies, 79
In-house advertising, 173
In-store sales promotions, 246–48
Incentive, 42
Influencers, 64
Inherent drama, 116, 214, 220
Inside-out, 7, 162
Integrated brand communication, 71
Integrated brand promotion, 244
Integrated marketing communication, 6, 11, 13,
    18, 71, 156, 162, 173, 184, 190, 199, 202, 206,
    239, 244, 245, 251, 252, 254, 25, 258, 268, 277,
    285, 286
Interactive, 6, 10, 171, 220, 259, 263, 265, 268,
    270, 287
Interactive agencies, 41
Interactive television, 215, 266
Internal audiences, 154, 158, 237
International advertising, 21, 39, 41, 93, 95, 155
Internet marketing, 256, 267
Internet use, 10, 182, 235–37

Jingles, 203, 204, 206, 207, 209

Key consumer benefit, 84, 112, 116, 122, 126, 127,
    130, 175, 159, 162, 183, 199, 202, 206, 207,
    222, 239, 241, 253, 259, 271, 273, 286

LED outdoor boards, 193
Legibility, 124, 137, 138, 200, 273
Life-Cycle phases, 66, 82, 99, 131, 254
Line screens, 141
Lobbyists, 23
Local advertising, 21, 28, 39, 41, 93, 95, 105, 155,
    169, 183, 193, 196, 202, 203, 209, 217
Logo, 88, 121
Low involvement, 101

M-Commerce, 265
Magazine advertising, 178, 205, 219, 237
Maintenance advertising, 68, 100, 196, 204, 252,
    286, 214, 227, 228, 252
Mainstream products, 67
Marketer, 18, 46, 154
Marketing, 18
Marketing mix, 78, 79
Marketing objectives, 77, 79
Marketing plan, 76, 79
Marketing public relations, 154
Marketing strategy, 77
Mass media. See Traditional advertising
Mechanical, 134, 143
Mechanical director, 136
Media buyer, 38, 104, 176, 187, 197, 200, 210,
    227
Media buying, 41
Media convergence, 94
Media mix, 14, 100, 161, 168, 171, 176, 199, 203,
    206, 215, 231, 239, 258, 285, 287, 288
Media multitasking, 284
Media objectives, 95, 96, 98, 99, 103, 104
Media plan, 95
Media planner, 38, 93, 113
Media planning, 93
Media strategy, 99
Media tactics, 103
Media waste, 101
Message weight, 98
Mixed media approach, 100
Mobile marketing, 264
Multichanneling, 258
Multiple selling proposition, 84

National advertising, 21, 28, 39, 41, 93, 95, 155,
    209, 219, 223
Network television, 217
New product launch, 66, 157, 171, 190, 196, 204,
    214, 222, 228, 241, 252, 253, 286
Newspaper advertising, 168, 182, 204, 219, 237,
    287
New media. See Alternative media
News release, 164, 171
Niche marketing, 52, 69, 205, 268–70
Nontraditional advertising, 92, 100, 106

Opt-in marketing, 262
Out-of-home, 190, 220, 237
Out-of-store promotions, 248–50
Outbound telemarketing, 236
Outdoor boards, 191
Outside-in, 7
Outside influencers, 56

Paid Search ads, 261
Painted bulletins, 192
Pantone matching system, 142
Pay Per click, 261

Permission marketing. *See* Opt-in marketing
Phishing, 262
Pixel, 140, 141
Planned contact, 8, 95
Political influence, 23
Positioning, 68, 69, 83, 86, 131, 156, 239, 279
Poster panels, 192
Posters, 192
Postproduction, 148, 209, 223, 238
Posttesting, 47
Preferred position, 176
Preproduction, 137, 209, 223, 238
Press kits, 165
Press proofs, 148
Press run, 146
Pretesting, 47
Primary research, 46, 160
Primary target, 56, 239
Print production manager, 136, 143, 146–8
Product approach, 206, 272
Product features and benefits, 7, 20, 22, 32, 58, 66, 68, 71, 79, 81, 83, 87, 88, 99, 127, 134, 202, 207, 208, 234
Product placement, 277, 278
Product usage, 96
Production, 209, 223
Production art. *See* Digital prepress
Production artist, 39, 136, 143
Promotional advertising, 105
Promotional mix, 10, 13, 158, 162–4, 171, 199, 202, 203, 205, 206, 221, 231, 239, 241, 245, 251, 253, 254, 271, 276, 286
Psychographic profiles, 48, 49, 204, 230, 231, 264
Psychological research, 46
Public relations, 14, 98, 154, 204, 219, 237, 250, 251, 253, 271, 287
Publicity, 166, 182, 280
Puffery, 28, 37, 129

Qualitative data, 47, 104
Quantitative data, 47, 104

Radio, 202, 219, 220
Radio execution techniques, 207–9
Radio scripts, 209
Rational needs, 58, 87, 99, 129, 178, 206, 239
Reach, 7, 96, 192, 195, 197, 199, 210, 220, 232, 270
Readability, 124, 137, 138, 200, 273
Reinforcing brand image, 286
Reinvented products, 67, 222, 228, 241, 245, 248, 253
Relationship building, 159
Relationship marketing. *See* Integrated marketing communication
Reminder advertising, 94, 100, 129, 190, 204, 214, 227, 241, 254, 286
Repositioning, 71, 214, 248, 253
Research, 10, 163

Retail advertising, 168
Return on investment, 16, 105, 164, 277, 285
Roughs, 118

Sales promotion, 15, 171, 182, 231, 244
Scheduling, 101
Script, 223–25
Secondary data, 46
Secondary target, 56, 239
Segmenting, 48, 78
Service mark, 63
Shock message, 26
Situation analysis, 77
Slogan, 88, 130
Sociological research, 46
Soft proof, 144
Spam, 262, 283
Special interest publications, 179, 180
Spokesperson, 72, 121
Sponsored educational messages, 34
Spot color, 120, 138
Spread ad, 150
Stakeholder, 154, 160
Standard Rate and Data System, 144
Stealth marketing, 281
Stock art, 120
Storyboard, 222–4
Strategic research, 47
Strategy, 10, 79, 86, 159, 162, 184, 186, 199, 206, 221–23, 237, 239, 241, 244, 253, 254, 273, 286, 288
Strategy statement, 80
Streaming audio and video, 257, 259, 263
Super comprehensives, 118
Supplemental advertising, 170
Support statement, 88
Support vehicle, 190, 194, 202, 203, 210, 239, 256

Tagline, 88, 131
Target audience, 10, 82
Target market analysis, 78
Telemarketing, 236
Television advertising, 205, 214, 220, 237
Thumbnails, 118
Tone, 87, 125, 127, 130, 154, 159, 221, 241
Tone of voice. *See* Tone
Trademark, 63
Traditional advertising, 7, 13, 14, 17, 92, 100, 106, 168, 216, 219, 230, 241, 258, 263, 271
Traffic manager, 39, 137
Transit advertising, 194
Trend, 67, 215, 220
Two-way communication, 4, 6, 11, 100, 155, 158, 159

Unique selling proposition, 84
Unplanned contact, 8, 95
U.S. Commerce Department, 25

Value-Added programs, 104
Values and lifestyles questionnaire, 49
Viral e-mail, 283
Viral marketing, 277, 280, 282, 283
Viral messages, 283
Virtual marketing, 15
Visual/Verbal identity, 66

Visual/Verbal message, 13, 36, 80, 81, 83, 84, 87,
    99, 113, 121, 126, 131, 136, 174, 175,178, 184,
    192, 202, 210, 241, 254, 273, 281, 284, 285, 286

Wireless communication. *See* Mobil marketing
Word of mouth, 4, 15, 62, 67, 95, 98, 155, 163,
    227, 250, 257, 267, 277–79, 282–83, 286

About the Author

Robyn Blakeman received her bachelor's degree from the University of Nebraska in 1980 and her master's from Southern Methodist University in Dallas, Texas, in 1996.

Upon graduation in 1980, she moved to Texas, where she began her career as a designer for an architectural magazine. She next took a position as mechanical director for one of the top advertising agencies in Dallas, eventually leaving to work as a freelance designer.

Professor Blakeman began teaching advertising and graphic design in 1987, first with the Art Institutes and then as an assistant professor of advertising, teaching both graphic and computer design, at Southern Methodist University. As an assistant professor of advertising at West Virginia University, she developed the creative track in layout and design. She was also responsible for designing and developing the first online integrated marketing communication graduate certificate and online integrated marketing communication graduate programs in the country. While at West Virginia University, she held several positions, including Advertising Program chair, coordinator of the Integrated Marketing Communication Online Graduate Certificate Program, and coordinator of Student Affairs and Curriculum.

In 2002–2005 Professor Blakeman was nominated by former students for inclusion in *Who's Who among America's Teachers*. In 2003–2006 she was included in *Who's Who in America*. She has received the Kappa Tau Alpha honorary from her peers and was voted P. I. Reed School of Journalism professor of the year for 2001–2002.

In October 2004 her first book, *The Bare Bones of Advertising Print Design*, was published, and a second, *Integrated Marketing Communication: Creative Strategy from Idea to Implementation*, was published in March 2007. As a part of a collaborative effort, Blakeman has a fourth book due out in 2009, tentatively titled *The Brains Behind the Great Ad Campaigns: Copywriters and Art Directors . . . How Do They Come Up With This Stuff*. Professor Blakeman currently teaches advertising design at the University of Tennessee, Knoxville.